Natural Resource Management and Policy

Volume NA

There is a growing awareness to the role that natural resources, such as water, land, forests and environmental amenities, play in our lives. There are many competing uses for natural resources, and society is challenged to manage them for improving social well-being. Furthermore, there may be dire consequences to natural resources mismanagement. Renewable resources, such as water, land and the environment are linked, and decisions made with regard to one may affect the others. Policy and management of natural resources now require interdisciplinary approaches including natural and social sciences to correctly address our society preferences.This series provides a collection of works containing most recent findings on economics, management and policy of renewable biological resources, such as water, land, crop protection, sustainable agriculture, technology, and environmental health. It incorporates modern thinking and techniques of economics and management. Books in this series will incorporate knowledge and models of natural phenomena with economics and managerial decision frameworks to assess alternative options for managing natural resources and environment.

Nicholas Guehlstorf
Editor

Environmental Policy Science's Exploration for Innovative Data

Springer

Editor
Nicholas Guehlstorf
Department of Environmental Sciences
Southern Illinois University
Edwardsville, IL, USA

ISSN 0929-127X ISSN 2511-8560 (electronic)
Natural Resource Management and Policy
ISBN 978-3-031-90888-0 ISBN 978-3-031-90889-7 (eBook)
https://doi.org/10.1007/978-3-031-90889-7

This Springer imprint is published by the registered company Springer Nature Switzerland AG
The registered company address is: Gewerbestrasse 11, 6330 Cham, Switzerland

Acknowledgements

My first book, published when I was an assistant professor, was simply in recognition of my professors and wife. Unexpectedly, I am still impacted by my esteemed mentor, Robert Bartlett. His guidance, wisdom, and work ethic—even in retirement—have shaped this book and my career. Also, this publication, and everything in my life, is a testament to my wife's trust in me. My second book, as an associate professor, was dedicated to my academic peers, children, and wife. Again, nothing has changed, as obviously this edited book would not be possible if not for my academic colleagues, most of whom are not my friends, rather young scholars with big ideas taking risks. Additionally, my beloved partner and four children are my principal supporters and most unwavering critics. Notwithstanding publishing with a handful of students over the years, I would like to acknowledge that my research would not have occurred without my students who have walked, managed, and cleared this path of environmental scholarship alongside me. Thank you for your curiosity and energy. Not all my work is pathfinding but please continue my endless pursuit of knowledge. Generally, my undergraduates and graduates have been guiding my academic insights as their collective passions have inspired this book. Specifically, Arta and Courtney, your dedication to the pursuit of sustainability and conservation endures to fuel my own. This book is as much a testament to my own efforts as it is to your contributions. Arta Cavazos, your persistent search for quality and your attention to detail have been an encouragement as you might be the only person to have read almost every word in this edited book. Courtney Breckenridge, your co-author donations without patience and predictability have been a motivator for my change to deliberate on new designs and data, and for that, I am grateful. Finally, this third book, as a professor, is dedicated to my wife, Kristin, who fills my life with joy and purpose, and for your career that has provided me with much opportunity.

Contents

Chapter 1
Introduction: Challenges and Opportunities for Social Scientists Working on Environmental Policy Today

Nicholas Guehlstorf

It should be noted that the title of this book, *"Environmental Policy Science's Exploration for Innovative Data,"* is not profound and was crafted with little thought and perhaps less time. The title does, however, originate from a lot of participation in and introspection about novel academic scholarship at the intersection of public policy analysis and environmental administrative decision-making. In over two decades of studying environmental policy, I have grown to realize that today's scholarship about pollution abatement and resource management is an evolving journey. The best work available today takes risks, as scholars in the twenty-first century must be daring by considering new machine learning methods and computational techniques from other disciplines while remaining wary of social data as literature at the same time. The controlling narrative of this book is that researchers involved in natural resource administrative investigations and pollution control policy analysis must be entrepreneurial. They must find and implement data sets that go beyond nationally available federal programs' assessments, original but local surveys, and case studies on collaborations with or about stakeholder groups. New environmental investigations must be bold and pathfinding to be relevant and taken seriously by scientists and administrators.

I have always found awkward pleasure in reading, watching, and listening to new environmental public policy. Unlike many of the graduate students and collaborators who attend academic conferences only to present, I enjoy taking the time to join multiple panels per day because I like to be intimidated by the scope and depth of the methods employed as well as the data used. Too often, the production of my own research has felt pleasurable yet routine as it infrequently takes risks. In contrast, I frequently find the work of others that captivates and catapults my thoughts to be

N. Guehlstorf (✉)
Southern Illinois University Edwardsville, Edwardsville, IL, USA
e-mail: nguehls@siue.edu

N. Guehlstorf (ed.), *Environmental Policy Science's Exploration for Innovative Data*, Natural Resource Management and Policy NA,
https://doi.org/10.1007/978-3-031-90889-7_1

both breathtaking and inspiring. Like a restaurant cook, bored with preparing the same unimaginative menu every night, who finds enjoyment in other kitchens by appreciating the innovation, formation, and construction of others. Similarly, in my academic work, I publish on commonly used research designs because they are legitimate and accepted but have realized I find more gratitude and passion for new research that makes unique attempts. My motivation for creating and editing this book is from that appreciation, and my goal is that others will start engaging in research, data, and literature that is not easy and simply based on past experiences.

When I first started researching environmental policy in graduate school, I was like a cook following a recipe. I associated with a policy science typology—such as advocacy coalition, multiple streams, or diffusion—just as a cook takes on a culinary style characterized by specific ingredients and associated with a distinctive culture and geographic region. Once committed to a cuisine (or typology), I followed with predictable techniques, starting with selection of a dish (or hypothesis creation). There was little ingenuity as I purchased the ingredients for the recipe and performed the same regression analysis and theoretical interpretation as every other junior scholar who used the same cookbook. Over the years, I learned new methods of statistical analysis, studied different environmental issues, and worked with new collaborators but only the processes changed. Much like deciding between broiling, roasting, grilling, or baking, the end product—regardless of technique—is acceptable but is likely similar to other works. Over the decades of my evolution in the policy sciences, I have realized the scholars who I most appreciate are not cooks like myself but chefs. A chef does not simply find a recipe and carry out instructions, but rather, a chef expertly identifies the highest quality ingredients available and then creates something new, resulting in an output that exceeds the inputs.

This book is inspired by environmental policy scholars who work in the same way a chef creates new dishes: they look at the available data from unique sources and then produce a hypothesis or research question to be tested. As such, this text is an anthology that can be separated neatly into six components with similar ideas, but different research designs and outputs. My research contribution to innovative data in twenty-first century environmental policy scholarship, exemplified in this book, is primarily an attempt to organize the variety of new analytical processes for assessing sustainability in natural resource management. The secondary focus of this anthology is to earnestly question if this era of environmental policy research is uniquely different than previous shifts in scholarship. That is, scholars must ensure creative efforts to learn about the environmental world are not an inference of logic that deserves more attention than traditional techniques.

Over twenty years ago, when I was a graduate student learning theories, models, and designs of environmental policy analysis, statistics professors advised that social scientists must always have a hypothesis prior to "running the numbers" of a data set to find relationships. In fact, it is only within the last couple of semesters as a research mentor to my own students that I have stopped cautioning about "datamining" because many of the limitations associated with the typical uses of regression, correlation, and other statistical tests with deductive learning are more obvious when compared to machine learning that can predict outcomes with much greater accuracy. I am not a formal modeler who defends inductive learning. In fact, I think deductive hypothesis testing saves time and is well suited for literature reviews and theoretical designs. Nonetheless, I am less rigid than the deductive defiance formerly required among environmental policy scholars and not afraid of "P hacking" to find the best causal inference. As a scholar who started out researching and publishing on environmental political theory and ethics, I have always been impressed by the ingenuity of positivist social scientists who use analytical chemistry, biological sampling, meteorological data, and agricultural statistics to test natural resource and pollution policy questions. In fact, as my career has evolved, so have my research methods and now, much of my work is done in teams with environmental scientists with predictive analytical assistance.

As such, my covetous appreciation of empirical environmental sciences has reached new heights because scholars today are using huge data sets from Twitter (X), images from satellites, Tik Tok, Geographical Information Systems (GIS), and elsewhere to examine policy relevant questions. Please note, this edited volume is not attempting to be a cookbook that explains technical methods such as brilliant books by Murphy (2021), Einstein (2019), and Silge and Robinson (2017). Truthfully, none has been more comprehensive and helpful to me and my students than Grimmer, Roberts, and Stewart's *Text as Data: A New Framework for Machine Learning and the Social Sciences* (2022). Instead, my authorial optimism is that the collaborators in this book inspire other environmental scholars to be creative and reflective of the same spirit I discovered after reading the most exciting piece of research in the last decade: Guber, Bohr, and Dunlap's "Time to Wake Up: Climate Change Advocacy in a Polarized Congress" in *Environmental Politics* (Guber et al., 2021). This anthology celebrates this use of social text as data and attempts to evaluate if this new method of conducting policy analysis is valid in environmental sciences. It was briefly after reading this article that I witnessed a young assistant professor, Dr. Costie, give a presentation on using Twitter to explain how the state of New York banned fracking and it was at that moment I was inspired to change my research agenda and write this edited book.

Chapter 2: "Tracking Variation in Activity in Unconventional Oil and Gas Subsystems: Advocacy Coalitions in the Twittersphere" is written by Dr. Daniel Costie at Eastern Oregon University. With the increased role of social media in political discourse, civic engagement through online deliberation is becoming more accessible and more common in Western democracies. Through observing trends in online behavior, it is possible to examine how coalition members align discursive strategies, such as participating in an on-line venue, for the purpose of shaping the policy agenda. Discursive strategies are particularly important to study in adversarial policy domains because when there is narrow space for compromise, conflicting interests compete over how policy issues are discussed. Coalition members often take advantage of major events by highlighting certain aspects of a problem, thereby shifting how a policy issue is perceived by the public and policymakers. If a coalition can take advantage of these opportunities to shape public discourse, they stand a better chance of having their interests translated into policy. This work poses the following general question: How do coalition strategies manifest in an online discursive venue and how do strategies change after a major policy change? To explore this question, Dr. Costie investigates which coalition members are participating in the popular online discursive venues. In this research, Costie compares pro- and anti- coalition participation as it relates to the unconventional oil and gas subsystems of New York, USA. Like many young twenty-first-century researchers, Costie finds a sizable number of policy actors active on Twitter (X), representing a diverse set of interests, and that while issue expansion did not occur leading up to a major policy change, participation did drop dramatically over the long term. The internet generally, and Twitter (X) specifically, have made acquisition of natural resources data easier and cheaper than older techniques of interviews, surveys, or publicly available data about biological and/or chemical indicators of policy analysis but due to volume of social media scholarship, extensive analysis is required for the data to be relevant.

Chapter 3: "Tweeting to Conserve: An Analysis of Water District Messaging during the California Drought" by Dr. Colin Kuehl at Northern Illinois University is a public administration evaluation of citizen efficacy using social media data from Twitter (X). Public service providers, like water districts, rely on effective public messaging to persuade their users to adopt preferred environmental behaviors, such as conserving water. As one component of their broader outreach efforts, government agencies increasingly rely on social media outlets to disseminate information and, hopefully, change the public's behavior. This paper examines the social media outreach via Twitter (X) by California water districts in their efforts to promote voluntary water conservation. It categorizes a random selection of the approximately 100,000 tweets from water providers between 2012 and 2022. Results show districts most often simply provided information about the presence of drought and the need for conservation, and rarely used Twitter (X) to communicate the presence of drought regulations or the financial benefits of water use reductions. The chapter concludes with a discussion of the implications of these results in relation to best practices from behavioral science, as well as the use of social media data as a means of understanding government agency messaging.

Chapter 4: "Taking Notice: The ECHO Network, integrated watershed governance, and TikTok" by Drs. Lars K. Hallstrom, Lanie Parr, and Nick Yarmey, from the University of Lethbridge, is an anthropological and sociological analysis of how the use of social media can facilitate science communication. In 2016, a large network of environmental, Indigenous, public health, and community researchers and practitioners received a two million dollar grant to create the Environment, Community, Health Observatory Network (ECHO). One of the key study sites for this network is the Battle River Watershed—a prairie fed river in East Central Alberta, Canada, that covers just under 50,000 sq. km and is home to significant energy, agricultural, municipal, and trade activity. To further develop the state of the watershed reporting in Alberta, the study partners developed a unique, multi-sectoral indicator framework and then used this framework to create an extensive series of maps, policy analyses, and data visualizations. This series (now published as a "Health in the Watershed Atlas") was designed and intended to inform policy and decision-making at a watershed scale, while retaining relevance to the scope and mandates of provincial, local, and federal jurisdictions. A corresponding series of short, educational summary videos was also created and posted on TikTok. Since their inception, these videos have received thousands of views. As such, they present a unique opportunity to better understand how much media may facilitate science and evidence-communication, as well as, to which audiences, and under which conditions. This chapter examines these dynamics while situating them within a complex array of social, cultural, and political contexts currently shaping the provincial discourses of science in public policy, of expertise "on tap, or on top" and the challenges of linking social, economic, ecological, and water-specific data at the watershed scale. As such, this research is ever evolving in scope and complexity while striving to be novel in function.

Chapter 5: "Exploring the Limitations of Traditional Public Policy Analysis and the Potential of Big Data: A Case Study of Social Media Discourse on the Renewable Fuel Standard" is from Ph.D. candidate Courtney Breckenridge at Southern Illinois University Carbondale and Dr. Nicholas Guehlstorf, Southern Illinois University Edwardsville. This work examines policy discourse around the Renewable Fuel Standard (RFS), which was established through the 2005 *Energy Policy Act* and expanded by the 2007 *Energy Security and Independence Act*. Unlike the other chapters in this book, this study includes a micro-analysis of hand coding and regression analysis performed for a previous study and includes a macro-analysis of machine learning to illustrate how research can learn from itself. This chapter examines policy discourse around the RFS, namely how themes of energy independence, positive environmental impacts, national security, and economic stability for rural communities initially garnered bipartisan support, but, in recent years, have become the subject of intense debate among various stakeholders, including government officials, trade organizations, agricultural interests, and the public. In response to this ongoing policy discourse, stakeholders have increasingly turned to social media platforms to express their support for or objections to the RFS. Kingdon's Multiple Streams Framework (MSF) provides a useful lens for analysis of social media policy discourse, particularly as the RFS has continued despite the end of Congressionally mandated statutory obligations in 2022.

In this chapter, the advocacy and framing of elected officials' discourse on Twitter (X) is compared with additional variables, such as lawmakers' geographical region, political party affiliation, characteristics of their Congressional district, and scorecard rankings generated by interest groups. Machine learning techniques are employed not only to increase the volume of Tweets able to be analyzed but also to increase the study's capacity for analysis. The result enabled the uncovering of new and stronger correlations not identified in earlier work performed with manual coding. This chapter, located in the middle of the book, is the last in which the authors use Twitter (X) as a data source but the first to explain the research trajectory of machine learning and artificial intelligence in social science research. In fact, this chapter exemplifies the journey I have embarked on as the first half of the work uses traditional regression analysis while the end of the scholarship uses unsupervised machine techniques to illustrate the future of natural resources policy research. This nicely sets up the themes of the subsequent chapters of this anthology.

Chapter 6: "Saving Little Jumper: Further Examination of the Effectiveness of Kinship Appeals in Conservation Efforts" is by Drs. David S. Morris and Hector N. Qirko, from the College of Charleston. Morris and Qirko are sociologists, not political scientists, so they come at policy research from a non-traditional perspective. Emerging research provides some evidence that presenting non-human species as related to humans using kin terms and other kinship cues promotes a willingness to contribute to their conservation. However, much is still unknown about who responds to kinship appeals in conservation marketing and why. To address gaps in our understanding of kinship appeals in conservation efforts, Morris and Qirko use survey experiments with a vignette design on a sample of over 1500 respondents. The authors use these data to analyze how variations in the presentation of kinship appeals (e.g., by sex and degree of neoteny and anthropomorphism in portrayals of different species) and variations in audience characteristics when such appeals are made (e.g., attitudes about the environment and political perspectives) are associated with the willingness to support conservation efforts. Unlike traditional surveys, Morris and Qirko are conducting an online experiment with pre- and post-test analysis or responses almost like psychology studies.

Dr. Carolyn Butts-Wilmsmeyer, a biologist and statistical geneticist at Southern Illinois University Edwardsville, has the most methodologically robust contribution in this book. Chapter 7 is titled: "Climate Change and Food Security: The Role of Natural Language Processing and Machine Learning in Automating the Analysis of Social Media Data to Discern Public Opinion of Agriculture's Impact on the Environment." In this chapter, Dr. Butts-Wilmsmeyer argues that the future of agricultural production is inextricably linked to policies, often contained in "Farm Bills," that are designed to mitigate climate change and the impact of agriculture on the environment. While these policies are crafted with the long-term goal of ensuring a sustainable food supply, there is often concern that they may threaten food security in the interim. Conversely, proponents of more progressive climate change mitigative measures have criticized current Farm Bills as doing "too little, too late." Understanding public sentiment of climate change as it relates to agricultural production is imperative to developing effective policies that address both climate change concerns and ensure a stable food supply. With the goal of improved understanding of public sentiment surrounding climate change in general, Reddit released the "Reddit Climate Change Dataset" which contains 262,476 comments that reference agriculture or food security and their relationship with climate change directly. While this comprehensive dataset is exciting and offers substantial insight into public opinion, its size requires the incorporation of natural language processing (NLP) and machine learning (ML) techniques to automate and expedite the analysis of these data. In this chapter, Dr. Butts-Wilmsmeyer presents the use of NLP and ML to identify how ideas and public sentiment surrounding themes of issue framing have changed over time. Furthermore, different ML classification algorithms were compared to determine if NLP and ML can be used to classify social media comments into stakeholder categories, and then subsequently to identify the themes that are of most importance or of greatest concern for each group.

This book may influence scholars to embrace these new processes, research designs, and data by celebrating the variety of contributions to our understanding of environmental politics in what may eventually be identified as an era of data revolution of the twenty-first-century environmental policy. Too many scholars like myself are attempting to define the new era of environmental policy scholarship, while instead we should just be outstanding researchers who conduct and participate in investigations and allow historians to define the epoch. We are 25 years into the twenty-first century and discussions on sustainable development, environmental justice, market-based incentives, and public-private partnerships are as hyperbolic and ubiquitous as ever. The authors in this volume are noteworthy for creating scholarship from novel data sources and pioneering analysis in efforts to identify new typologies. It is my hope that this policy scholarship will be taken seriously by other academics, public administrators, industry leaders, and governmental decisionmakers. As data science and social media becomes more commonplace in academia with the increasing emphasis on digital humanities and artificial intelligence methods, political science and public administration academics must celebrate these innovations.

The final chapter in this book, which is probably the most theoretical, attempts to answer my second question about the relevancy of policy sciences for natural resource managers. Simply, will creative predictions with casual inference have real-world applications and earnestly challenge social science academia? Chap. 8 directly addresses this question but leaves an evolving answer. That is, I think Kalmbach and Ralston are correct in the final chapter of this book, is that making science-based policy is not as simple as "following the science." Policy makers have to grapple with tradeoffs and must recognize that science is only one data point when developing equitable and efficient policy solutions for natural resource problems. This is because scientists need to be aware of the "possibilities and perils when engaging in the political process as well as the limits of the information they provide decision makers" (Chap. 8, pgs. 25–26). The second question of this book might be answered as new scholars address and utilize new data sources but at this juncture regardless of whether the science is derived from traditional techniques, or the innovative techniques covered in this anthology, policy sciences scholarship will continue to be only one element considered when developing policy.

Chapter 8: "The Possibilities and Perils of Research Engagement with Policymakers" is by Dr. Jason Kalmbach, National Coalition of Independent Scholars, and Dr. Jonah Ralston, University of Wisconsin Whitewater. If public policies are intended to remedy public problems, then it is critical that decision-makers understand the root cause(s) of the problem as well as the intended (and unintended) consequences of the interventions available to society. Scientists play a key role in this process through the research they undertake. This research may involve identifying a problem (e.g., an increase in cancer rates), isolating the root cause(s) of the problem (e.g., examining environmental contaminants and their biological connection to the increased cancer rates), and/or exploring the feasibility of solutions by studying similar policy interventions carried out elsewhere. Understanding the scope and extent of a problem is critical for the problem to attract the attention of both the public as well as governmental actors. Multiple Streams Framework conceptualizes experts as a source of information for bureaucrats, but the use of their information is contingent on the opening of a policy window. Elsewhere, newer scholarship has categorized the various roles scientists can play, noting that some scientists take on an advocacy role, trying to pry open a policy window so that their preferred policy is implemented. Throughout this concluding chapter, the authors consider the challenges scientists face when developing and presenting research to decision-makers. An innovative case study is utilized to illustrate an instance when a scientist was able to successfully navigate a solution onto the agenda and before decision-makers for a vote. The chapter concludes by identifying the implications for environmental scientists who are interested in greater engagement with policymakers using non-traditional datasets in their research.

This anthology reveals that many social scientists are utilizing non-traditional data sets from various new sources. These social scientists are exploring a new landscape of data that must be taken seriously. The work presented in this anthology goes far beyond simply recycling old policy theories, models, and typologies with new data from the internet and machine learning methodologies. My conclusion is that social scientists must continue to be more creative with research designs for natural resource management assessments because we must acknowledge that we are not rudimentarily unfolding and rejuvenating tired theories with original data sets. There is increased interest in computational text analysis and interdisciplinary data as this book is one of the first examinations of policy analysis of natural resource management that needs to be sampled and digested. Ideally, this work will act as a catalyst for shifting the paradigm towards innovative environmental policy research using groundbreaking data sources and alternative analytical tools. Quite simply, I hope the featured research in this book will inspire other figurative cooks, like myself, to become chefs. This text is not a cookbook but a sample of daring researchers who are attempting to create something different to be critiqued and further developed.

References

Einstein, J. (2019). *Introduction to natural language processing*. MIT Press.

Grimmer, J., Roberts, M. E., & Stewart, B. M. (2022). *Text as data: A new framework for machine learning and the social sciences*. Princeton University Press.

Guber, L. D., Boher, J., & Dunlap, R. E. (2021). Time to wake up: climate change advocacy in a polarized congress, 1996–2015. *Environmental Politics, 30*(4), 538–558. https://doi.org/10.1080/09644016.2020.1786333

Murphy, K. P. (2021). *Probabilistic machine learning: An introduction*. MIT Press.

Silge, J., & Robinson, R. (2017). *Text mining with R: A tidy approach*. O'Reilley Media.

Chapter 2
Advocacy Coalitions in the 'Twittersphere:' Tracking Variation in Activity in Unconventional Oil and Gas Subsystems

Daniel P. Costie

With the increased role of social media in political discourse, online civic participation is becoming more accessible and more common within democratic political landscapes. The proliferation of social media has catalyzed the process of turning personalized messaging into political participation (Bennett, 2012). Toward political ends, community stakeholders and interest groups use digital technology, such as X (formerly Twitter) and Facebook, to gather relevant information, shape public discourse, and organize online for coordinated action offline. Because traditional decision-making venues are not accessible to many and because of the low cost of engagement, a variety of organizations can use social media as an alternative venue for shaping the policy agenda. A theoretical framework that allows scholars to recognize this pluralism is the Advocacy Coalition Framework (ACF). The ACF argues that like-minded organizations coalesce around shared policy beliefs. These coalitions utilize a variety of venues to advocate and associate, including online venues such as X. Large-scale coordinated strategies employed online are evidenced in the migrant rights movement, Occupy Wall Street, and the Arab Spring (Agarwal et al., 2014; Costanza-Chock, 2008; Steinert-Threlkeld et al., 2015).

Because of social networking sites, a large, diverse set of policy actors, theoretically, are able to participate because of the low cost of entry. Political organizations, both large and small, are active in these online discursive venues, representing a diverse set of interests and policy preferences. Its ubiquity results in a discourse composed of policy actors with notoriety and resources, intermixing with those with fewer resources, who have been traditionally left out of the 'conversation.' Exactly which policy actors are active in these venues is less clear and is the objective of this work.

D. P. Costie (✉)
Eastern Oregon University, La Grande, OR, USA
e-mail: dcostie@eou.edu

N. Guehlstorf (ed.), *Environmental Policy Science's Exploration for Innovative Data*, Natural Resource Management and Policy NA,
https://doi.org/10.1007/978-3-031-90889-7_2

Salient events can impact the make-up of coalitions by intensifying conflict, shifting social constructions, or changing the priorities set out on the policy agenda. One type of such events are major policy changes. These are events that dramatically impact a central practice or feature within a policy domain, or as policy process scholars refer to it, the 'policy subsystem.' These major policy changes can lead to an entirely new political equilibrium when it significantly redistributes costs and benefits to different interests. In the face of a major policy change, it is unclear how coalitions will change their strategy. Schattschneider (1975) argues that the losing coalition will work to expand the issue while the winning coalition will work to restrict mobilization. However, in online discursive venues where the cost of participation is low, it is reasonable that both coalitions would be incentivized to expand the issue, leading up to an anticipated policy change. This expectation would lead scholars to believe that there would be a major increase in online activity leading up to a major policy change. This work poses the following question: Which policy actors influencing the policy process offline are active via X and how does participation change after a major policy change?

Through this analysis, I find that a significant portion of pro- and anti-unconventional oil and gas development (more colloquially referred to as hydraulic fracturing or 'fracking') coalition members, as well as many unaffiliated actors, are active on X and that they represent a variety of interests. Organizational affiliation is found to be strongly associated with policy position. Also, while many policy actors were identified, a small few contributed a very large share of the tweets. Lastly, participation did not increase leading up to a major policy change and both coalitions' activity decreased significantly over the two years following the policy change.

This work will begin by discussing how advocacy coalitions have been traditionally studied. It will then explore the role that major policy change plays in discursive political strategy and how they may expand or constrain mobilization around a policy issue. Next, I will provide relevant background information on the policy subsystem in New York. The Chapter will conclude with the presentation of results, interpretation of key findings, the limitations of my work, the contributions this study made towards a better understanding of online coalition participation, and some potential avenues to build off this research.

Tracking Participation Through Advocacy Coalitions

The Advocacy Coalition Framework (ACF) is an analytical approach used to understand how politics inform public policies (and vice versa). More traditional approaches focus on the iron triangle: the dynamics within and between legislatures, the executive branch, and special interests (Hayden, 2002). Past research tends to overlook the complexity of the policy process by only focusing on formal governing institutions (e.g., a single government decision-making venue) while the ACF recognizes the value in incorporating a more diverse set of actors. Similar to scholarship observing 'issue networks' (Heclo, 1978) and 'policy communities' (Guber & Bosso, 2013), the study of advocacy coalitions seeks to broaden the aforementioned iron triangle by asserting that actors outside of the US Congress, resource-rich interest groups, and the bureaucracy can be relevant. Furthermore, scholars must endeavor to study the motivations of a broader set of actors, how they coordinate action (through the formation of advocacy coalitions), what strategies they employ and the spaces they engage to influence policy outcomes (Ingold, 2011; Jenkins-Smith et al., 1991; Matti & Sandström, 2011; Sabatier, 1988).

The ACF recognizes that meaningful action influencing the policy process involves the actions of individuals but is most often conducted when affiliated with an organization embedded within an advocacy coalition. The ACF also argues that participation manifests through a variety of practices and tactics and cannot be simply reduced to citizens voting for elected officials and elected officials voting for policy. Political and civic participation is exercised in a variety of ways by a variety of policy actors, with a diverse set of values and incentives. This is a central attribute of pluralist, western democracies and is evidenced through activities such as donating to a cause, door knocking for an elected official, providing testimony to a legislative committee, or expressing policy preferences on one's social media page. Smith (1984) calls this public participation and defines it as 'any action taken by an interested public (individual or group) to influence a decision, plan, or policy beyond that of voting in elections.'

In the scholarship, it is largely assumed that participation is positively correlated with increased social benefits and thus implicitly or explicitly championed by policy scholars. Undergirding such normative assumptions are several rationales for why participation should be encouraged. First, decision-makers are not experts in a variety of issues that are within their purview to govern and thus need specialized information from experts (May et al., 2016). Second, there is an additional assumption that inclusive decision-making is a core democratic practice that must be relentlessly championed. Third, the only way to match problems with effective solutions, especially for problems acutely impacting those traditionally written out of the decision-making process, is to empower local organizations and encourage civic engagement to more effectively advocate for local interests (Fung, 2008).

Those rationales inform the objectives of political participation. These objectives include information sharing, involving the community in decision-making, taking community aspirations into consideration, accessing local knowledge, broadening the range of potential solutions, avoiding litigation, enabling sustainability, strengthening individual and community empowerment, among others (Momtaz & Gladstone, 2008; Stewart & Sinclair, 2007). Objectives related to the transmission of information are particularly relevant to studies of participation because a basic level of knowledge is a prerequisite to engage in collective action through coalitions and employ aligned discursive strategies.

Low cost of access attracts many groups to online activism, especially for those left out of formal decision-making processes. As most social networking sites (SNS) do not charge for basic membership, many minority voices are finding their way into the collective discourse, which often gets transmitted to other platforms. These voices can compete with the messaging of similar resource-rich allies as well as their political opponents. X, particularly, allows traditionally excluded groups to engage in political discourse like few discursive venues have. O'Faircheallaigh (2010) argues that broadening the discourse to allow the participation of such groups is important for policymaking as it provides an alternative set of information that can contest established convention and interpretation of the policy process. Traditional studies of advocacy coalitions have not used SNS to build a better understanding of what constitutes a coalition and thus likely misses key policy actors in the subsystem.

In addition, if traditional sources of information provided to policymakers have been co-opted by one coalition to the exclusion of others, there is little push back should the information be used to obfuscate or exaggerate key facts surrounding a policy conflict. For instance, if local and state policymakers are learning about problems related to unconventional oil and gas development, and potential policy solutions are all championed by industry and pro-oil and gas interest groups, the discourse will be disproportionately constructed through the lens of their priorities. Environmental groups, if given the opportunity, would likely pursue alternative sources and types of information and would likely interpret findings differently.

Issue Expansion and Containment in an Adversarial Subsystem

The space within which these policy actors interact is called the policy subsystem. A policy subsystem is a semi-autonomous network of policy actors, confined by the policy topic and geographic area in which the policy actors make decisions (Jenkins-Smith et al., 1991; Sabatier, 1987). Adversarial subsystems are characterized by a high degree of policy belief divergence and a very narrow set of available policy solutions. Because there is little room for compromise in these settings, coalitions compete over how to frame the issue (Weible & Sabatier, 2009). It is assumed that as these coalitions compete, they will take on strategies of conflict expansion and containment. Schattschneider (1975) argues that different groups will engage the subsystem differently depending on their position within the subsystem as either the 'winning' or 'losing' coalition at any given point in time. The winning coalition will be incentivized to contain the issue by mobilizing their existing constituency but uninclined to advance that support beyond its current base. The losing, or minority, coalition has the opposite incentive. They will want to expand the issue to mobilize interested but unaffiliated policy actors and to energize latent coalition members (Olofsson, 2022). Issue expansion involves changing or diversifying symbols, imagery, and discursive framing to appeal to a large set of stakeholders.

However, the ease with which social media allows coalition members to engage their allies and supporters and shape the policy agenda may have changed the incentive structure of winning coalitions. Typically, such coalitions work to maintain and not expand their base. This is a calculated move; the result of putting their limited and valuable time and energy into strategies that have already proven to be successful. However, compared to other similar forms of discursive strategies, participation in these online venues is a low-cost endeavor, relative to the potential benefits attributed to impacting the subsystem discourse. It is expected that leading up to an anticipated major policy change, both coalitions would increase their participation to mobilize their supporters and attract potential members to their mission.

Impact of Major Policy Change on Participation

Advocacy coalitions tend to be stable through a combination of entrenched institutional forces (such as rules and norms), especially when there is a dominant coalition with resource superiority and control over subsystem politics (Sabatier, 1991; Sabatier & Weible, 2016). However, instability can manifest after a major policy change as such changes often favor one coalition over another, altering resource distribution by providing a favored coalition with, among other things, new legal authorities, new streams of financial resources, or access to types of political venues not available to the coalition before (Costie et al., 2018).

Major policy changes may take time to reshape the political arena but often immediate changes in coalition activity are evidenced if the impending policy is anticipated and if the losing coalition organizes in response. How large of a shift is unclear and likely context dependent. What we do know is that salient events give significant advantage to groups who can mobilize around a policy change, but sustained influence is not a certainty. The window of exploitation is short lived unless skilled actors, such as policy entrepreneurs, create smart strategies to amplify their message (Downs, 1972; Heikkila et al., 2014). After a short period of time, the salience of the issue dies down as actors no longer want to invest further resources when they see no movement has been made. It is also impacted by the fact that attention is limited and often divided amongst many issues (Jones & Baumgartner, 2012). This will frequently translate into instability, especially within the coalition, as activity and coordination will temporarily heighten due to increases in issue salience but will die down soon after.

While short term instability is possible, there are also instances where a major policy change ushers in a new 'normal' as changes to institutional rules and norms indefinitely shift access to resources. Policies can in and of themselves create shifts whereby the mandates included in a policy influences political arrangements in the subsystem through a policy feedback loop (Pierson, 1993). If the new distribution of resources is too uneven and it proves too costly for policy actors to use coalitions to pursue their interests, the coalition may significantly weaken or may even dissolve. The winning coalition may also reduce their activity if the weakening of a competing coalition is coupled with a decrease in the intensity of conflict that characterizes the subsystem. If there is no organized competition, there is less incentive to mobilize. While this work holds the expectation that strategies of issue expansion will occur before a major policy change, it is unclear if this increase will be sustained over time. This chapter represents exploratory research aimed at observing how a major policy change influences the long-term participation of the coalitions.

Unconventional Oil and Gas Development in New York

Hydraulic fracturing, often associated with horizontal drilling, refers to a completion technique that injects high pressure liquid into a rock formation until it fractures (Cook et al., 2018). Due to technological innovation, high global energy prices, and a desire to increase national energy independence, these formerly off-limits shale beds have become accessible and economical (Finkel & Hays, 2013). With the increased use of hydraulic fracturing, the United States has been the world's top producer of oil and gas since 2009 (Cook et al., 2018).

In New York, influence of policy actors and impacted areas are not distributed evenly. Eighty-four trillion cubic feet of natural gas can be found in the western region of the state called the Southern Tier (Esch, 2012). At the turn of the century, there was a lot of enthusiasm around the prospect of unconventional oil and gas development, particularly in the economically deprived western region. The shale boom was expected to bring in 54,000 jobs and increase state and local revenues by \$32–126 million (Arnold & Neupane, 2017). By 2003, land leases to oil and gas companies were being signed (Dodge & Jeongyoon, 2017).

The promise of extraction would prove to be short lived. Governor Paterson imposed a moratorium on unconventional oil and gas development in 2008. After 2008, there was a significant increase in policies and resolutions related to unconventional oil and gas development at the local level and at least 200 anti-unconventional oil and gas development groups were formed (Arnold et al., 2017). In December of 2014, that was followed up with a total ban on unconventional oil and gas development in New York, making the state only one of two to have banned it (Sabatier & Weible, 2016). Unconventional oil and gas development had been one of the most divisive issues in New York politics in years. While conflict may be high, it is clear that institutional support and mobilization of anti-unconventional oil and gas interests are behind the most significant policy change around unconventional oil and gas in United States history and is the major policy change under observation.

Methods and Research Design

Source This research studies the composition of coalition members in a discursive venue, the frequency of their participation, and how that participation changes over time. X will represent the discursive venue and coalition member tweets will be the primary data source for this work. According to X's website, their priorities are to protect security and privacy as well as ensure civic integrity (Twitter, n.d.).[1] As of 2023, X self-reported 540 million users worldwide (Al Jazeera, 2023). Studies of X data have found that there is variation in user behavior and connectivity across social media sites. X is used frequently to share information on what is in the news. Kwak et al.'s (2010) study found that over 85% of topics are about headline or 'persistent' news. In addition, connectivity on Facebook has a stronger association with one's smaller off-line social network. On X, users 'follow' what Buccafurri et al. (2015) refer to as 'power users:' influential individuals that have many more followers the average user. Because of this, information is more easily accessible for people outside of one's off-line network on X than on Facebook. Lastly, the data are discursive in nature but utilize a variety of communication tools such as 'Mentions,' 'Likes,' and 'Retweets.'

Case Selection The unconventional oil and gas subsystem of New York will be the focus of this study. Following Seawright and Gerring (2008)'s Purposive Case Selection method, I am interested in focusing on an 'extreme' case; cases that are unusual or special, assessed by variation in the independent variable. The extreme characteristic (and independent variable) related to my research question is a major policy change. In New York, the policy process led to an outright ban of hydraulic fracturing. In this respect, the case study represents participation within an adversarial subsystem; with the 'extreme' case resulting in an outright ban of the subsystem's central practice and resulting in a clear losing coalition. In line with the aforementioned scholars, such an approach is exploratory in nature: to understand how an extreme treatment impacts coalition member participation over the long term.

Data Collection Data collection occurred in three steps. The first step involved identifying the sample frame. I identified policy actors *a priori* using the results of a sampling process conducted by the Workshop on Policy Process Research (WOPPR) at the University of Colorado Denver in 2017. WOPPR is a research lab focused on using diverse theoretical lenses and methodological approaches to understand how public policy is designed and implemented. The purpose of one project was to capture and analyze actors who were actively involved or knowledgeable about unconventional oil and gas development in New York. Through a purposive sampling approach based on evidence in media reports, online reports, public hearings, testimony and recommendations from interviews, 379 policy actors were identified in New York (Heikkila & Weible, 2015; Heikkila et al., 2017; Pierce, 2013). Those identified policy actors were used as the preliminary sample. During this step, both individuals and organizations were captured.

[1] This mission has changed from the original mission of 'to give everyone the power to create and share ideas and information instantly, without barriers'.

During the second step, I cross referenced those individuals and organizations to identify which of those policy actors had active X accounts.[2] Of the 379, 94 accounts were identified.[3] The last step utilized programming software created by a computer programmer at University of Colorado Denver to 'call up' tweets from X's Application Programming Interface based on a set of parameters. The X 'handles' of the 94 policy actors were then paired with keywords 'hydraulic fracturing,' 'unconventional oil and gas development,' 'unconventional oil and gas,' 'shale gas,' 'shale oil,' 'unconventional oil,' 'unconventional gas,' and 'stimulation.' Keywords were selected based on the most common ways in which hydraulic fracturing is discussed in the news media and referenced in scientific reports. The queries then collected all tweets with the aforementioned keywords made by the identified X accounts from 2009 to 2016.[4]

Measurement The unit of observation and analysis are tweets of coalition members (representing organizations) in the unconventional oil and gas subsystem of New York. Recognizing that not all those who tweet about this topic are policy actors, I limit my observations to those identified through the WOPPR survey design described above. Coalition members were further organized by their organizational affiliation. Organizational affiliations were determined by following the link provided on the organization's X page or their organization's web page.[5] Aggregating by this attribute and not capturing individuals within the organization is more valuable because organizational affiliation enables individuals to overcome constraints on their time and resources, project legitimacy, and are more likely to be used to engage a discursive venue (Weible & Ingold, 2018). Organization by affiliation also works as a proxy for capturing group interests and their missions. The categories were created *a priori* as *academics and consultants*, *organized citizen groups*, *environmental organizations*, *community-based organizations*, *formal alliances*, *industry*, *business and trade associations*, *media organizations*, and *public agencies and legislators*. See Table 2.1 for conceptual definitions of these categories.

---

[2] Individuals and organizations can have inactive or 'zombie' X accounts that are either unattended or not used to post Tweets. Those accounts are excluded from this work.

[3] In the original 'snowball' approach, individuals that worked at the same organization were separated out. Because this study is more interested in the organizational affiliation of policy actors on X, those individuals were aggregated into a singular policy actor. Actors without an organizational affiliation were omitted.

[4] This work focuses on a seven-year period (or smaller increments therein) around the major policy change. This covers the time period 2009–2016. While I recognize that policy actors 'come and go' from the subsystem, it is a reasonable assumption to make that those identified in the survey during 2017 in New York would also be present from 2012 to 2016. Their activity is not assumed but rather evidenced in their frequency of tweets that included content about unconventional oil and gas.

[5] If their X page did not reveal their organizational affiliation, the link they provide to their home page was used. These pages often led to an 'about us' page where their services were used to make an organizational determination.

Table 2.1 Organizational affiliation definitions

Organizational affiliation	Definition	Examples
Academics and consultants	Organizations that provide scientific and technical support to other coalition members. They include universities, research institutes, law firms, and public relation firms	Cornell University; Center for Natural Resources Development and Protection; Institute for Energy Research
Organized citizen groups	Grass-roots organizations directed at a specific problem. Organizations building local support among 'concerned citizens' populate this category	Working Families Party; CREDO Action; Frack Action
Environmental organizations	Organizations whose primary mission is environmental protection	The Nature Conservancy in NY; Natural Resources Defense Council; Earthworks
Community-based organizations	Organizations that advocate for an issue or community but prioritize non-environmental issues. They may advocate for a pro-environment agenda in so far as it aligns with a broader set of issues or represents the interests of a constituency such as labor or criminal justice	Slow Food NYC; Center for Health, Environment, and Justice; Brooklyn for Peace
Formal alliances	Organizations that collectively work together on a common agenda. These entities tend to have the word 'coalition' or 'alliance' in their title	New Yorkers Against Fracking; Stop the Frack Attack; Citizens' Environmental Coalition
Industry	Organizations that are direct service providers related to the exploitation of unconventional oil and gas through hydraulic fracturing	Chevron; Chesapeake Energy Corp.; Marcellus Shale Coalition
Business and trade associations	Organizations that represent collective interests of individual companies and are composed of a much narrower cross-section of economic interests and tend to have interests aligned with the oil and gas industry	American Petroleum Institute; Independent Petroleum Association of America; Business Council of New York State, Inc.
Media organizations	Journalism outlets discussing some aspect of unconventional oil and gas	ProPublica; New York Times; Times Union
Public agencies and legislators	Government bodies at the local, state, and Federal level	US Geological Survey; Senator Gillibrand; NY Governor's office

Coalition membership was measured by identifying a policy position in the content of an original post within two years of the major policy change or by evaluating their mission statement on their website as of August of 2019.[6] It is assumed that policy core beliefs such as support or opposition to unconventional oil and gas are relatively stable. Because of this, one instance of a policy position was sufficient to

[6] Retweets and Likes were not used to identify policy position. An original tweet is a post on X that came directly from the primary source.

determine coalition membership. Policy actors were coded as pro-, anti-, or unaffiliated based on their policy position related to unconventional oil and gas development, also referred to as hydraulic fracturing or 'fracking.' Unaffiliated policy actors were those that did not express support or opposition to the practice.

A 'pro-coalition' member would be coded if the actor expresses in a tweet that they were supportive of unconventional oil and gas development. A supportive tweet can come in the form of stating that the actor wants to see unconventional oil and gas continued or expanded. It could also be through their professed actions. Supportive actions can be identified if the policy actors talk about engaging in drilling or unconventional oil and gas wells, investing in unconventional oil and gas businesses, collaborating with the oil and gas industry on researching unconventional oil and gas technologies, exploring a shale formation, or taking political actions that represent support (e.g. testifying in a public hearing that unconventional oil and gas is beneficial, safe, or 'good' in some way), etc.

The 'anti-coalition' policy position would be coded if the actor expresses in the tweet that they are in opposition to the level of unconventional oil and gas development, want to see the practice ended entirely, or if the tweet describes the actor's actions in a way that makes it clear that the actor is opposed. For example, an 'opposing' tweet could come in the form of stating that no more wells should be drilled, or they support an end to fracking. Opposing 'actions' would be identified if the author talks about attempts to stop or limit unconventional oil and gas such as protesting at a public event, by testifying before Congress on problems related to unconventional oil and gas or talking about collaborating with other organizations.

Results

The composition of coalition members in the New York subsystem is illustrated by Fig. 2.1. It shows early indications of coalition activity occurring on X. Ninety-four coalition members are captured in the New York subsystem. Looking at participation across the lifespan of this venue, the anti-coalitions have more members than the pro-coalition. In addition to identifying two coalitions, this research also finds strong representation of unaffiliated actors; those that participate in the discourse but do not take a clear policy position. Unaffiliated policy actors are more common in the New York subsystem than the pro-coalition.

Policy position was strongly aligned with organizational affiliation. Organized citizen groups and environmental organizations are the most active types of organizations. These organizations only expressed neutral or anti-unconventional oil and gas development sentiments. A similar trend was identified in the pro-coalition. Industry and business/trade associations exclusively expressed neutral or pro-development rhetoric. Academics and consultants make up the vast majority of unaffiliated policy actors. While academics and consultants did not exclusively author neutral tweets, the vast majority did not take a policy position.

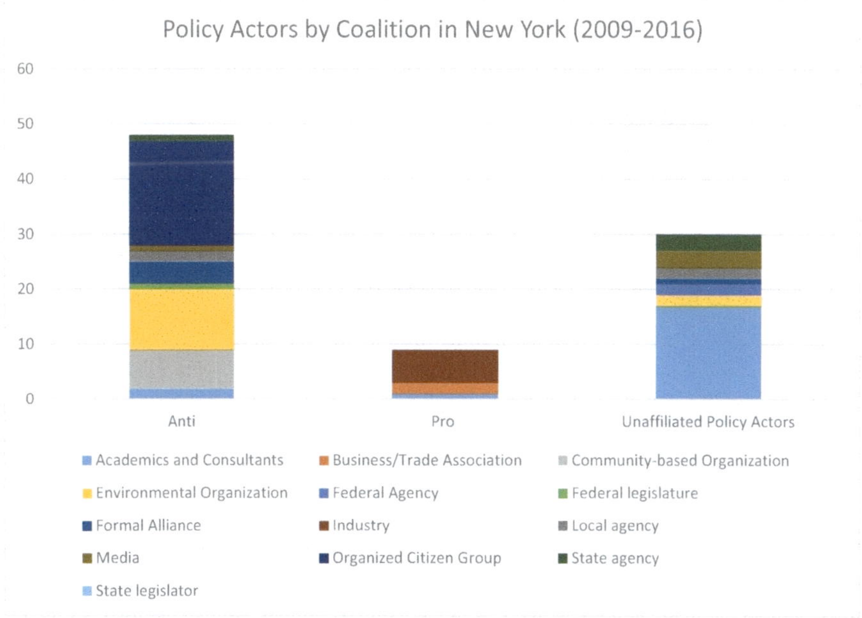

Fig. 2.1 Policy actors on X

Figure 2.2 provides a snapshot of overall activity. In total, the anti-coalition in New York subsystem had significantly more activity than the pro-coalition.[7] Environmental organizations and business and trade associations are by far the most prolific 'tweeters' in their respective coalition. While unaffiliated actors were identified in the subsystem, their activity is much lower than either the anti- or pro-coalitions.

Table 2.2 provides the most active coalition members in the New York subsystem. Of all total tweets by all identified actors, these 10 organizations make up 48% of activity. Members of the anti-coalition are represented by all but one organization (American Petroleum Institute) listed in Table 2.2. Among the most active coalition members, those representing environmental organizations and business and trade associations dominate the conversation on X. Looking closer at the most prolific individual policy actors, two names emerge: Earthworks and American Petroleum Institute. Earthworks is a 501(c)3 non-profit that works with communities and grass roots groups to reform government policies to discourage mining and oil and gas development. Their mission is to protect 'communities and the environment from the adverse impacts of mineral and energy development while promoting sustainable solutions' (Earthworks, 2024). American Petroleum Institute (API) is a national trade association that represents both up- and down-stream oil and gas development. Their mission is 'to promote safety across the industry globally and to influence

[7] Both 'tweets' and 'retweets' are included in this total.

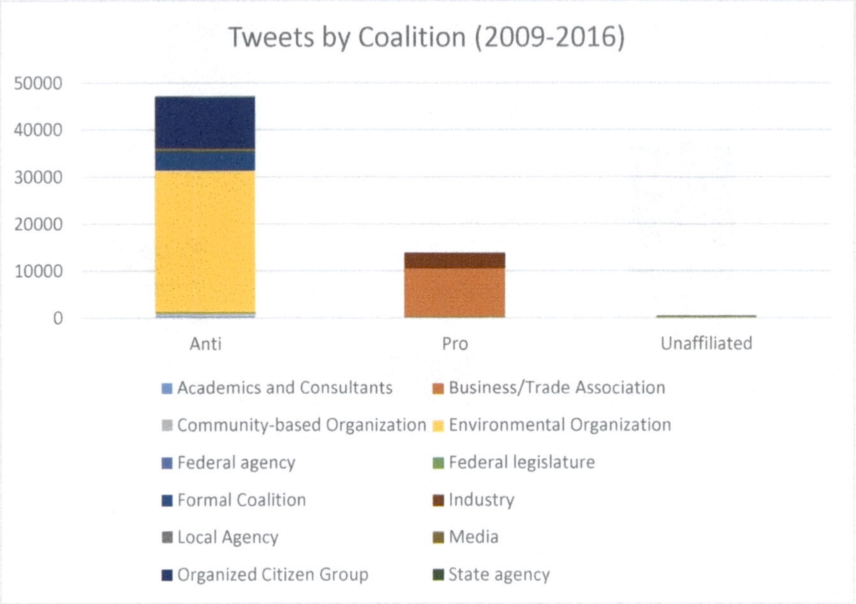

Fig. 2.2 Tweets by coalition membership

Table 2.2 Top tweeters in the New York subsystem

New York (2009–2016)		
Organization name	Organizational affiliation	# of tweets
1. Earthworks.	Environmental organization	20,376
2. American Petroleum Institute.	Business/trade association	9123
3. Frack Action.	Organized citizen group	4132
4. Marcellus Shale Coalition.	Industry	2625
5. Food & Water Watch.	Environmental organization	2387
6. New Yorkers Against Fracking.	Formal alliance	2356
7. Environmental Advocates of NY.	Environmental organization	2000
8. Chefs for the Marcellus.	Organized citizen group	1890
9. Stop the Frack Attack.	Formal alliance	1672
10. Earthjustice.	Environmental organization	1555
	Total	48,116

public policy in support of a strong viable US oil and natural gas industry.' API works to influence policy change on behalf of the oil and gas industry in the United States (American Petroleum Institute, 2024). Frack Action is the third most active organization on X. Their mission is 'to protect our water, air, and public health from the dangerous practice of gas drilling and fracking.' Frack Action is a 501(c) 3 organization that works with partner organizations to conduct awareness campaigns around the aforementioned practices (Frack Action, 2023). All of the aforementioned organizations demonstrate that their online activity is complemented by offline activity within the subsystem.

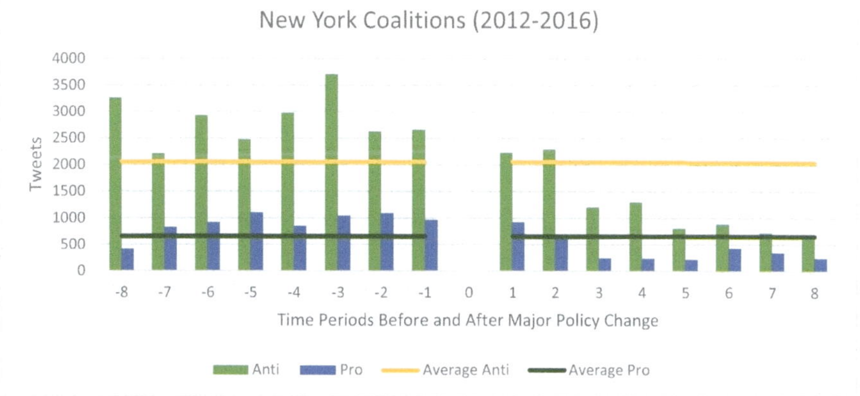

Fig. 2.3 Participation over four years (2012–2016)

Lastly, I wanted to 'zoom in' and analyze frequency of tweets over a four-year period. Figure 2.3 shows tweets captured between December 17th, 2012 and December 16th, 2016, broken down into three-month increments. Periods '−8' to '−1' each represent 3-month periods over the two years leading up to the major policy change. Periods '1' to '8' each represent 3-month periods over the two years following the major policy change. Figure 2.3 also displays the average number of tweets over the four-year period for both coalitions. The dark green line represents the average number of tweets for the pro-coalition in three month increments over the four years surrounding the policy change. The yellow line represents the average number of tweets for the anti-coalition in three month increments over the four years surrounding the policy change. In both subsystems, there is a steady reduction in activity over time. Over this four-year time span, the anti-coalition tweets an average of 2063 tweets every three months. The pro-coalition tweets an average of 657 times during that same period. The analysis also shows that several time periods pass before the number of tweets begin to deviate significantly from the mean. For the anti-coalition, we see that after period two (June 16th, 2015), there was a dramatic shift away from the average.

Discussion

This work sought to explore which coalition members were using X as a discursive venue and how that changed over time. Several important findings were identified in this analysis. First, many policy actors that are influential in the subsystem were also engaging on X, with more anti-members participating than pro-members. This composition may be due to the low cost of participation through social networking sites such as X. The presence of unaffiliated policy actors contributing to the discourse may indicate that the subsystem includes policy actors playing the roles of policy entrepreneurs and brokers. These parties work to mitigate conflict, to find compromise, and share information (Weible et al., 2020).

Second, while a great variety of interests were represented in the data, organizational affiliation is found to be associated with policy position. Environmental groups and community organizations are exclusively anti-unconventional oil and gas. Industry and business and trade associations are exclusively pro-unconventional oil and gas. Also, a large share of tweets are the contributions of a much narrower set of coalition members. The discursive dominance of Earthworks and API in both subsystems, along with their stated missions to impact policy, indicate that national level organizations are attempting to utilize X for diametrically opposed policy positions at the state and local levels. What is also noteworthy is that the industry at the heart of this subsystem is relatively inactive. The presence of business and trade associations, in the absence of industry, may speak to a broader strategy among pro-coalition of centralizing lobbying and advocacy work within organizations with more explicitly political functions.

Third, testing the basic assumption of issue expansion that informs how the ACF understands the ebb and flow of political discourse, I must reject the notion that strategies of online discursive venues reflect the desire or ability of interested parties to expand the issue in this context. I find no evidence that there is a significant increase in participation immediately before the policy change. Only a small increase in participation is observed leading up to the ban in New York on December 16th, 2014, by any coalition. This may be a result of an effective ban in the form of a moratorium or the reactionary nature of participation on X. The subsystem, however, does experience a major spike in the week *after* the policy change. This indicates that participation in this instance is not proactive as had been presumed. In other words, the foreknowledge of an internal shock does not influence frequency of participation in the lead up to the event. This is particularly interesting as almost 20% of tweets prior to the policy change include the word 'ban.' The coalitions may not have been strategizing to expand the issue as the ACF would expect. For the pro-coalition, this is particularly unexpected and may be evidence of a coalition that is not trying to expand the issue beforehand but may have directed their attention to venues in other jurisdictions where they have a greater likelihood of advancing their interests.

Lastly, over the long term, the policy change would have a long-term impact on the overall activity of all coalitions in both subsystems. While a lagged response to the ban is identified over three-month increments, the frequency of participation never reaches pre-policy change levels, and it rarely hits the mean of participation over the four-year period. This finding is evidence that the ban had created a new 'normal,' at least within this discursive venue. This lends some credence to the idea that a major policy change can impact the distribution of authority and resources so extraordinarily that both coalitions will participate at dramatically less as the losing coalition is significantly weakened and the winning coalition no longer has to compete as vigorously.

Conclusion

While this exploratory work offers insight into activity and coalition composition on social networking sites, there are several noteworthy limitations. One limitation of this research is the extent to which social media reflects meaningful association and coordination. Information transfer amongst policy actors may be overstated. One lingering weakness of the ACF is its inability to draw the line between what is meaningful coordination and what is not. More explicit and visible displays of collective action are easily identified but there are many other behaviors of successful coalitions that are not as easy to measure. However, as more and more people shift their civic engagement to online platforms, the more likely that those associations will manifest into real changes to the policy agenda vis-à-vis shifts in public opinion.

A second limitation is that this analysis grouped organizations by a single policy core belief. This meets the operational standard of the ACF, but it does not recognize the more nuanced positions actors hold or the complexity of decision-making that comes with 'layering' policy positions onto each other. This means that we are making assumptions about the degree to which unconventional oil and gas or the regulation of unconventional oil and gas would be tolerated by the various coalition members involved. I do not expect secondary beliefs to be uniform across all members, however, these groups have taken a firm stance and are much more likely to coordinate with those holding the same firm stance, and thus can be organized accordingly.

A final limitation relates to the impact of exogenous factors on changes observed. An external factor that could have played a role in the major reduction in activity after the policy change is dynamics of the energy market more broadly. Between 2014 and 2015, the price of a barrel of oil dropped from 87.39 USD to 44.39 USD (Bruel, 2016). With such low prices, hydraulic fracturing had become less economically tenable in many parts of the country. Fewer wells were being drilled and the conflicts associated with such development may be neutered for the time. Such changes could have reduced salience of the issue. However, drilled wells continue to be active, and the domestic production of crude oil has grown significantly since 2016 (U.S. Energy Information Administration, 2024). This has placed more pressure on the domestic energy sector to explore unconventional oil and gas even further.

This work contributes to a more comprehensive understanding of the policy process in a variety of ways. First, I am looking at discursive strategies employed through a commonly overlooked alternative venue of the policy process: social networking sites. Strategies in discursive online venues are likely different than those captured in news media. As venues differ by rules of access and participation, it is not surprising that a different composition of interests is represented via X than is through news media. While in this research we see a great deal of community-led organizations and environmental organizations, this representation is not reflected in newspapers. Past scholarship observing newspapers have found strong representation of pro-coalitions and industry actors and little representation of anti-coalitions and NGOs (Olofsson et al., 2018; Heikkila et al., 2019). By only analyzing social media or news media, one would come away with a different understanding of the coalitional composition of these subsystems. This research works to demonstrate that smaller, less known organizations who are not included in more conventional venues are finding a platform to participate in the conversation and advance their policy agenda.

Second, it provides additional insight into how the ACF should conceptualize a policy subsystem. While all politics may be local, those politics can be strategically used across subsystems, blurring the boundaries between them. National players such as the American Petroleum Institute and Earthworks have influence in discursive venues even if they are not ones with local knowledge or 'boots on the ground.' Discursive venues like X allow for events in different geographic locations relevant to policy actors in the New York subsystem to be distributed through the coalition's network. While the adage that 'all politics are local' is still true, it is often being recontextualized and used strategically in different subsystems. Jones and Jenkins-Smith (2009) refer to the 'permeable' nature of subsystems and offers the term 'trans-subsystem' to highlight the interrelationships among similar subsystems. As the use of the internet increases, the physical boundaries separating subsystems may need to be rethought or perhaps rejected entirely.

Thirdly, this study was only made possible due to the relatively accessible data that Twitter had provided. Under the leadership of Elon Musk, X has significantly restricted access to social media content as analyzable data. In February of 2023, Twitter informed the world that it would no longer offer academics free access to the programming interface which had been the standard data collection method for scholars. Twitter, once a platform that offered public interest researchers reasonable access to its data, has erected monetary barriers functionally inhibiting a research design such as this in the future. This lack of access (and the potential for litigation against data analysts) makes the dataset that informs this research even more valuable to those interested in understanding online political discourse (Dang, 2023).

This research represents the first step in a broader research agenda to better understand how political discourse is used as collective action strategies in alternative policy venues. Lasswell (1956) argues that the purpose of studying the policy process is to improve democracy. In order to do that, we need to identify better, more efficient, and more innovative ways to include a broader range of interests in the policy process. Social media platforms have historically facilitated inclusion and will likely continue to grow in popularity. Still, more work needs to be done to have a better understanding of the relationship between conflict and inclusion and how online discursive venues demonstrate promise at bringing attention to disenfranchised voices so that their interests can be represented through policy. Next steps in this research portfolio are to understand how political frames are used in the subsystem and how coalition members construct their social networks online.

References

Agarwal, S. D., Lance Bennett, W., Johnson, C. N., & Walker, S. (2014). A model of crowd-enabled organization: Theory and methods for understanding the role of Twitter in the occupy protests. *International Journal of Communication, 8*(1), 646–672. https://ijoc.org/index.php/ijoc/article/view/2068/1091

Al Jazeera. (2023, August 16). *Musk says X monthly users reach "new high"*. Retrieved from https://www.aljazeera.com/economy/2023/7/28/musk-says-x-monthly-users-reach-new-high

American Petroleum Institute. (2024). *About API*. https://www.api.org/about

Arnold, G., & Neupane, K. W. (2017). Determinants of pro-Fracking measure adoption by New York Southern Tier Municipalities. *Review of Policy Research, 34*(2), 208–232. https://doi.org/10.1111/ropr.12212

Arnold, G., Nguyen Long, L. A., & Gottlieb, M. (2017). Social networks and policy entrepreneurship. How relationships shape municipal decision making about high-volume hydraulic fracturing. *Policy Studies Journal, 45*(3), 414–441. https://doi.org/10.1111/psj.12175

Bennett, W. L. (2012). The personalization of politics: Political identity, social media, and changing patterns of participation. *Annals of the American Academy of Political and Social Science, 644*(1), 20–39. https://doi.org/10.1177/0002716212451428

Bruel, H. (2016, January 6). *Crude oil prices started 2015 relatively low, ended the year lower*. U.S. Energy Information Administration. https://www.eia.gov/todayinenergy/detail.php?id=24432.

Buccafurri, F., Lax, G., Nicolazzo, S., & Nocera, A. (2015). Comparing Twitter and Facebook user behavior: Privacy and other aspects. *Computers in Human Behavior, 52*, 87–95. https://doi.org/10.1016/j.chb.2015.05.045

Cook, T., Perrin, J., Van Wagener, D. (2018, January 30). *Hydraulic fractured horizontal wells account for most new oil and natural gas wells*. U.S. Energy Information Administration https://www.eia.gov/todayinenergy/detail.php?id=34732

Costanza-Chock, S. (2008). The immigrant rights movement on the net: Between 'Web 2.0' and comunicación popular. *American Quarterly, 60*(3), 851–864. https://doi.org/10.1353/aq.0.0029

Costie, D. P., Holm, F., & Berardo, R. (2018). Hydraulic fracturing, coalition activity and shock: Assessing the potential for coalition-based collective action in Argentina's Vaca Muerta formation. *The Extractive Industries and Society, 5*(4), 499–507. https://doi.org/10.1016/j.exis.2018.08.003

Dang, S. (2023, November 6). *Exclusive: Elon Musk's X restructuring curtails disinformation research, Spurs legal fears*. Reuters. https://www.reuters.com/technology/elon-musks-x-restructuring-curtails-disinformation-research-spurs-legal-fears-2023-11-06/

Dodge, J., & Jeongyoon, L. (2017). Framing dynamics and political gridlock: The curious case of hydraulic fracturing in New York. *Journal of Environmental Policy and Planning, 19*(1), 14–34. https://doi.org/10.1080/1523908X.2015.1116378

Downs, A. (1972). Up and down with ecology-the issue-attention cycle. *Public Interest, 28*(Summer), 38.

Earthworks. (2024). *What we do*. https://earthworks.org/what-we-do/

Esch, M. (2012, May 13). Gas Drillers Wrangle over New York limitations, Bans. *Akron Beacon Journal*. https://www.beaconjournal.com/story/news/nation-world/2012/05/13/gas-drillers-wrangle-over-n/10649662007/

Finkel, M. L., & Hays, J. (2013). The implications of unconventional drilling for natural gas: A global public health concern. *Public Health, 127*(10), 889–893. https://doi.org/10.1016/j.puhe.2013.07.005

Frack Action. (2023). *About*. https://www.frackaction.com/about/

Fung, A. (2008). Democratizing the policy process. In *The Oxford handbook of public policy* (pp. 669–686). Oxford University Press. https://doi.org/10.1093/oxfordhb/9780199548453.001.0001. Retrieved 2018.

Guber, D. L., & Bosso, C. J. (2013). Issue framing, agenda setting, and environmental discourse. In *The Oxford handbook of U.S. environmental policy* (pp. 437–460). Oxford University Press. https://doi.org/10.1093/oxfordhb/9780199744671.001.0001

Hayden, F. G. (2002). Policymaking network of the Iron-triangle subgovernment for licensing hazardous waste facilities. *Journal of Economic Issues, 36*(2), 477–484. https://doi.org/10.1080/00213624.2002.11506492

Heclo, H. (1978). Issue networks and the executive establishment. In A. King (Ed.), *The new American political system* (pp. 263–287). American Enterprise Institute.

Heikkila, T., Berardo, R., Weible, C. M., & Yi, H. (2019). A comparative view of advocacy coalitions: Exploring shale development politics in the United States, Argentina, and China. *Journal of Comparative Policy Analysis: Research and Practice, 21*(2), 151–166. https://doi.org/10.1080/13876988.2017.1405551

Heikkila, T., & Weible, C. M. (2015). *A summary report of a 2015 survey of the politics of oil and gas development using hydraulic fracturing in Colorado*. School of Public Affairs, University of Colorado Denver.

Heikkila, T., Weible, C. M., & Olofsson, K. (2017). Lessons from state-level and national-level policy conflicts over U.S. Shale development. *Environment: Science and Policy for Sustainable Development, 59*(3), 4–13. https://doi.org/10.1080/00139157.2017.1301165

Heikkila, T., Weible, C. M., & Pierce, J. J. (2014). Exploring the policy narratives and politics of hydraulic fracturing in New York. In M. D. Jones, E. A. Shanahan, & M. K. McBeth (Eds.), *The science of stories: Applications of the narrative policy framework in public policy analysis* (pp. 185–207). Palgrave Macmillan. https://doi.org/10.1057/9781137485861_9

Ingold, K. (2011). Network structures within policy processes: Coalitions, power, and brokerage in Swiss climate policy. *Policy Studies Journal, 39*(3), 435–459. https://doi.org/10.1111/j.1541-0072.2011.00416.x

Jenkins-Smith, H. C., St. Clair, G. K., & Woods, B. (1991). Explaining change in policy subsystems: Analysis of coalition stability and defection over time. *American Journal of Political Science, 35*(4), 851–880. https://doi.org/10.2307/2111497

Jones, B. D., & Baumgartner, F. R. (2012). From there to here: Punctuated equilibrium to the general punctuation thesis to a theory of government information processing. *Policy Studies Journal, 40*(1), 1–20. https://doi.org/10.1111/j.1541-0072.2011.00431.x

Jones, M. D., & Jenkins-Smith, H. C. (2009). Trans-subsystem dynamics: Policy topography, mass opinion, and policy change. *Policy Studies Journal, 37*(1), 37–58. https://doi.org/10.1111/j.1541-0072.2008.00294.x

Kwak, H., Lee, C., Park, H., & Moon, S. (2010). What is Twitter, a social network or a news media? In *Proceedings of the 19th international conference on World wide web* (pp. 591–600). https://doi.org/10.1145/1772690.1772751

Lasswell, H. D. (1956). The political science of science: An inquiry into the possible reconciliation of mastery and freedom. *American Political Science Review, 50*(4), 961–979. https://doi.org/10.2307/1951330

Matti, S., & Sandström, A. (2011). The rationale determining advocacy coalitions: Examining coordination networks and corresponding beliefs. *Policy Studies Journal, 39*(3), 385–410. https://doi.org/10.1111/j.1541-0072.2011.00414.x

May, P. J., Koski, C., & Stramp, N. (2016). Issue expertise in policymaking. *Journal of Public Policy, 36*(2), 195–218. https://doi.org/10.1016/j.eiar.2007.03.001

Momtaz, S., & Gladstone, W. (2008). Ban on commercial fishing in the estuarine waters of New South Wales, Australia: Community consultation and social impacts. *Environmental Impact Assessment Review, 28*(2–3), 214–225. https://doi.org/10.1016/j.eiar.2007.03.001

O'Faircheallaigh, C. (2010). Public participation and environmental impact assessment: Purposes, implications, and lessons for public policy making. *Environmental Impact Assessment Review, 30*(1), 19–27. https://doi.org/10.1016/j.eiar.2009.05.001

Olofsson, K. L. (2022). Winners and losers: Conflict management through strategic policy engagement. *Review of Policy Research, 39*(1), 73–89. https://doi.org/10.1111/ropr.12453

Olofsson, K. L., Katz, J., Costie, D. P., Heikkila, T., & Weible, C. M. (2018). A dominant coalition and policy change: An analysis of shale oil and gas politics in India. *Journal of Environmental Policy & Planning, 20*(5), 645–660. https://doi.org/10.1080/1523908X.2018.1493984

Pierce, J. (2013). *A summary report of perceptions of the politics and regulation of hydraulic fracturing in Colorado*. Produced by the School of Public Affairs at the University of Colorado Denver. https://libcat.colorado.edu/Record/b10145692

Pierson, P. (1993). When cause becomes effect: Policy feedback and political change. *World Politics, 45*(4), 595–628. https://doi.org/10.2307/2950710

Sabatier, P. A. (1987). Knowledge, policy-oriented learning, and policy change. *Knowledge, 8*(4), 649–692. https://doi.org/10.1177/016402598700800400

Sabatier, P. A. (1988). An advocacy coalition framework of policy change and the role of policy-oriented learning therein. *Policy Sciences, 21*, 129–168. https://doi.org/10.1007/BF00136406

Sabatier, P. A. (1991). Toward better theories of the policy process. *PS: Political Science & Politics, 24*(2), 147–156. https://doi.org/10.2307/419923

Sabatier, P. A., & Weible, C. M. (2016). *Theories of the policy process*. Westview Press.

Schattschneider, E. E. (1975). *The semi-Sovereign people: A realist's view of democracy in America*. Dryden Press.

Seawright, J., & Gerring, J. (2008). Case selection techniques in case study research: A menu of qualitative and quantitative options. *Political Research Quarterly, 61*(2), 294–308. https://doi.org/10.1177/1065912907313077

Smith, L. G. (1984). Public participation in policy making: The state-of-the-art in Canada. *Geoforum, 15*(2), 253–259. https://doi.org/10.1016/0016-7185(84)90036-8

Steinert-Threlkeld, Z. C., Mocanu, D., Vespignani, A., & Fowler, J. (2015). Online social networks and offline protest. *EPJ Data Science, 4*(1), 1–9. https://doi.org/10.1140/epjds/s13688-015-0056-y

Stewart, J. M., & Sinclair, A. J. (2007). Meaningful public participation in environmental assessment: Perspectives from Canadian participants, proponents, and government. *Journal of Environmental Assessment Policy and Management, 9*(02), 161–183. https://doi.org/10.1142/S1464333207002743

Twitter. (n.d.). *About X: Our company and priorities*. About Twitter. https://about.x.com/en

U.S. Energy Information Administration. (2024). "U.S. field production of crude oil (thousand barrels per day)." *eia.gov*. https://www.eia.gov/dnav/pet/hist/LeafHandler.ashx?n=pet&s=mcrfpus2&f=m

Weible, C. M., & Ingold, K. (2018). Why advocacy coalitions matter and practical insights about them. *Policy & Politics, 46*(2), 325–343. https://doi.org/10.1332/030557318X15230061739399

Weible, C. M., Ingold, K., Nohrstedt, D., Henry, A. D., & Jenkins-Smith, H. C. (2020). Sharpening advocacy coalitions. *Policy Studies Journal, 48*(4), 1054–1081. https://doi.org/10.1111/psj.12360

Weible, C. M., & Sabatier, P. A. (2009). Coalitions, science, and belief change: Comparing adversarial and collaborative policy subsystems. *Policy Studies Journal, 37*(2), 195–212. https://doi.org/10.1111/j.1541-0072.2009.00310.x

Chapter 3
Tweeting to Conserve: An Analysis of Water District Messaging During the California Drought

Colin Kuehl

In 2015, California's water districts each faced a monumental task. In the face of an historic drought, water supplies across the state were at all-time lows and Governor Jerry Brown mandated that all districts reduce water consumption by at least 25% compared to 2012 levels (Brown, 2015). To reach these ambitious goals, water districts needed the public to quickly and meaningfully reduce their water use. A central component of that outreach, as has become increasingly common, was the use of social media. The use of social media allowed water districts to communicate directly to citizens—their customers—about the need to conserve. However, the strategies used by water districts to promote conservation weren't necessarily the most effective for changing citizens' behavior.

At the time, the drought that hit California and other Southwestern states from 2010 to 2017 was viewed as unprecedented; however, the situation districts found themselves in is not unusual. Government agencies are often put in situations where they rely on the public's help in producing public goods, known as coproduction. Increased variability caused by climate change not only makes drought in California more likely, but it is also expected to increase the likelihood of both drought and flooding as well as a number of other disasters around the world (Intergovernmental Panel on Climate Change, 2008). Similarly, during the Covid-19 pandemic, governments relied on the public to voluntarily adopt public health practices to reduce the spread of the infection. In each of these cases, government agencies relied on the public to quickly and voluntarily make significant behavior changes to benefit society as a whole. To achieve those changes, governments relied on effective outreach through social media. Accordingly, it is crucial to understand the messaging

C. Kuehl (✉)
Department of Political Science & Institute for the Study of the Environment, Sustainability and Energy, Northern Illinois University, DeKalb, IL, USA
e-mail: ckuehl@niu.edu

N. Guehlstorf (ed.), *Environmental Policy Science's Exploration for Innovative Data*, Natural Resource Management and Policy NA,
https://doi.org/10.1007/978-3-031-90889-7_3

approaches government entities use when communicating with their citizens, their choice of strategies, and where their outreach diverges from what might be considered best practice.

This chapter provides an in-depth descriptive analysis of the strategies California water districts used to encourage citizens to reduce their water use between 2012 and 2022. It uses a coded sample of 10,000 tweets obtained from a population of over 250,000 tweets sent by water districts during the drought period. It finds that districts overwhelmingly relied on behavioral interventions in their outreach. Despite important changes, mentions of changes to policy or the use of economic incentives were minimal. Furthermore, within the tweets that focused on voluntary behavior change, the vast majority simply provided users with information about the presence of drought or the need for conservation. This is in contrast to best practices from the academic literature that suggest information is most effective when paired with motivation and behavioral skills. It concludes with a broader discussion of the role of social media messaging in government agencies in situations of coproduction.

Public Agencies and Social Media

Governments at all levels increasingly use social media to communicate with the public (Barberá & Zeitzoff, 2018; Mergel & Bretschneider, 2013). According to one calculation, 94% of local governments already had some form of social media presence as of 2013 (Norris & Reddick, 2013). While there is tremendous variation in how governments use social media, generally, it is a means to convey information to the public (Campbell et al., 2014). However, in most cases, there is little actual reciprocity from citizens (Feeney & Porumbescu, 2021; Stone & Can, 2020; Wukich, 2021). Agencies use social media in different ways. For some, it is a way to increase participation and civic engagement in ways that help government decision-makers with increased citizen input (Lee & Kim, 2018; Mergel & Bretschneider, 2013; Tai et al., 2020). Others have examined the role of government social media accounts in communicating information to citizens quickly during natural disasters (Olson et al., 2019).

Of growing importance is governments' use of social media to promote behavior change among citizens, particularly in ways that are beneficial to the whole community. This was vividly demonstrated during the Covid-19 pandemic when government agencies, such as public health departments, used social media to communicate the value of social distancing, masking, and other safety measures (Li et al., 2021; Wang et al., 2021). Unlike environmental goods, extensive literature in public health has long examined the role of social media in messaging (Heldman et al., 2013) with some evidence that social media plays a positive role in minimizing health crises (Graham et al., 2015). While a wide variety of policy tools were used to minimize the spread COVID-19, a central component was voluntary behavior change from citizens with the goal of improving overall public health.

This process, in which citizens become actively involved in the provision of public goods, rather than expecting governmental authority to provide the good itself, is known as coproduction (Ostrom, 1996). The broad concept of coproduction includes a variety of processes in which citizens are directly involved in the design, delivery, monitoring, and evaluation of public policy alongside professional administrators (Jo & Nabatchi, 2016; Parks et al., 1981). In the case discussed in this chapter, citizens are taking responsibility for voluntarily conserving water in order to help government authorities, water districts, achieve their conservation goals. Co-production can take a wide variety of forms. The focus here is on scenarios in which citizens are actively helping a public service provider co-deliver a public good (Bovaird, 2007), in this case, an adequate supply of water. The use of social media has the potential to play a particularly important role in this form of coproduction given how inexpensively it provides an opportunity for citizens to self-organize and for governments to communicate widely (Linders, 2012).

For some scholars, coproduction and codelivery are core to a broader pattern in which a wide variety of services previously viewed as in the exclusive domain of public agencies are now being produced by users and their communities. Broadly, governments face growing interest in steering citizens towards socially beneficial actions. In domains ranging from preventative healthcare, community service, and ethical consumption, softer policy tools that encourage behavioral shifts rather than coercive mandates are increasingly being used (Lehner et al., 2016). These efforts to effectively promote voluntary behavior change, sometimes referred to as nudges (Thaler & Sunstein, 2008), are becoming an important aspect of how government agencies encourage coproduction and the use of social media is essential to, and indicative of, these efforts. For scholars of public administration, this reflects a shift from policy relying almost exclusively on coercion (Lowi, 1964), to one that acknowledges the power of suasion (Anderson, 1997) as an effective policy tool.

Water Districts and the Push for Conservation

Coproduction, and thus the enhanced use of tools like social media, was particularly important during the California drought for several reasons. With water levels hitting record lows within a few years, long-term infrastructure investments to increase supply were not a timely solution. While greater longer-term supply solutions such as reservoir storage or desalinization plants were discussed and, in some cases built, they were not available to respond to the immediate need during the drought. With the ability to increase supplies limited, both by precipitation and infrastructure, water managers primarily relied on decreasing demand to maintain adequate water supplies. The 25% reduction mandate from Governor Brown was statewide, but it was up to water managers to decide what combination of policy tools they would use. As a result, a wide variety of changes to local laws and price changes were implemented across the state. These changes were accompanied by a number of information campaigns imploring citizens to increase their conservation.

These public outreach campaigns were essential to water providers' campaigns, given the limits on other policy tools intended to increase conservation. While increasing regulations have been shown to be effective and may be the preferred choice of water managers (Hall, 2009; Teodoro, 2010), they can be politically unpopular, challenging to pass, and difficult to implement. Similar political constraints limited the ability of districts to aggressively implement price changes to increase the cost of excessive water use and incentivize conservation. While the use of market mechanisms can increase water savings (Olmstead & Stavins, 2009), they can also be regressive and place an undue burden on low-income residents (Rachunok & Fletcher, 2023).

On the other hand, voluntary behavior changes, in the service of coproduction, can be achieved quickly and implemented with less cost than the alternative options. This led to efforts by water districts across the state to encourage voluntary behavior change by customers. In addition, the value of inducing voluntary behavior has led to significant academic research in recent years within social psychology, behavioral economics, and other social sciences on the most effective behavioral interventions to increase water conservation (Ehret et al., 2019; Fielding et al., 2013; Liang et al., 2018; Russell & Fielding, 2010). Using a wide variety of experimental methods, researchers have uncovered a number of theoretical insights on what can induce individuals to perform the pro-environmental behavior of increasing their conservation. However, existing research has not connected insights from these studies to what water district messaging actually contains. Extant literature has examined various forms of public outreach, particularly on social media. For example, Boyer et al. (2021) use a case study in Arizona to examine how Twitter affected the discourse around water conservation. Others have used content analysis to examine the use of public service announcements to increase water conservation (Krajewski et al., 2019). To date, research has not analyzed social media for its connection to best practices from behavioral science.

For water districts, successfully encouraging individuals to change their behavior without resorting to changing laws or costs has clear advantages. Conservation campaigns can be implemented very quickly, they are cheap and effective. However, for individuals, the decision to adopt conservation behaviors is a classic example of a collective action problem. While it is clear the community and state are better off from actions to reduce water use, such as taking a shorter shower or letting a lawn go brown, the benefits do not accrue to the individual. Accordingly, it is individually rational for citizens to be unwilling to take on the additional cost, whether time, money, or inconvenience, of conserving water. Presumably, if it was cheaper or easier to reduce their water use, they would have done so already. This all suggests there are strong reasons to be a free-rider. To overcome this reasoning, water districts employed a wide assortment of techniques to convince citizens to voluntarily reduce their water use.

This study uses the information, motivation, behavioral skills (IMB) model to better understand and classify the messages focused on voluntary behavior change. Originally developed for communications around public health (Fisher et al., 2014), the IMB model has more recently been adapted to environmental behaviors (Seacat

& Northrup, 2010) and specifically the issue of water conservation (Ehret et al., 2019; Hodges et al., 2020). Simply put, the IMB model suggests that for individuals to change their behavior they must be informed about a problem, motivated to take action, and have the skills necessary to make and maintain that change. In the IMB model, "information" refers to whether individuals have accurate knowledge of a problem and its consequences, and so the information component in this context refers specifically to problem awareness. In this case that is references to the presence of drought or the need to conserve water. Motivation (M) refers to internal drives or goals that direct and energize an individual to engage in a behavior (Pittman, 1998). A wide variety of interventions that rely on motivations are often based on social norms, identity, or other tools that have been explored in the water conservation literature (Goldstein et al., 2008). Behavioral skills (B) reflect an individual's objective and perceived ability to engage in a target behavior. Even when informed and motivated, individuals may not know what to do; messaging can provide those behavioral skills. These could be the specific tips about how not to use water around the house or a drought-resistant plant for yards. While increases in each IMB component increase the likelihood of taking action, messages are expected to be the most effective when they contain all three. In other words, as suggested in Fig. 3.1, each component is necessary, but likely not sufficient for behavior change.

While this study focuses on Twitter, clearly the use of social media remains just one of many ways governments can communicate with their constituents. In the context of the California drought, physical mailings, emails, billboards, yard signs,

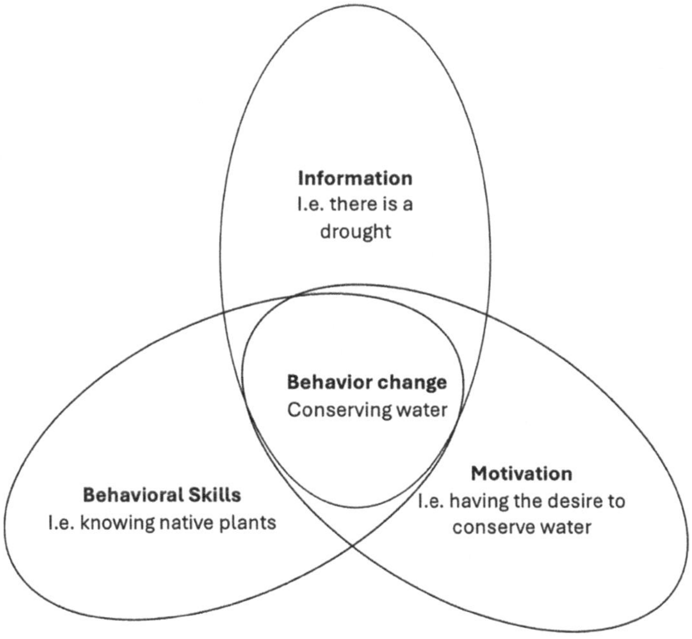

Fig. 3.1 The information-motivation-behavioral skills model

emails, and even television ads were all used in a broader effort to encourage conservation. Though there is likely to be a difference, social media messaging, specifically through Twitter, is assumed to largely be mirrored in the other forms of outreach. For example, many tweets linked to TV ads or borrowed imagery from district flyers.[1] Accordingly, it is assumed that the broad trends of Twitter content discussed below are largely applicable to the water district messaging as a whole. Empirically, tweets have the advantage of providing a uniquely accessible and, given its broad popularity, comprehensive view of how California water districts responded to this environmental challenge (Steinert-Threlkeld, 2018).

The 2010s drought in California provides an excellent case to study these dynamics because of the extent of the necessary water use reductions, the size and diversity of the state, and its relatively high social media uptake, but it is far from unique in terms of both having to adopt ambitious conservation goals quickly and its use of messaging to encourage residential water conservation. Countries around the world have faced similar challenges in recent decades with corresponding research focused on messaging strategies. Recent examples include the Cape Town water crisis (2015–2018) (Brick et al., 2023), Australia's millennium drought (Addo et al., 2019), Spain's recent drought (March et al., 2013), as well as ongoing water scarcity challenges in Israel (Katz et al., 2016), India (Vasilaky et al., 2023), China (Zhuang et al., 2018), and Latin America (Sánchez et al., 2024).

California Water Districts on Twitter

To better understand how government agencies use messaging on social media to achieve coproduction, this study systematically categorizes water conservation tweets from California water districts during a ten-year period of extended drought. The final dataset consists of a randomly sampled subset of tweets posted by California water districts coded to provide a picture of both the broad strategies of district outreach and specifically the efforts to induce voluntary conservation.

There are 413 entities designated by the State of California as water providers. Of these 138 are classified as a special district. The remainder are a mix of for-profit companies (67), or water is provided as one aspect of city utility districts (208). By exclusively focusing on water districts rather than all water providers, this study can more exclusively focus on comparable units. There is also a wide variety of priorities for a city utility and differing incentive structures that make categorization unreliable (Mullin, 2009), for example, profit maximization for private water companies. In addition, further analysis of these tweets revealed that the for-profit entities tend to rarely tweet, and when part of broader city utility districts, water conservation

[1] Actor Danny Trujillo's ad for Palmdale water district is a great example: https://www.youtube.com/watch?v=GPHuOEITeUw

was rarely mentioned. Rather these accounts focused on other utility issues and broader city-wide concerns.

Of the 138 special districts, 82 (60%) of the water districts had a Twitter account linked on their official website or that was easily accessible as of Fall 2022. A Twitter Application Programming Interface (API) was then used to download (Kearney, 2019) all tweets from these accounts between October first, 2012, just as the drought was starting to impact large portions of the state, and October first, 2022. Later that same month the purchase of Twitter was completed by Elon Musk. His ownership has since resulted in many changes to the platform including a name change to X and other choices that have led to decreasing usage and the loss of major advertisers. These changes, along with the decreased prevalence of drought at the time, suggest that activity may have changed on the platform after the purchase and thus tweets after the change in ownership are excluded from the sample.

All together the water districts tweeted 254,571 times over the study's time period. Given the large size of the full population of tweets, a sample of 10,000 tweets was randomly drawn for this study. To begin, a team of coders coded all tweets as drought-focused or not. Tweets were considered to be drought-focused if they contained references to the ongoing drought, water conservation, or changes to water supplies. Accordingly, only about 35% (for a total sample size of 3543) of tweets within the sample were drought related. Other commonly discussed issues were assurances of water quality, district governance issues like meeting times, or other items relevant to the community without a direct connection to water scarcity issues.

Water districts varied widely in their use of Twitter to communicate about the drought. Within the sample, four districts had over 200 tweets focused on conservation. Expanded to the full population, this equates to an average of two tweets per day over the ten-year period. About half the Twitter handles in the full population didn't show up in the sample at all. This suggests that they rarely, if ever, were using social media, or at least Twitter, to communicate with citizens. This variation likely reflects broader differences across districts in their outreach efforts and broader resources. In most cases active social media usage is likely proportional to other forms of outreach. However, it is possible that some districts may be very active in communicating in other ways and may just not be as active on Twitter.[2]

Figure 3.2 shows that larger districts, as measured by the number of people that they serve, are associated with more drought related tweets. A basic linear regression model suggests that within the sample, an additional 2500 residents are associated with one additional drought related tweet ($\beta = 0.41$, $p < 0.001$). Larger districts presumably have larger budgets and more staff increasing their capacity to be active on social media. In Fig. 3.2, water districts in southern California[3] are represented by triangle symbols districts in the northern half of the state are represented by

[2] Many districts also use Facebook though in many cases the posts are the same. Facebook and parent company Meta, however, does not provide access to its data.

[3] In this case Southern California is defined as the five furthest southern hydrologic regions—Central Coast, Tulare Lake, South Lahontan, South Coast, and Colorado River. The five regions of

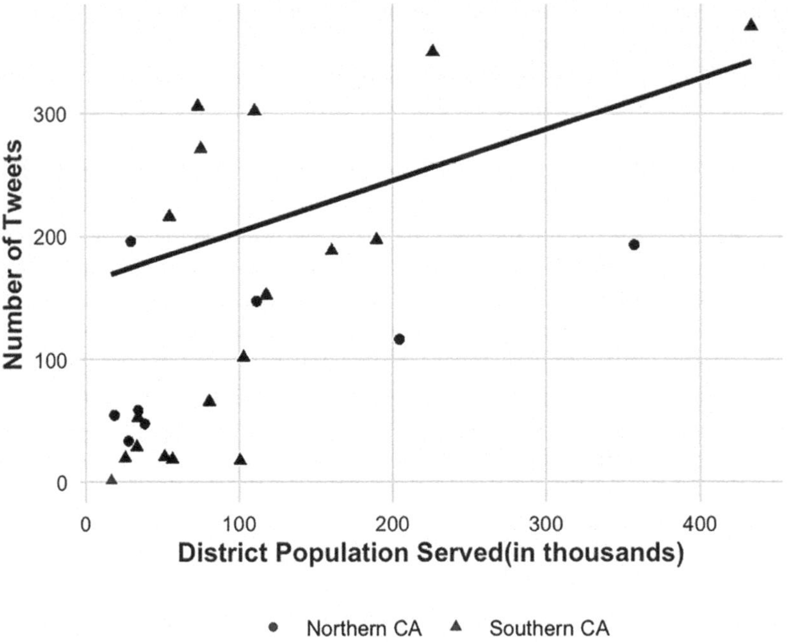

Fig. 3.2 District size and count of drought tweets in sample

circles. While there are more Southern California accounts in the sample generally, they also were more likely to tweet ($\beta = 115.7$, $p < 0.001$). This is consistent with expectations given that Southern California generally has less available water and is more susceptible to drought.

Figure 3.3 shows the relationship between the number of tweets in the sample in a given month and the percentage of the state in severe drought as defined by the USGS. It shows an increase in activity as the drought continued to worsen throughout the state from 2013 to 2015. Tweet levels then stayed fairly consistent, even as the percentage of the state in drought decreased in 2017 and 2018. Overall, districts stayed fairly consistent in their efforts to communicate about water conservation across the study period, though there are clear differences from month to month and across seasons.

North coast, Sacramento river, north Lahontan, San Francisco Bay, and San Joaquin river, are considered northern.

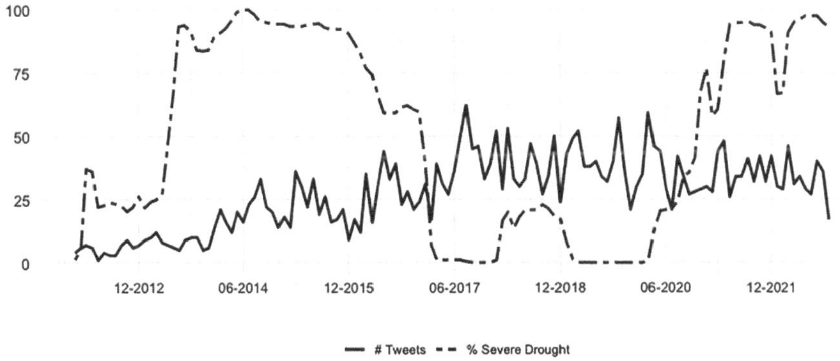

Fig. 3.3 Tweet counts within the sample and percentage of California in severe drought over time

Broad Strategies

In the second step of this study, each drought-related tweet was then coded based on both the content of the message and the overarching strategy of the water district. As discussed previously, when it comes to achieving water conservation goals, as well as other public goods provisions, water utilities have three broad strategies. The first is placing increased regulations or enforcing mandatory restrictions on water use. Second, they can change prices to incentivize decreased use. Finally, they can rely on their customers to voluntarily change their conservation. Behavioral tweets were then further categorized according to the IMB framework. The full categorization structure is shown in Fig. 3.4 and examples of tweets within each category are shown in Table 3.1.

The first strategy, "Laws and Regulation," focuses on using the power of the state to force citizens to reduce water use. As mentioned previously, California Governor Brown issued an executive order in 2015 requiring water providers to reduce their water by 25% (Brown, 2015). How providers achieved that goal was up to the provider. Some providers passed local ordinances, many prior to the Governor's declaration, that restricted water use and applied harsh penalties for those that did not comply. Across the state, laws were passed restricting outdoor watering to certain days, outlawing washing cars at home, limits on swimming pools, and other mandated restrictions on water use. Tweets categorized as regulation generally focused on providing information about new restrictions, reminded residents of existing restrictions, or gave updates on state or other relevant local policy changes. A few, like the one provided as an example in Table 3.1, mentioned penalties for breaking rules, but these were generally rare.

The second strategy, "Incentives," centers on the use of price changes and other market-based mechanisms to increase conservation. Though implementation varied widely, generally water providers used incentives to either make the use of water more expensive through rate hikes or the adoption of conservation-friendly technology or infrastructure cheaper. On Twitter, while water providers occasionally

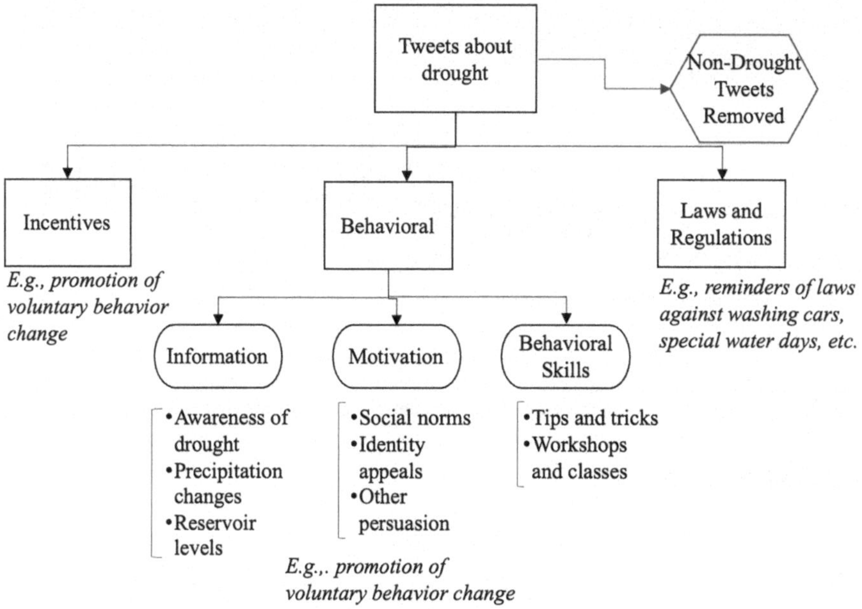

Fig. 3.4 The full categorization scheme used in this study

reminded residents of rate hikes, they were much more likely to remind users of the cost-saving benefits of reduced usage. More common were references to the variety of subsidies providers offered in an effort to encourage adoption of new technologies, like automatic sprinklers or new appliances, or particularly in switching yards from traditional turfgrass to drought-friendly landscaping.

Finally, the third strategy, "Behavioral Skills," refers to voluntary behavior change. In other words, citizens do not change their behavior because they are forced to, as with laws and regulations, or because it benefits them financially, as with incentives, but because they are simply willing to take on the cost of conserving water. Though the benefits don't accrue to them personally, they are willing to help provide the public good.

Water districts used varying combinations of these different strategies in response to drought. As shown in Fig. 3.5, the vast majority of tweets focused on voluntary behavior change. Fully 91% of tweets were focused on residents willingly changing their behavior. Despite the widespread adoption of both changing incentives and new regulations by water providers across the state, these strategies were rarely discussed on Twitter with only 11% of tweets mentioning pocketbook concerns and 5% mentioning regulations. It should be noted that these categories are not mutually exclusive, and, in some cases, tweets fit multiple categories. For example, a tweet for taking advantage of subsidies to replace a lawn for the common good of the community contains both incentives and motivation.

While the actual variation in the implementation of these broad strategies across different water districts is beyond the scope of this study, this figure exhibits the

Table 3.1 Example tweets by categorization

Category	Example tweet
Incentives	"@CCWD customers can earn rebates up to $400 per toilet, and a lot of water, with our new rebates" —*@CCWD – 2/19/2014*
Regulations	"Have you spotted water waste? We want to know about it! Use our online reporting tool to give us details" —*@SanJuanWtrDist – 11/23/2014*
Information	"The newly released California drought map indicates 81.71% of the state to be in abnormally dry conditions; down slightly from 81.73% from last week. However, the severe drought designation grew significantly to 19.98% up from 6.39% last week. #socalwater #drought #conservation" —*@LVMWD – 2/15/2018*
Motivation	"Happy Monday! Here's a fresh selection of #ShowerSongs! #MervynMusicMondays" —*@LongBeachWater – 12/18/2017*
Behavioral skills	"Water Tip Tuesday: Repair leaks at home. Save up to 190 gallons a month." —*@ElisonoreEddie – 8/7/2013*
Information + Motivation	"If you can eat kale in your smoothie you can #savewater! There's nothing bitter about saving a little more when were in a drought for a blend of water saving tips visit bewaterwise.com" — *@Otaywater – 11/1/2021*
Information + Behavioral skills	"As the weather warms up, so does the possibility of overwatering your lawn. EVWD wants to help customers improve their outdoor water use by upgrading old irrigation controllers to one that adjusts to the weather." —*@eastvallywater – 4/12/2019*
Information + Motivation + Behavioral skills	"It's all hands on deck #California. We need to consider every step we can take to conserve our previous water supply in a severe drought. Try this easy tip from our friends at @valley water to recycle water at home" —*@IRWDnews – 7/12/2021*

degree to which water districts emphasized the different strategies in their communication with the public. Others have examined the relative effectiveness of these differing strategies (Browne et al., 2021; Maas et al., 2024). By examining the tweets, we are able to focus on the relative importance given to different approaches. The conclusion is quite clear. In their social media communications, water districts overwhelmingly relied on voluntary behavior change to reach their conservation goals.

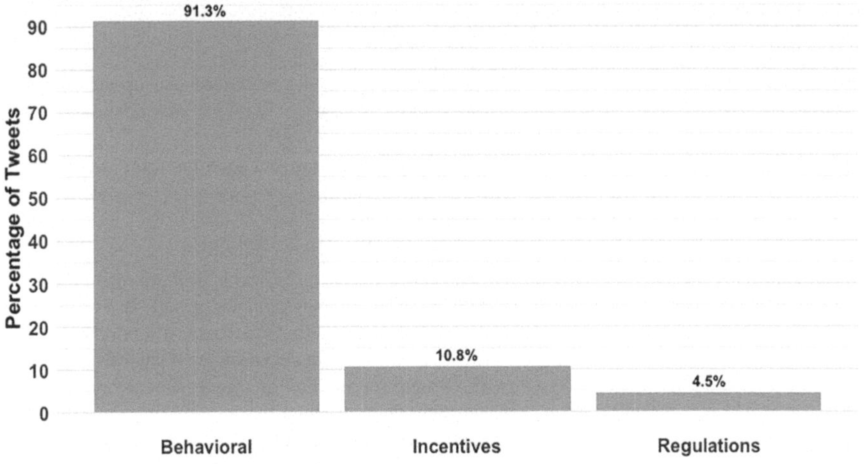

Fig. 3.5 Breakdown of tweet categorization by broad strategy

Behavioral Interventions

As a second stage of coding, all behavioral tweets were categorized using the information-motivation-behavior skills framework discussed above. Recall that existing experimental work has shown that messaging containing all three components is most effective at reducing residential water use. However, as shown in Fig. 3.6, only one percent of water district tweets focused on behavioral skills contained all three IMB components. Instead, the greatest portion, nearly half, simply provided information about the existence of drought or other aspects of the need to conserve water. The second largest category only focused on behavioral skills. Obviously, a focus on behavioral skills, such as outdoor watering versus consuming less drinking water, is crucial to meaningful conservation. Public managers focus on behavioral skills because they may assume that citizens are already aware of the drought and just don't know what to do about it. However, in the sample, tweets focusing on behavioral skills were only paired with motivation 3.5% of the time. If citizens aren't motivated, then are less likely to actually employ the skills. Indeed, it is noteworthy that fully 88.6% of the behavioral tweets only contain one IMB component. Though tweets, by their nature, are intended to be short and to the point, the variation present in the sample suggests this is not a constraint. Accordingly, the IMB model would suggest tweets containing multiple components, even if not all three, are likely to be more effective at eliciting conservation than those containing only a single component.

The results of logistic regression models with the presence of multiple IMB components (1) versus only a single component (0) among the behavioral tweets are shown in Table 3.2. To aid in interpretation, the first three models contain only binary explanatory variables. This exploratory analysis provides a basic idea of what factors may be associated with more effective drought messaging on social

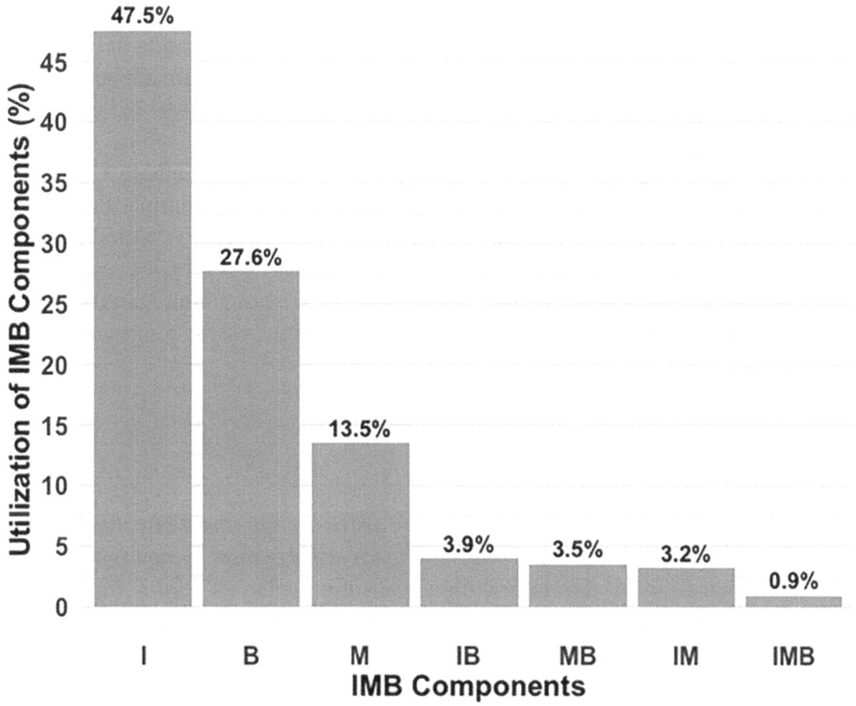

Fig. 3.6 Percentages of behavioral tweets in each IMB category

Table 3.2 Logit models

	(1)	(2)	(3)	(4)
Dependent variable: tweet contains multiple IMB components				
Large district	0.154	0.168	0.161	0.187*
	(0.112)	(0.113)	(0.113)	(0.113)
Southern CA		−0.245*	−0.244*	−0.198
		(0.138)	(0.138)	(0.139)
Summer months			−0.186	−0.190
			(0.121)	(0.121)
Year				−0.056**
				(0.023)
Constant	1.952***	2.135***	2.192***	114.313**
	(0.086)	(0.136)	(0.141)	(45.502)
Observations	3211	3211	3211	3211
Log likelihood	−1142.303	−1140.651	−1139.502	−1136.421
Akaike Inf. Crit.	2288.606	2287.303	2287.004	2282.843

Note: $^{*}p < 0.1$; $^{**}p < 0.05$; $^{***}p < 0.01$

media. Large districts are those with over 100,000 residents. While coefficients are positive, as might be expected for districts with greater resources, it is only significant in Model 4 at the $p < 0.1$ level. This suggests larger districts are not necessarily employing effective messaging strategies than smaller ones. As was the case with the previous section, Southern California is defined as the five most southerly hydrologic regions within the state. Models 2 and 3 suggest Southern California districts were actually less likely to tweet about drought using multiple IMB components. Summer months is a dummy variable for if the tweet was posted in June, July, or August. In neither model does the time of year appear to be significant. Finally, the value for year is negative, suggesting as the drought increased districts were more likely to tweet containing messages with only a single component.

Discussion

The results of this analysis suggest that water districts could more effectively communicate to citizens to maximize potential water conservation by combining multiple components from the information-motivation-behavior skills framework. Naturally, these tweets are not observed by citizens in isolation. Citizens are exposed to broader information campaigns that may contain all three components or tweets in combination may contain multiple components, potentially negating some of the impacts of lack of combination observed in these results. However, the wide discrepancies between what previous experimental research has shown as the most effective and results shown here is striking.

The broad focus on behavior suggest that districts viewed water conservation as an outcome that could be achieved through co-production. Rather than relying heavily on communicating about changes to laws or prices, both which are more traditional tools used to achieve policy outcomes, they focused heavily on promoting voluntary behavior change. As mentioned previously, given the relatively short time period and logistical as well as political challenges, this makes sense. However, it is also indicative of broader efforts by municipalities to promote voluntary behavior change to provide public goods outcomes that previously would have been assumed to be achieved through government efforts alone.

Within the tweets focused on voluntary behavior change, exploratory regression analysis did not show clear patterns in what makes districts more likely to combine IMB components in their messaging, rather than containing only one component. Some evidence suggests larger districts were more likely to include multiple components, but Southern California districts, the portion of the state with the greatest need for conservation, were more likely to use basic messaging. This suggests a need for more work on the decision-making of public managers in how they choose to craft their social media messaging.

Conclusion

In response to Governor Brown's 2015 order, California water providers were successful in reducing residential water use by 25% statewide. Though public outreach was only one aspect of their response, it is clear these efforts, particularly messaging to promote voluntary conservation, was a key component of their strategy. This chapter has analyzed tweets from California water districts during this period of sustained drought to better understand how conservation communications were actually implemented. The use of social media allows for a quantification and systematic comparison of these efforts. Specifically, in the case presented here, tweets provide a unique and easily accessible source of data from across the state allowing for analysis that would be impossible or prohibitively time-consuming if focused on alternative messaging mediums like mailers or advertisements. Though this analysis has largely assumed these online messaging strategies are similar to these alternatives, future work is needed to empirically assess the overlap.

In addition to identifying broad messaging strategy, tweets focused on behavioral skills were coded using the IMB framework. IMB was developed in psychology and was not originally intended as a coding scheme. This presents challenges for coders that an alternative approach built inductively from the sample may avoid (Liang et al., 2018). However, because the utility of the IMB framework for water conservation has previously been validated using experimental studies, we know what messaging works. Results presented here show that in many ways reductions may have been even greater if California water district communications more effectively combined elements of information, motivation, and behavioral skills.

Citizen involvement in the production of a variety of public goods is an issue of growing importance for public managers across a variety of domains. As agencies increasingly rely on their citizens to manage resources and provide other public goods, the use of social media to encourage behavior change is likely to only increase. While scholars have pointed to the importance of this dynamic, few have examined the actual content of the messaging and its relative effectiveness. This chapter has provided an initial case study of one state, on one social media platform, using one categorization schema to understand these dynamics. The results provide some initial answers but also point to several fruitful avenues for future research.

First, this review only examined a small sample of the total tweets in the population of California tweets during the drought. Work using machine learning and natural language models could potentially categorize the full corpus of tweets from all water providers in California. This broader dataset could provide a much more in-depth look at spatial and temporal heterogeneity within the data. Of course, other actors are also interested in promoting conservation, so gathering data using hashtags or other approaches could allow for a fuller picture of the messaging the public is exposed to. It could also facilitate the gathering of data and categorization in different areas and different time periods. California is not the only region impacted by drought, and additional work could analyze the degree to which similar dynamics have played out elsewhere.

Second, more theoretical and empirical work could be done to better understand the motivations of government agencies and the employees actually composing tweets when using social media. Public managers doing to the day-to-day work composing these tweets are likely to perform a wide variety of tasks. Understanding how they conceive of achieving behavior change and their goals when crafting this messaging could help clarify the outcomes observed in this study.

Finally, future work could overcome the substantial endogeneity problems and connect district messaging to actual conservation outcomes. Given the wide variety of factors that influence water use at the household level, not to mention the district level, this will be challenging. It is clear water district employees believe these campaigns are important. Identifying what messaging broadly, and social media specifically, has on behavior change will be a crucial question moving forward.

References

Addo, I. B., Thoms, M. C., & Parsons, M. (2019). The influence of water-conservation messages on reducing household water use. *Applied Water Science, 9*, 126. https://doi.org/10.1007/s13201-019-1002-0

Anderson, J. L. (1997). Governmental suasion: Refocusing the Lowi policy typology. *Policy Studies Journal, 25*(2), 266–282. https://doi.org/10.1111/j.1541-0072.1997.tb00020.x

Barberá, P., & Zeitzoff, T. (2018). The new public address system: Why do world leaders adopt social media? *International Studies Quarterly, 62*(1), 121–130. https://doi.org/10.1093/isq/sqx047

Bovaird, T. (2007). Beyond engagement and participation: User and community coproduction of public services. *Public Administration Review, 67*(5), 846–860. https://doi.org/10.1111/j.1540-6210.2007.00773.x

Boyer, A.-L., Vaudor, L., Le Lay, Y.-F., & Marty, P. (2021). Building consensus? The production of a water conservation discourse through Twitter: The water use it wisely campaign in Arizona. *Environmental Communication, 15*(3), 285–300. https://doi.org/10.1080/17524032.2020.1821743

Brick, K., De Martino, S., & Visser, M. (2023). Behavioural nudges for water conservation in unequal settings: Experimental evidence from Cape Town. *Journal of Environmental Economics and Management, 121*, 102852. https://doi.org/10.1016/j.jeem.2023.102852

Brown, E. G. J. (2015). Executive order B-29-15.

Browne, O. R., Gazze, L., & Greenstone, M. (2021). Do conservation policies work? Evidence from residential water use. *Environmental and Energy Policy and the Economy, 2*, 190–225. https://doi.org/10.1086/711310

Campbell, D. A., Lambright, K. T., & Wells, C. J. (2014). Looking for friends, fans, and followers? Social media use in public and nonprofit human services. *Public Administration Review, 74*(5), 655–663. https://doi.org/10.1111/puar.12261

Ehret, P. J., Hodges, H. E., Kuehl, C., Brick, C., Mueller, S., & Anderson, S. E. (2019). Systematic review of household water conservation interventions using the information–motivation–behavioral skills model. *Environment and Behavior, 53*(5), 485–519. https://doi.org/10.1177/0013916519896868

Feeney, M. K., & Porumbescu, G. (2021). The limits of social media for public administration research and practice. *Public Administration Review, 81*(4), 787–792. https://doi.org/10.1111/puar.13276

Fielding, K. S., Spinks, A., Russell, S., McCrea, R., Stewart, R., & Gardner, J. (2013). An experimental test of voluntary strategies to promote urban water demand management. *Journal of Environmental Management, 114*, 343–351. https://doi.org/10.1016/j.jenvman.2012.10.027

Fisher, W. A., Fisher, J. D., & Shuper, P. A. (2014). Chapter 3—Social psychology and the fight against AIDS: An information–Motivation–Behavioral skills model for the prediction and promotion of health behavior change. In J. M. Olson & M. P. Zanna (Eds.), *Advances in experimental social psychology* (Vol. 50, pp. 105–193). Academic Press.

Goldstein, N. J., Cialdini, R. B., & Griskevicius, V. (2008). A room with a viewpoint: Using social norms to motivate environmental conservation in hotels. *Journal of Consumer Research, 35*(3), 472–482. https://doi.org/10.1086/586910

Graham, M. W., Avery, E. J., & Park, S. (2015). The role of social media in local government crisis communications. *Public Relations Review, 41*(3), 386–394. https://doi.org/10.1016/j.pubrev.2015.02.001

Hall, D. C. (2009). Politically feasible, revenue sufficient, and economically efficient municipal water rates. *Contemporary Economic Policy, 27*(4), 539–554. https://doi.org/10.1111/j.1465-7287.2009.00164.x

Heldman, A. B., Schindelar, J., & Weaver, J. B. (2013). Social media engagement and public health communication: Implications for public health organizations being truly "social". *Public Health Reviews, 35*, 13. https://doi.org/10.1007/BF03391698

Hodges, H. E., Kuehl, C., Anderson, S. E., Ehret, P. J., & Brick, C. (2020). How managers can reduce household water use through communication: A field experiment. *Journal of Policy Analysis and Management, 39*(5), 1076–1099. https://doi.org/10.1002/pam.22246

Intergovernmental Panel on Climate Change. (2008). *Climate change and water*. https://archive.ipcc.ch/pdf/technical-papers/climate-change-water-en.pdf

Jo, S., & Nabatchi, T. (2016). Getting back to basics: Advancing the study and practice of coproduction. *International Journal of Public Administration, 39*(13), 1101–1108. https://doi.org/10.1080/01900692.2016.1177840

Katz, D., Grinstein, A., Kronrod, A., & Nisan, U. (2016). Evaluating the effectiveness of a water conservation campaign: Combining experimental and field methods. *Journal of Environmental Management, 180*, 335–343. https://doi.org/10.1016/j.jenvman.2016.05.049

Kearney, M. W. (2019). rtweet: Collecting and analyzing Twitter data. *Journal of OpenSource Software, 4*(42), 1829. https://doi.org/10.21105/joss.01829

Krajewski, J. M. T., Schumacher, A. C., & Dalrymple, K. E. (2019). Just turn on the faucet: A content analysis of PSAs about the global water crisis on YouTube. *Environmental Communication, 13*(2), 255–275. https://doi.org/10.1080/17524032.2017.1373137

Lee, J., & Kim, S. (2018). Citizens' e-participation on agenda setting in local governance: Do individual social capital and e-participation management matter? *Public Management Review, 20*(6), 873–895. https://doi.org/10.1080/14719037.2017.1340507

Lehner, M., Mont, O., & Heiskanen, E. (2016). Nudging – A promising tool for sustainable consumption behaviour? *Journal of Cleaner Production, 134*, 166–177. https://doi.org/10.1016/j.jclepro.2015.11.086

Li, Y., Guan, M., Hammond, P., & Berrey, L. E. (2021). Communicating COVID-19 information on TikTok: A content analysis of TikTok videos from official accounts featured in the COVID-19 information hub. *Health Education Research, 36*(3), 261–271. https://doi.org/10.1093/her/cyab010

Liang, Y., Henderson, L. K., & Kee, K. F. (2018). Running out of water! Developing a message typology and evaluating message effects on attitude toward water conservation. *Environmental Communication, 12*(4), 541–557. https://doi.org/10.1080/17524032.2017.1288648

Linders, D. (2012). From e-government to we-government: Defining a typology for citizen coproduction in the age of social media. *Government Information Quarterly, 29*(4), 446–454. https://doi.org/10.1016/j.giq.2012.06.003

Lowi, T. J. (1964). American business, public policy, case-studies, and political theory. *World Politics, 16*(4), 677–715. https://doi.org/10.2307/2009452

Maas, A., Puri, R., & Goemans, C. (2024). A review of residential water conservation policies and attempts to measure their effectiveness. *PLOS Water, 3*(8), e0000278. https://doi.org/10.1371/journal.pwat.0000278

March, H., Doménech, L., & Saurí, D. (2013). Water conservation campaigns and citizen perceptions: The drought of 2007–2008 in the Metropolitan Area of Barcelona. *Natural Hazards, 65*, 1951–1966. https://doi.org/10.1007/s11069-012-0456-2

Mergel, I., & Bretschneider, S. I. (2013). A three-stage adoption process for social media use in government. *Public Administration Review, 73*(3), 390–400.

Mullin, M. (2009). *Governing the tap: Special district governance and the new local politics of water*. MIT Press.

Norris, D. F., & Reddick, C. G. (2013). Local E-Government in the United States: Transformation or incremental change? *Public Administration Review, 73*(1), 165–175. https://doi.org/10.1111/j.1540-6210.2012.02647.x

Olmstead, S. M., & Stavins, R. N. (2009). Comparing price and nonprice approaches to urban water conservation. *Water Resources Research, 45*(4), W04301. https://doi.org/10.1029/2008WR007227

Olson, M. K., Sutton, J., Vos, S. C., Prestley, R., Renshaw, S. L., & Butts, C. T. (2019). Build community before the storm: The National Weather Service's social media engagement. *Journal of Contingencies and Crisis Management, 27*(4), 359–373. https://doi.org/10.1111/1468-5973.12267

Ostrom, E. (1996). Crossing the great divide: Coproduction, synergy, and development. *World Development, 24*(6), 1073–1087. https://doi.org/10.1016/0305-750X(96)00023-X

Parks, R. B., Baker, P. C., Kiser, L., Oakerson, R., Ostrom, E., Ostrom, V., Percy, S. L., Vandivort, M. B., Whitaker, G. P., & Wilson, R. (1981). Consumers as coproducers of public services: Some economic and institutional considerations. *Policy Studies Journal, 9*(7), 1001–1011. https://doi.org/10.1111/j.1541-0072.1981.tb01208.x

Pittman, T. S. (1998). Motivation. In D. T. Gilbert, S. T. Fiske, & G. Linzey (Eds.), *The Handbook of social psychology* (4th ed., pp. 549–590). McGraw-Hill.

Rachunok, B., & Fletcher, S. (2023). Socio-hydrological drought impacts on urban water affordability. *Nature Water, 1*, 83–94. https://doi.org/10.1038/s44221-022-00009-w

Russell, S., & Fielding, K. (2010). Water demand management research: A psychological perspective. *Water Resources Research, 46*(5), W05302. https://doi.org/10.1029/2009WR008408

Sánchez, C., Bianchi, E. C., Rodriguez-Sanchez, C., & Sancho-Esper, F. (2024). Are advertising campaigns for water conservation in Latin America persuasive? A mixed-method approach. *International Review on Public and Nonprofit Marketing, 21*, 341–369. https://doi.org/10.1007/s12208-023-00386-2

Seacat, J. D., & Northrup, D. (2010). An information–motivation–behavioral skills assessment of curbside recycling behavior. *Journal of Environmental Psychology, 30*(4), 393–401. https://doi.org/10.1016/j.jenvp.2010.02.002

Steinert-Threlkeld, Z. C. (2018). *Twitter as data*. Cambridge University Press.

Stone, J. A., & Can, S. H. (2020). Linguistic analysis of municipal twitter feeds: Factors influencing frequency and engagement. *Government Information Quarterly, 37*(4), 101468. https://doi.org/10.1016/j.giq.2020.101468

Tai, K.-T., Porumbescu, G., & Shon, J. (2020). Can e-participation stimulate offline citizen participation: An empirical test with practical implications. *Public Management Review, 22*(2), 278–296. https://doi.org/10.1080/14719037.2019.1584233

Teodoro, M. P. (2010). The institutional politics of water conservation. *Journal – American Water Works Association, 102*(2), 98–111. https://doi.org/10.1002/j.1551-8833.2010.tb10055.x

Thaler, R. H., & Sunstein, C. R. (2008). *Nudge: Improving decisions about health, wealth, and happiness*. Yale University Press.

Vasilaky, K., Harou, A., Alfredo, K., & Kapur, I. (2023). What works for water conservation? Evidence from a field experiment in India. *Journal of Environmental Economics and Management, 119*, 102802. https://doi.org/10.1016/j.jeem.2023.102802

Wang, Y., Hao, H., & Platt, L. S. (2021). Examining risk and crisis communications of government agencies and stakeholders during early-stages of COVID-19 on Twitter. *Computers in Human Behavior, 114*, 106568. https://doi.org/10.1016/j.chb.2020.106568

Wukich, C. (2021). Government social media engagement strategies and public roles. *Public Performance & Management Review, 44*(1), 187–215. https://doi.org/10.1080/15309576.2020.1851266

Zhuang, J., Lapinski, M. K., & Peng, W. (2018). Crafting messages to promote water conservation: Using time-framed messages to boost conservation actions in the United States and China. *Journal of Applied Social Psychology, 48*(5), 248–256. https://doi.org/10.1111/jasp.12509

Chapter 4
Taking Notice: The ECHO Network, Integrated Watershed Governance, and TikTok/YouTube

Lars K. Hallstrom, Lanie Parr, and Nicholas Yarmey

The intersection between the natural environment and the health of human populations is a long-standing foundation to public health. In fact, it embodies a very real dynamic that has clear implications for global economies, populations, agriculture and the movement and mobility of people around the world. As the COVID-19 pandemic demonstrated, and as the recent concern about avian flu (Dye & Barclay, 2024) reinforces, it is impossible to separate the health and well-being of human beings from the environment upon which we rely, and then which we live.

While the foundation and establishment of public health as a practice and field of study did in fact hinge on the intersection between water, wastewater, and built environments, the reality of the last several decades has clearly shown that anthropogenic climate change, globalization, patterns of human consumption, human security considerations, and population health define the contemporary realities of the twenty-first century. Even as Canada continues to struggle with balancing the need for immigration with the realities of urbanization and employment, or the implications of anthropogenic climate change for critical policy sectors such as water supply, agriculture, or even the security of Arctic Canada, it has also become very clear that political action and public responses are both polarized and polarizing.

In many cases, and despite attempts to gain or retain a global reputation as an environmental and equity leader, Canada has a remarkably poor record when it comes to policy innovation. This reality extends far from just the accusation of policy greenwashing (see for example the book Green-Lite by Doern et al. (2015)),

L. K. Hallstrom (✉) · L. Parr · N. Yarmey
University of Lethbridge, Lethbridge, AB, Canada
e-mail: lars.hallstrom@uleth.ca; nick.yarmey@uleth.ca; nick.yarmey@uleth.ca

N. Guehlstorf (ed.), *Environmental Policy Science's Exploration for Innovative Data*, Natural Resource Management and Policy NA,
https://doi.org/10.1007/978-3-031-90889-7_4

and extends into the reality of (1) highly differentiated political rhetoric from policy implementation and inaction on climate change or sustainability-based indicators (Hallstrom et al., 2021); (2) a long-standing tendency to marginalize or "forget" challenges for rural communities; and (3) a broader sociocultural and economic mindset that is embedded in the joint mythologies of abundance, perpetuity, and equity when we consider the extensive natural resources of the country (Hatt et al., 2005).

While there has been a long-standing trend of (often justly) questioning the science that underlies public policy in any number of different sectors, that trend is particularly pronounced within environmental policy (see, for example, the extensive literature regarding climate change denial, peak oil, or genetic modified foods (Leiss, 2003; Guehlstorf, 2004; Guehlstorf & Hallstrom, 2005) and is most certainly present within contemporary public health contexts. For example, Alberta, Canada, was both the site of a major border blockade triggered by the implementation of COVID-19-related restrictions and was also the "source province" for a major anti-COVID-19 convoy and protest that occupied the capital city of Ottawa for several weeks in 2022. Similarly, in June 2024, members of the provincial government from Calgary, Alberta, hosted an event called, "An Injection of Truth" in order to provide a platform for suspended physicians to present their perspective on the negative health impacts of COVID-19 mRNA vaccines on children (it should be noted that the medical and public health community were very much opposed to this event, and the Alberta Public Health Association publicly stated the same). In other words, while environmental, municipal, and health policy more broadly are very much embedded in a reliance upon evidence and good science to support decisions, there are also very powerful populist, religious, and politically conservative groups and organizations that object not only to the science that underlies public decision-making, but may also object to the very exercise of political authority that is required by those decisions.

This political reality is an important contextual element for this chapter: while the functionality of educational science content (ESC) disseminated through contemporary social media platforms is the focus, the politics of Alberta (which hinge upon long-standing economic dependencies upon both conventional oil and gas, but which also extend to a consistent and persistent tension between environmentalism and environmentalists (Parkins, May 2024)) inform both public opinion, and public policy. As a result, while much of the attention focused on water and water supply in the province is driven by the "news of the day", there is a secondary function for such forms of science communication. As noted by Habibi and Salim (2021), there is a key engagement audience in youth, facilitated in great part by TikTok, which has a younger audience base than other platforms (10–29 years old). While younger citizens may demonstrate shorter attention spans (Rein, 2023) when engaging with social media content, they also present both the next generation of scientists, as well as a community that often views "the past" in an almost ahistorical light. In the politically polarized context of Alberta, both ecological and political knowledge, especially when situated in a historical context, are important for that next generation of science, and for the next generation of policy and political "problem solving".

When coupled with the proliferation of social media content, it is perhaps understandable that short, dynamic, "punchy" videos demonstrate the most effective form of audience "capture", particularly when compared to conventional print media and lectures. At the same time, platforms such as TikTok and YouTube also present an archival and therefore function that facilitates storage, and potentially even recall, of scientific content in the future. In fact, both YouTube and particularly TikTok rely upon the maintenance of video content for the push algorithm to function. As a result, these platforms (at least for the time being) present a storage function for billions of videos (almost 4 billion on YouTube in 2024, and over 8 billion on TikTok).

This storage function is an important component for the videos created and analysed for this chapter. Like many governments, the Province of Alberta has made significant investments in online "dashboards" that provide relatively easy access to key indicators for the province across multiple sectors and ministries (such dashboards include community health, regional data, economic and migration data, and other data collected by either Statistics Canada, the Province itself, or in some cases by the private sector). Unfortunately, what has emerged in recent years are significant challenges in the maintenance, accuracy, and validity of such dashboards—in some cases they may rely upon now obsolete or irrelevant cross-sectional data collected several years ago, and in other cases they may contain clearly incorrect data (often as a result of how, or by whom, the data were collected). As a result, the videos created from the "Health in the Watershed" Atlas, described later in this chapter, are not only much more broadly available (particularly when compared to a print version that costs almost $200/unit, or even a Portable Document Format (PDF) that exceeds easy circulation by email), but also stored in a way that transcends both political control of data and data accessibility, as well as the uncertainties of research funding and university-based content management systems.

Integrating Social Media, Engagement, and Science Communication

As noted above, neither the politicization of science, nor the clear intersections between environment, economy, society, and health are new. In fact, the Ottawa Charter put forward this very assertion in 1986 (WHO, 1986). Since then, there has been a global acknowledgement of the social determinants of health (WHO, 2006), continued pressure (and in some cases, action) to address the anthropogenic causes of climate change and their very real social and health implications (Gupta, 2010; UN, 2015) beginning the early 1990s, and a number of both practitioner and academic movements that have sought to clarify and address the artificial delineation between environment and health.

Whether embodied within initiatives such as EcoHealth or One Health (see for example Charron, 2012 and the WHO, 2017), calls for more integrated approaches to impact assessment, natural resource management, agriculture, and epidemiology are all broadly consistent in their emphasis upon more holistic, systems based, and intersectoral paradigms, as well as the importance of policy design (Bobrow & Dryzek, 1987) that values both equity (broadly defined) and a foundational role for scientifically generated and accessible evidence. In other words, perspectives that seek to reconcile social, economic, and health inequities with systemic levels of functionality very much draw from not only the primacy of evidence-based practice in medicine, but also the primacy of scientific knowledge in public policy and public decision-making. That primacy was first articulated by Harold Lasswell as part of the "Policy Sciences" in the 1930s (Lasswell, 1936, 1971), and while it is very clear that science alone cannot solve complex policy problems (Head, 2022; Hallstrom et al., 2015), there is no question that as we continue to face and acknowledge the impact that we as a species have both upon the planet and in turn, upon ourselves; we must find viable methods to bring science to public policy. As the waves of misinformation and disinformation regarding any number of political and scientific issues continue to mount, there is clearly a need for making science more accessible to the public. There is a need to support the skills and competencies of the general public, and of course, children and youth, to better understand the complexities, interactions, and both proximal and distal causal chains that actually shape the policy problems our institutions struggle to manage. While social media is often, and correctly, noted for its negative effect upon the mental health, physical activity, and social dynamics of younger generations, it also holds great opportunity. Not only does the relative accessibility and ease of use for social media platforms provide almost unprecedented reach (some videos can be viewed tens, hundreds, or even billions of times), they may also provide "digestible" and higher frequency opportunities for scientific communication, particularly when compared to academic articles of 6000–8000 words, often housed behind publisher paywalls.

In keeping with this need, this chapter is focused upon the work of the Environment, Community and Health Observatory (ECHO) Network, and specifically upon the use of both conventional and more recent and popular forms of knowledge mobilization. Utilizing a rather unique "Health in the Watershed Atlas" that explicitly sought to not only provide a more innovative and integrated approach to state of the watershed reporting, but also to increase the accessibility and usability of that same content in different ways, this chapter provides a retrospective assessment of media platforms such as TikTok and YouTube that may support the democratization of science and watershed reporting. It also seeks to situate both the atlas and the use of these platforms as a resource for watershed management that explicitly situates watersheds as not just a hydrological or geographic space, but also as a place where social, economic, ecological, political, cultural, and public health issues and activities all occur and intersect (Morrison et al., 2012).

This chapter proceeds in the following way. It begins with an overview of the ECHO Network and the different dynamics that led to its formation and funding by the Canadian Institutes for Health Research between 2016 and 2023. The ECHO Network includes a number of interrelated hubs, including engagement with youth, engagement with rural communities and populations, engagements with water and watersheds, as well as engagement with a wide range of public health, public policy, and related academic and practitioner fields. This overview of the Network sets the stage and context for the Health in the Watershed Atlas. As noted above, this atlas is positioned as a resource and potential teaching intervention for both watershed management and planning, as well as for a more integrated yet necessarily limited approach towards state of the watershed reporting. The case study of this atlas and its use within two different media platforms (TikTok and YouTube) forms the third component of this chapter. This is followed by an assessment and practical consideration of how using these platforms may, or may not, contribute to the democratization of watershed and sustainability-based science. Specifically, it examines the data generated regarding viewership and dissemination from those platforms. We also consider the shift in original goals (which hinged largely upon use in educational and curricular contexts) to the ways in which videographic media can and have been used to support broader community and Indigenous community engagement with state of watershed reporting, the social determinants of health, sustainability indicators, and approaches to communicating with both the public and policymakers (particularly at the municipal level) about both the intersectoral and integrative implications and meanings of those indicators.

This chapter concludes with a consideration of potential and desirable directions that such initiatives may follow. Those directions are placed explicitly within the political, environmental, and climatological context of 2024. In Alberta (the site of the Battle River Watershed and subject of the atlas), that context includes a wildfire season that began earlier than any other in the history of the province, very high likelihood of significant droughts across the province in both rural and urban environments, significant and related physical challenges for municipalities of all sizes, and increasing demands for both social and health supports related not only to the spillover effects of the COVID-19 pandemic, but also the significant population growth that the province experienced in the past two years. Given the notable environmental, economic, and social dynamics within the province, and a clearly populist, libertarian, and openly anti-science government, the province of Alberta has become an excellent location to better understand the intersections between environment, community, and health and well-being.

The ECHO Network and the Health in the Watershed Atlas

The ECHO Network emerged as a result of a series of long-term collaborations between academics, health practitioners, natural resource-based organizations like watershed management alliances, and other fields including educational institutions, Indigenous community groups, and environmental organizations. Underlying these collaborations, which often had roots in initiatives like EcoHealth and the Canadian Community of Practice in Ecosystem Approaches to Health (CoPEH-Canada), was both a scientific and practitioner-based goal of considering environment and health, both separately and together, in a new way.

Water and wastewater specifically were the original focus of intervention, and indeed for the creation, of the discipline and practice of public health. In turn, the common framing of environmental health emphasizes the risks that factors like pollution, contamination, toxins, and the like present to either individual or collective physiological health. However, with the growing attention given to the social determinants of health, and the growing understanding of how health inequities often correlate with environmental, social, and economic inequities, there has been increased attention to thinking in different ways about how both risk and benefit may manifest. This can extend to including different ways to think about science, agriculture, natural resource management, and the ways different economic and extractive practises can shape population health and well-being (see for example, the work of David Waltner Toews, James Kay, Henry Vennema, Martin Bunch, Karen Morrison, Margot Parkes, and many others).

Since approximately 2006, a group of scholars and practitioners based in Canada, but with networks around the world, has been examining different ways in which environment and population health can intersect. In terms of the development of the ECHO Network, that group included individuals from a wide range of disciplines (including engineering, watershed management, medicine, geography, veterinary medicine, and public policy), but with a common goal of bringing systems-based methods, complexity science, and interdisciplinary perspectives on how people, places, and activities (whether social, economic, or ecological) intersect to improve or worsen the health of the public. As the work of this group progressed (whether in the form of not-for profit organizations like NESH (Network for Ecosystem Sustainability and Health), or with funding from the Public Health Agency of Canada), two common and additional themes began to emerge. The first was an emphasis upon water and watersheds as both geographic and hydrological spaces that literally provide a catchment from which to consider population and public health. The second was an emphasis upon using water and watersheds as an integrative space and resource from which to consider how community dynamics (such as the social and structural determinants of health) intersect with the framing, use, and functionality of natural resources. Particularly in Canada, that functionality is historically understood within an extractive and anthropocentric paradigm that emphasizes the economic reliance of the country and its communities upon industries such as forestry, mining, fisheries, agriculture, and particularly in the second half of the twentieth century, both conventional and unconventional energy in the form of oil and gas.

These collaborations and areas of inquiry led to the formulation and successful funding of the ECHO Network in 2016. Comprised of over 40 academics, dozens of graduate students and post-doctoral students, as well as community partners from across Canada, the overarching goal of the ECHO Network was not simply to be an observatory. Rather, it was to be an observatory that could support political, practitioner, professional, academic, and policy responses; the dynamics observed; and their respective causal chains. The motto, in fact, for the Network was "taking notice in order to take action". As noted above, this goal was directly influenced by not only the practice of evidence-based medicine and policy science, but also the commonly articulated need to link academic and policy expertise with community-based experiences, perspectives, and priorities. Of particular importance for this Network was the engagement of Indigenous communities (particularly in British Columbia and Maritime Canada), the recognition of Indigenous community and Elder-based wisdom, as well as the inclusion of younger community members (such as high school students) who will form the next generation of health scientists, policy analysts, physicians, and teachers.

The ECHO Network consisted of both geographic and thematic hubs, with the core funding being held and administered at the University of Northern British Columbia. Other partners included faculty working at Simon Fraser University, the University of Alberta, and the University of Moncton in New Brunswick. Thematic areas of work included watersheds, rural communities, measurement and indicators, spatial data and modelling, intersectoral action, youth and education, and art and healing.

Over its nearly eight-year lifespan, the ECHO Network generated a very diverse range of projects, knowledge products, events, and collaborations. These extended to spinoff projects, such as the cumulative impact assessment of resource extraction on the eastern slopes of the Rocky Mountains. The Network also facilitated the creation and completion of innovative projects that sought to directly assist, support, and inform the work of community-based partners, including organizations like the Battle River Watershed Planning and Advisory Council (WPAC) and the Cocagne Watershed in New Brunswick.

State of the Watershed Reporting and the Battle River/ Sounding Creek "Health in the Watershed Atlas"

The Battle River is a rather unique watershed located in East Central Alberta. It extends from headwaters at Battle Lake and runs east across aspen parkland to the provincial border with Saskatchewan, after which it joins the North Saskatchewan River. Unlike the other rivers in Alberta, the Battle River and Sounding Creek watershed is not glacier-fed. Rather, it is reliant upon precipitation in the form of rain and snow that falls throughout the year. It is, therefore, considered a prairie-fed river, but is often located within a much larger river valley that was created thousands of years ago. The watershed covers approximately 30,000 km^2, the vast majority of which (83%) is in Alberta.

The geography of the watershed consists of a blend of aspen parkland and prairie lands, with a heavy industrial footprint in the form of agriculture, oil, gas, and coal mining, as well as significant infrastructure in the form of small to midsize rural communities, a large military installation, and substantial roadway and train infrastructure. It is home to approximately 130,000 people of all ages, and while many do live on farms that may have been homesteaded at the turn of the twentieth century, many others live in communities ranging from a few hundred to almost 20,000.

These larger communities often act as service hubs for the surrounding agricultural and industrial activities, and provide not only economic resources, such as sales and supplies, but also financial, cultural, and educational services.

As one of 11 watershed planning and advisory councils in the province, the Battle River and Sounding Creek watershed is under the stewardship of a council which in turn seeks to build consensus on land and water resource management strategies through collaboration with a wide range of stakeholders. Stakeholders may include different levels of government, industry, ecological and conservation groups, Indigenous communities, the research community, and, of course, the general public itself. There are nonprofit organizations that are designated by the provincial government to lead collaborative planning, facilitate education and stewardship activities, and to report on the status of the watershed on a regular basis.

These reports, known as state of the watershed reports, are very common in North American water stewardship. In Alberta, reports are historically structured by the 2008 Handbook for State of the Watershed Reporting which "introduces users to the concept of watershed-scale assessments via watershed health indicators" (Government of Alberta, 2008, Preface), and also provide insight into the process by which the screening of the physical features, conditions, and resources of a watershed may be conducted. Conventionally, these reports are conducted every 10 years and are limited to the catchment or watershed in question. In other words, no province-wide state of the watershed reporting is conducted. As a result, there is often both similarity and difference between both what the watersheds report upon as well as when councils conduct and release that reporting. In general, state of the watershed reporting is historically focused upon assessing the quality and quantity of water within a watershed and is intended to provide a baseline rating system to support decision-making and planning. In Alberta, and many other places where state of the watershed reporting is utilized, the emphasis is typically upon anthropogenic activities (stressors), their impact upon the condition of the watershed, and potentially the ways in which management activities (responses) may drive those conditions.

As a result of the work noted above between public health, public policy, and water researchers, the formation and resources of the ECHO Network provided a unique opportunity to support a largely rural watershed (it lies to the southeast of the capital city of Edmonton) in expanding the scope and the paradigm of state of the watershed reporting in a new way. Following a lengthy and extensive development and design process that included a review of comparable attempts elsewhere in the world (including the Orinoco and Mississippi Rivers), what emerged was an attempt to reflect the different sectors relevant to integrated watershed management in a way that extended human action beyond being a causal variable. The ECHO project instead sought to position human health and well-being across multiple different sectors as both cause and effect. Such an approach was both consistent with the broader body of work within the ECHO network that emphasized systems dynamics, both proximal and distal causation (causes of the causes), recursivity, and the benefits of supporting watershed management in ways that reflected the different systems at play within those geographic and hydrologic spaces.

The result of this work was a multi-year project that created "Taking Notice to Take Action: Integrating Environment, Community and Health—A Health in the Watershed Atlas of the Battle River and Sounding Creek Watersheds" (2022). The atlas was co-authored by a research, authorial, and editorial team led by one of the ECHO Co-Principal Investigators (Lars Hallstrom) and was "co-designed" with the staff of the Battle River Watershed Alliance. All authors of this chapter contributed to the creation of the atlas. It has been formally adopted by the council as the second state of the watershed report for the Battle River watershed (the first was released in 2011 (BRWA, 2011)). The design approach to the atlas was multifaceted. Specifically, while the atlas needed to reflect and include the conventional measures specific to water and the watershed's hydrological quality and quantity-relevant dynamics, it also needed to reflect how those dynamics intersect with five other sectors (ecosystems and biodiversity; personal well-being; weather and climate; people and community; and economy and land management). Each of the sectors is then divided into three or four measures, which in turn then lead to more specific indicators related to watershed performance, impacts, and effects.

The atlas was designed to not only expand the scope and performance of condition assessment, but also to facilitate public engagement and community involvement in watershed management and related activities as well as assist practitioners and decision-makers working outside of watershed management such as municipal counsellors and planners, economic development officers, public health practitioners, and even those working in industry, agriculture, and infrastructure. The atlas was also intended to be a potential support for education and research. In addition to providing a unique collection of cross-sectional data and maps for the 44 indicators that form the backbone of the atlas, there is a wealth of explanatory text to help the reader understand not only the state of the watershed, but the causal dynamics and factors leading to that state across all the included sectors.

Given this emphasis upon educational support and finding ways to make the atlas accessible to different audiences and to different levels of environmental health and policy literacy, the publication of the atlas was supported by three somewhat independent knowledge mobilization streams. The first was to make the atlas widely available in both print and digital form. As a hardcopy book, the atlas is almost 400 pages long and would retail for hundreds of dollars. Fortunately, the combination of the ECHO Network and the Prentice Institute for Global Population and Economy at the University of Lethbridge was able to provide funding to disseminate several hundred hardcopy texts to school divisions and research libraries across the province. Copies were also distributed to all the watershed planning and advisory councils.

The second stream was focused upon public engagement and facilitating a public response to the atlas as a state of the watershed report. This work was undertaken by the Battle River Watershed Planning and Advisory Council (BR-WPAC) and has consisted of a wide range of community-based events, workshops, feedback sessions, and briefing meetings to not just present the content and design intention of the atlas, but also to trigger conversations about the different economic, human, and environmental footprints and relationships at play within the watershed.

The third stream, which will comprise the focus of the remainder of this chapter, was an attempt to take advantage of the long-standing history of documentary film-making related to rural Canada agriculture, the colonial and Indigenous experience of country, and the sociocultural realities of that experience. At the same time and given both the educational and broader engagement goals underlying the atlas, the intention was not to create a 50-to-90-minute film that translated the atlas into images and sound. Rather, the intention was to utilize relatively new and very widely popular and accessible digital media platforms to disseminate the content of the atlas in visually appealing, informative, and short videos that could be viewed by any of the millions of users of TikTok and YouTube. The short-form videos can also be included as a primer for public engagement or classroom-based activities related to any of the sectors found in the atlas.

As the analytic and authorial work of the atlas progressed between 2019 and 2022, TikToks emerged as an increasingly popular short-form video format used for entertainment, comedy, and, increasingly, for entertainment, informational, or sales products. The app currently has over 4.7 billion downloads (as of February 2024) and is available in 150 markets and more than 50 languages (Howarth, 2024). It is particularly used by those under the age of 24. TikTok has over 100 million users in the United States alone. In Canada (which has a population of just over 40 million citizens), there are 3.2 million active monthly users, and the vast majority (70%) are under the age of 40. Globally, 60% of TikTok users are from Generation Z (meaning they were born between 1995 and 2009) and are between the ages of 15 and 30 years old.

TikTok presented a unique opportunity to attempt to both democratize more conventional forms of print and text-based research and to extend the reach of the atlas in terms of geographic, demographic, and stakeholder-based audiences. This hope was tempered by realism and the experience of the authorial and editorial teams—although the atlas is a substantial and very rigorous document, it is necessarily limited in geographic scope and applicability. In other words, while the atlas could be replicated in any watershed around the world, depending on availability and quality of relevant data, the truth of the atlas is that its relevance is largely limited to the 130,000 people living within the watershed itself.

At the same time, it is all too important to acknowledge that public consumption of academic materials similar to this atlas is historically limited. While some of that limitation has been the result of housing academic text first in university and research libraries and more recently behind publisher pay walls, the increased availability of academic text through platforms such as Google Scholar or Research Gate must be tempered with demand, interest, and the technical, methodological, or educational competencies that are often needed to access and use scientific and social scientific research. In other words, even when material is available in the public domain, there is no guarantee that it will be read, cited, or utilized in education, decision-making, planning, or public policy and the like. As a result, the hope was never for the atlas to "go viral" since the likelihood of doing so was infinitely small. Creating and sharing videos was instead a way to further stretch the reach and accessibility of the atlas in both those younger consumers who comprise such a large portion of the TikTok viewership, as well as for instructors in a wide range of educational settings.

Translating Cartography and Text to Film and Sound

Work began on creating a series of TikTok videos in 2020. Research staff affiliated with the project were able to combine locally recorded footage from throughout the Battle River watershed with scripted voiceover and interview-style commentary from research staff who generated the material itself. In some cases, virtual and in-person interviews were recorded to complement other visualizations within the videos, but a number emphasize the content, maps, and related videos of the watershed and surrounding environments, with the human presence limited to voice-over narration. Video was almost always recorded on an iPhone or similar (with a 12 Mega-Pixel capacity) and were usually shot in 1080p (at 60fps). Footage was then edited and refined using iMovie (an Apple application that is readily available to Macintosh users).

The TikTok account "ECHO_RuralAB" was created to house this content, and the work followed the general structure and model of the atlas itself. One of the key limitations in the early phases of this undertaking was the time constraint to only 90 s per video. Originally the platform limited videos to 15 s, and that was increased to 60 in 2017. That constraint was a real challenge for knowledge mobilization—finding ways to condense and yet still articulate meaningful content in such a short period of time was difficult. For example, at an adult reading rate of 180 words per minute out loud it would take approximately twelve hours, or 480 90-second TikToks, to read the atlas in its entirety to an audience.

The series includes introductory videos about the (Alberta) ECHO Atlas, with an emphasis on the Health in the Watershed Assessment Framework which includes Sectors, Measures, and Indicators. An overview video was created for each of the 6 sectors: Personal Wellbeing, Weather and Climate, People and Community, Water, Economy and Land Management, and Ecosystems and Biodiversity and videos were also created for measures under each sector. For example, in the Water Sector, there are 4 measures, each with several indicators. There is an overview video of Water, explaining what measures and indicators were used, followed by a video for each measure. For example, Water-Related Advisories is a measure within the Water sector (and is also a chapter in the atlas), and the indicators used for that measure then form the subject matter for the videos: drinking water advisories; algae advisories; fecal coliform and *E. coli* advisories.

In recognition of cultural sensitivity and the importance of sacred sites and areas of historical importance for Indigenous peoples within the watershed, the creators explicitly and deliberately chose not to use any potentially sensitive content. As a result, video content does not include any footage of sites or areas where people leave offerings (such as sweetgrass, tobacco, coins, etc.), sacred objects (such as the

RibStones near the small community of Viking in central Alberta), or sacred ribbon trees.

In 2021, TikTok increased the length of videos to 3 min, which greatly simplified the editorial and film-making process. Over the next two years, a total of 48 videos were created and posted to the platform, and to date those videos have received individual views ranging from 68 to 1854, averaging a few hundred views per video (as of June 2024). Unfortunately, at the time of writing, there are two key challenges to using data about the use and viewership of these videos: (1) Despite a relatively high number of views (for academic material), the account has only 31 "followers"—in turn, as per TikTok policy, metadata related to the viewership of the videos is not available, and (2) the Chinese ownership of TikTok has introduced a political dimension into the viewership, both in terms of Canadian viewers but also those in other countries. Specifically, both the United States and Canadian governments have expressed concerns about the use of TikTok to collect data about and from its users. In early 2023, the Canadian Government found that TikTok presents "an unacceptable level of risk to privacy and security" (Deschamps, 2023) and in turn then required the removal of the app from all government-issued mobile devices. More recently, in May of 2024, the US government passed legislation that could force either the sale of the platform (a move already proposed under then-President Donald Trump in 2020) or an outright ban of the platform. As a result of this potential limitation or even banning of TikTok-based content, the videos were duplicated and moved to YouTube, a long-standing platform first created in 2005. It is the second-most searched website in the world, and is home to over 14 billion videos, being watched by 2.5+ billion monthly users (https://www.youtube.com/@prenticeinstitute1947)

Results—TikTok

As noted above, there are significant limitations to the analytics available from TikTok, particularly when the number of followers is below 100. Specifically, only basic descriptive data regarding views, likes, and shares are available. In this case, since TikTok was the original platform for media dissemination, it was anticipated that uptake (in the form of followers) would be greater than it was. As a result, the TikTok results are essentially only able to reflect "scope" within a number of key caveats regarding the usage of such platforms. However, we are able to balance those data with more detailed analytics from YouTube. Unfortunately, since YouTube was a secondary and delayed strategy for both storage and dissemination, the results are necessarily skewed since it is likely that most of the initial and therefore greatest viewership happened with the original videos when they were posted on TikTok.

Due to the relatively low number of followers, the TikTok data provide us with little more than an overview of audience and audience dynamics. Specifically, we can get a sense of how many times the videos were viewed, although we do not have data regarding unique views from TikTok. Similarly, we are able to treat the videos (there are 48) as a collective and, as seen in Table 4.1, can generate some standard indicators of central tendency regarding the videos as a whole. Other data points, such as who the viewership is, or where they might be located, are not available from TikTok.

In total, the 48 videos have been viewed just over 18,000 times, with the least watched video receiving 68 views and the most watched receiving almost 2000. Content for the videos reflects the structure and general outline of the atlas itself, with an emphasis upon indicators and measures within 6 policy sectors. The average number of views was 376, with the majority of videos receiving a modest number of likes and a few shares. In other words, given the readily small and narrow geographic focus of the atlas and the subsequent videos, it is perhaps not surprising that the videos received some viewership, but not necessarily a lot of dissemination. This reality is not unique to the ECHO videos—other bodies have released a range of both high-quality, professional grade production videos and most "grassroots" film related to watershed management, watershed reporting, and watershed indicators. A quick scan of such videos shows consistently low viewership (some videos may receive on 30–40 views despite being available for over a decade). This is likely indicative of both the relatively small potential audience for such content, and the asymmetrical emphasis upon social and other media platforms for entertainment purposes.

Given the original intention of utilizing the video platforms as both an educational support and a way to foster the availability and accessibility of the atlas content in different ways, a result of 18,000 views spread across 48 videos is rather respectable. Since the videos are short and necessarily concise in terms of content, those 18,000 views do reflect that there is an audience for such content, although we are not able to determine the geographic location or details of who actually constitutes that audience. Compared to the readership of peer reviewed research, especially within a relatively short timeframe of only a few years and a global pandemic, the use of such a platform may have some merit. Not only are the videos available at almost no tangible cost to the viewer, the video platforms provide an accessible storage platform for such content that is not necessarily subject to periodical subscription rates, library committee decisions, or the like. At the same time, however, one should be very aware of how fleeting a TikTok view may be (any viewer who pressed "play" is counted as a view, even if they only watch for 1 s). YouTube,

Table 4.1 Views, likes, and shares from TikTok

	Views	Likes	Shares
Mean	376.23	7.23	2.06
Median	243.00	6.00	2.00
Std. error of mean	47.59	4.53	3.04
Sum	18,059	347	99
Minimum	68	3	0
Maximum	1854	22	9
Range	1786	19	9

however, requires a viewer to spend at least 30 s with a video, and while repeat views do count, bots or spam views do not. Consequently, TikTok viewership results may be subject to a false positive effect, with "real" viewership (watching videos to the closing credits, for example) being quite a bit lower.

Results—YouTube

Fortunately, the analytics that are available from YouTube are quite a bit more robust. As noted above, the shift and replication from TikTok to YouTube was undertaken as a precaution given the possibility that TikTok could, at some point, be banned from North American markets. This means that the YouTube data are essentially an echo of the TikTok viewership, since we anticipate that the majority of views for this content occurred when first posted to that platform.

As a result, we are less concerned with the viewership data *per se*, and instead focus upon some of the other dynamics made available through YouTube. The videos are created as a playlist on the Prentice Institute YouTube channel. We were able to discern both the how and the why of viewers arriving at the content as well as some of the viewer behaviours in terms of viewing duration. What we see, which can perhaps be viewed as triangulated with the TikTok data, is that even though the content is now dated, it continues to attract new and unique viewers, and many of these viewers do in fact spend quite some time viewing the videos. While the length of the videos varies due to the platform policies of TikTok, we anticipate that such viewing patterns are a result of "engaged" viewers who are seeking this content as part of the activities of the Battle River Watershed Alliance, or perhaps seeking to understand or access such materials from an educational or research background. We can in fact confirm the latter to a degree, since one of the larger sources of viewership is a research university located in Eastern Canada.

In general, YouTube data presented in Table 4.2 reflect a number of different patterns. Specifically, the majority of users are viewing the videos on a desktop (which might imply an institutional or workplace setting) although second is mobile devices. Most users arrive at the content through YouTube itself, which means they are either being directed towards the content as a result of YouTube's preference algorithm or through previews. However, since we do not have data on how effective preview tiles are for this content, we do not see the preview function as being terribly important.

As might be expected, not all videos receive the same attention from viewers. In general, there is more interest or viewer time spent on introductory or overview videos, but we see a range in terms of content. The most watched video, which focused on the atlas sector measures and indicators, had an average view duration of 23 s. The majority of viewers for that video were at IP addresses located in the United States, and the majority of viewers were not subscribers. In second place for viewership was a video focused on heat-related illness, with an average view duration of 29 s. Again, the majority of viewers were from the United States. In third

Table 4.2 YouTube viewership analytics by Atlas Chapter (Sector), 2023 and 2024

Year	Video sector	Number of videos	Total views	Average views per video	Average view duration (sec)
2023	Year summary	38	782	20.58	41.29
	1. Personal wellbeing	4	42	10.50	45.25
	2. People and community	5	37	7.40	57.80
	3. Weather and climate	5	141	28.20	39.60
	4. Economy and land management	7	90	12.86	49.57
	5. Ecosystems and biodiversity	5	74	14.80	39.80
	6. Water	5	109	21.80	35.00
	General	*7*	*289*	*41.29*	*25.71*
2024	Year summary	32	174	5.44	47.19
	1. Personal wellbeing	3	9	3.00	37.00
	2. People and community	4	5	1.25	11.25
	3. Weather and climate	4	12	3.00	81.75
	4. Economy and land management	4	9	2.25	73.00
	5. Ecosystems and biodiversity	4	29	7.25	50.75
	6. Water	5	30	6.00	51.80
	General	*8*	*80*	*10.00*	*34.13*
	Grand total	70	956	13.66	43.99

place was the introductory video for the series, with an average view time of 25 s. The introductory video was directly followed by a video focused on water quality with the fourth highest number of views and the longest average watch time of 40 s.

In keeping with other work on science communication (Hababi & Salim, 2021), videos that featured people, rather than moving images with voice over, did garner a greater response rate in terms of views. However, that result was not always universal—in fact, one of the more popular videos (with almost 1200 views on TikTok) is focused on an overview of the atlas and atlas project and contains a "slide show" of both still imagery and film footage shot in the watershed. Similarly, while other variables that might predict increased viewership (for example, older videos have naturally been exposed to the potential audience for a longer period of time) show some "patterns", the viewership data are insufficient to actually support any such claims (as both the oldest and the newest videos are among the most watched).

In total, viewers have spent just under eight (7.88) hours watching atlas-based content with the majority of watch time not coming from the playlist but of individual video content. The most watched content varies across the different atlas sectors, with higher durations of viewership on videos related to air quality, water advisories, ecosystem services, agricultural land, fish health, wetlands, and personal well-being. In other words, the goal of the atlas and the ECHO Network of "taking notice to take action" may very well be supported by these usage patterns. While there is no way to assess if action is being taken, there is reason to believe that some individuals are at least "taking notice" as a result of this content, particularly since many of the views are not from within Alberta. As might be expected, the more conventional dynamics of state of the watershed reporting are reflected in the viewer data, but the addition of personal health and well-being data do attract viewers as well. On the whole, ecosystems, water, and economic indicators attracted more interest than content focused on health, community well-being, or weather and climate.

Conclusion

The Health in the Watershed Atlas, created for the Battle River Watershed Alliance, was a major undertaking that included large volumes of policy analysis, legislative and regulatory synthesis, data analysis, and spatial analysis. That atlas, as noted above, is several hundred pages long and contains a massive amount of both indicator-specific and policy-based content. As resolved, and as shown through the adoption of the atlas as the current state of the watershed report for the Battle River watershed, it is perhaps overwhelming, and potentially inaccessible due to both size, limited print run, and geographic/hydrological scope. The video series created for TikTok and then subsequently posted on YouTube was not created to replace the atlas nor the thousands of hours needed to create it. Instead, it was a deliberate attempt to support knowledge mobilization and usage beyond both the watershed management community and beyond the academy more generally. The videos were created with the goal of being visually interesting, capturing a sense of both the landscape and ecosystem characteristics of the watershed and the people and communities within it.

When placed within the broader context of YouTube and TikTok influencers, YouTube shorts, and similar, 18,000 views are completely irrelevant. The most viewed TikTok of all time has received over two billion views (Guinness World Records, 2022) with many other videos having received over 800 million views. On YouTube, the Baby Shark dance video has received over 15 billion views (Baby Shark, 2016) while many other videos have received over 5 billion views (as of 2024). However, it should be noted that none of these videos have anything to do with science, public policy, public health, watershed management, or community development. They are, in fact, music and entertainment. When we turn our attention to YouTube content focused on science, most have emphasized space and astrophysics, and most include content about specific subject matter, such as the God Particle (Einstein's theory), the theory of evolution, and fishing. These videos typically have over one million views. By comparison, a discussion of watershed reports from the World Wildlife Fund Canada has received 422 views (WWF-Canada, 2020), while a video about watershed health presented by The Conservation

Foundation has received 91 views (Gail Borden Public Library, 2024). A comparable video from the Ottawa River Keeper on healthy watershed has 1566 views (Ottawa Riverkeeper, 2021). This is not a criticism of these videos, their creators, nor their content. Rather, it is a stark reflection of both public interest and awareness in environmental services and policy more generally, and particularly in regard to state of the watershed reporting and watershed health.

Ultimately, the question that emerges is whether it is worthwhile for those working in environmental policy research, watershed management, or a similar disciplinary field such as EcoHealth to engage in such knowledge mobilization strategies. Generating such videos requires dedicated staff, time, and resources, and the ECHO Network was fortunate to be able to have such resources at hand. Given the relatively low viewership and relatively brief interactions with this content, one might be inclined to avoid or dismiss such strategies as part of broader patterns of democratizing science, engaging with citizens, and communicating about the intersections between people, communities, and ecosystems. Almost 20 years ago, Row and Foster (in Habibi & Salim, 2021) identified public engagement with science as consisting of three different things: (1) public consultation, (2) public participation, and (3) public communication. Given the general lack of feedback (comments) or responses from the public, it is doubtful that such videos extend far beyond public communication of science. There is little evidence of public participation (other than watching videos, which is a deeply passive activity), and little to suggest that the videos, or their content, are seen a controversial or contested. They provide, at best, an educational and watershed-focused "snapshot" of the watershed.

While that interpretation may appear disheartening, our results do also show that while there are costs to undertaking this work, it may have benefits that extend beyond simple publicity. Specifically, we do know that these videos have been used as part of public engagement strategies and activities by the Battle River Watershed Alliance. Similarly, such exposure by YouTube or TikTok may have driven some viewers to acquire the atlas in its digital form (we do not, unfortunately, have any data to confirm this possibility).

Perhaps most importantly, the combination of the atlas and videos provides a launching point for state of the watershed reporting and related public engagement in the future. Traditionally, watershed reports, including the atlas, are cross-sectional in nature, but they may increasingly be utilized to establish a baseline for more longitudinal assessment of change over time. Similarly, the atlas and videos may also help to expand the collection and accessibility of data related to state of the watershed reporting, as well as facilitate the generation of reports that track change at larger scales, including at a provincial level.

Ultimately, the usage and utility of these products rests with the public and with those engaged in watershed management. If there is uptake and interest at even a modest level, that interest is likely greater than the interest or engagement generated by the publication of a book, special edition, a journal, or a peer-reviewed article of 6000–8000 words. Creating such videos, or a comparable media and platform, may very well be an increasing requirement or "duty" for the scientific community. Particularly as both health and environmental policy continue to be politicized, initiatives such as these videos, and the atlas, can provide an important point of reference for the public, educators, and policymakers to consider not only the context within which they work, but also to ask the framing question of the ECHO Network: Are we taking notice? How are we taking action as a result?

Acknowledgements The authors would like to thank Carly Heck, Research Associate at the Prentice Institute for Global Population and Economy, for her editorial skills and assistance.

References

Baby Shark – Pinkfong Kids' Songs & Stories. (2016, June 17). *Baby Shark Dance* [Video]. YouTube. https://www.youtube.com/watch?v=XqZsoesa55w

Battle River Watershed Association (BRWA). (2011). *Our battle: State of the battle river and sounding creek watershed report 2011*. https://www.battleriverwatershed.ca/wp-content/uploads/2018/09/Battle-River-Watershed-Report.Web.pdf

Bobrow, D. B., & Dryzek, J. S. (1987). *Policy analysis by design*. University of Pittsburgh Press.

Charron, D. F. (2012). *Innovative applications of an ecosystem approach to health*. International Development Research Centre. Springer New York.

Deschamps, T. (2023, March 1). TikTok ban should make companies review social media, device policies, experts say. *Toronto Star*. https://www.thestar.com/business/tiktok-ban-should-make-companies-review-social-media-device-policies-experts-say/article_c0636b02-8766-5f27-b944-e5709573f11f.html

Doern, G. B., Auld, G., & Stoney, C. (2015). *Green-lite: Complexity in fifty years of Canadian environmental policy, governance, and democracy*. McGill-Queen's Press-MQUP.

Dye, C., & Barclay, W. S. (2024). Should we worry about a growing threat from "bird flu"? *BMJ*, 385q1199. https://doi.org/10.1136/bmj.q1199

Gail Borden Public Library. (2024, March 20). *Down to the creek series: Watershed health: What can i do at home?* [Video]. YouTube. https://www.youtube.com/watch?v=5oa7tvSFd5U

Government of Alberta. (2008). *Handbook for state of the watershed reporting: A guide for developing state of the watershed reports in Alberta*. https://open.alberta.ca/dataset/b149604a-28d6-46bd-8618-c283d36f1c0b/resource/1d095661-c668-4cf0-bd46-de81f0fd1cc7/download/handbookstatewatershedreporting-nov2008.pdf

Guehlstorf, N. P. (2004). *The political theories of risk analysis* (Vol. 4). Springer Science & Business Media.

Guehlstorf, N. P., & Hallstrom, L. K. (2005). The role of culture in risk regulations: A comparative case study of genetically modified corn in the United States of America and European Union. *Environmental Science & Policy, 8*(4), 327–342. https://doi.org/10.1016/j.envsci.2005.04.007

Guinness World Records. (2022, March 15). *Most viewed video on TikTok*. https://www.guinnessworldrecords.com/world-records/689105-most-viewed-video-on-tiktok#:~:text=The%20most%20viewed%20video%20on,TikTok%20on%2015%20March%202022

Gupta, J. (2010). A history of international climate change policy. *Wiley Interdisciplinary Reviews: Climate Change, 1*(5), 636–653. https://doi.org/10.1002/wcc.67

Habibi, S. A., & Salim, L. (2021). Static vs. dynamic methods of delivery for science communication: A critical analysis of user engagement with science on social media. PLoS ONE, 16(3), Article e0248507. https://doi.org/10.1371/journal.pone.0248507

Hallstrom, L. K., Haugen, S., Grant, P., & Emiloju, T. (2021). *Carrying capacity surveillance: Indicators and frameworks for equitable sustainability*. Prentice Institute, University of Lethbridge.

Hallstrom, L. K., Parkes, M. W., & Guehlstorf, N. P. (2015). Convergence and diversity: Integrating encounters with health, ecological and social concerns. In *Ecosystems, society and health: Pathways through diversity, convergence and integration* (pp. 3–28). McGill-Queen's University Press. https://doi.org/10.1515/9780773583122

Hatt, K., Davidson, D., & Lock, I. (2005). Power and sustainability. In *Consuming sustainability: Critical social analyses of ecological change* (pp. 8–46). Fernwood Publishing.

Head, B. W. (2022). *Wicked problems in public policy: Understanding and responding to complex challenges* (p. 176). Springer Nature.

Howarth, J. (2024, June 12). TikTok user age, gender, & demographics (2024). *Exploding Topics.* https://explodingtopics.com/blog/tiktok-demographics

Lasswell, H. D. (1936). The Encyclopedia of the social sciences in review. *International Journal of Ethics, 46*(3), 388–396. http://www.jstor.org/stable/2989274

Lasswell, H. D. (1971). *A pre-view of policy sciences.* Elsevier.

Leiss, W. (2003, April 4). *Kyoto Kerfuffle and the Citizen's dilemma: Figuring out what to believe about climate change* [Keynote address]. 3rd Annual conference on science, values and public policy. Wilfrid Laurier University, Brantford, Ontario.

Morrison, K., Parkes, M., Hallstrom, L., Neudoerffer, C., Bunch, M., & Venema, H. D. (2012). *Ecohealth and watersheds: Watersheds as settings for health and well-being in Canada.* IISD.Canada.https://policycommons.net/artifacts/615140/ecohealth-and-watersheds/1595605/

Ottawa Riverkeeper. (2021, December 11). *Chasing a healthy watershed* [Video]. YouTube. https://youtu.be/Ar7uKiEv3HA?si=0fzmpkov6D5XzpGx

Rein B. (2023). Making Science Education More Accessible: A Case Study of TikTok's Utility as a Science Communication Tool. Neuroscience. 530:192–200. https://doi.org/10.1016/j.neuroscience.2023.08.021. Epub 2023 Aug 26. PMID: 37640135.

United Nations (UN). (2015, December). Paris agreement. In *Report of the conference of the parties to the United Nations framework convention on climate change (21st session, 2015: Paris).*

World Health Organization (WHO). (2006). *Commission on social determinants of health.* https://www.who.int/publications/i/item/WHO-EIP-EQH-01-2006

World Health Organization (WHO). (2017, September 21). *One health.* https://www.who.int/news-room/questions-and-answers/item/one-health

World Health Organization (WHO), Health and Welfare Canada, Canadian Public Health Association. (1986). *Ottawa charter for health promotion.* https://iris.who.int/bitstream/handle/10665/53166/WH-1987-May-p16-17-eng.pdf?sequence=1

World Wildlife Fund Canada (WWF-Canada). (2020, November 9). *Discover Canada's watershed health – The watershed reports live 2020.* [Video]. YouTube. https://www.youtube.com/live/e8oVs2joSK4?si=2rOx8A8n39_GAaqv

Chapter 5
Exploring the Limitations of Traditional Public Policy Analysis and the Potential of Big Data: A Case Study of Social Media Discourse on the Renewable Fuel Standard

Courtney Breckenridge and Nicholas Guehlstorf

The advent of big data has introduced tremendous opportunities for researchers to harness methodological innovations to better answer complex research questions. While the definition varies across cultures, scholars, and disciplines, Favaretto et al. (2020) define big data as "a cluster concept that includes a plethora of sophisticated and evolving computing methodologies" (p. 17). For researchers studying public policy, big data allows social science researchers to exponentially increase the size and diversity of their research samples beyond the limitations of conventional data derived from federal program assessments, surveys, or stakeholder interviews.

This paper seeks to compare and validate big data methodologies to interpret public discourse surrounding the U.S. Renewable Fuel Standard (RFS). The RFS was established via a pair of amendments to the Clean Air Act (CAA) designed to increase U.S. energy independence and reduce greenhouse gas (GHG) emissions caused by the combustion of transportation fuels. Given the relatively small number of Congressional votes on the RFS itself, policymaker and interest group discussions provide a helpful proxy for legislative votes, stakeholders, and the public. This research uses a dataset collected from Twitter (now known as "X") to systematically track and measure the program's issue salience among policymakers.

Signed into law by President George W. Bush in the early 2000s, the RFS was established by the *Energy Policy Act of 2005* (EPAct05) and subsequently expanded through the *Energy Independence and Security Act of* 2007 (EISA07). The expansion, known as RFS2, set progressive targets for the integration of renewable fuels into the domestic transportation fuel supply.

C. Breckenridge
Southern Illinois University Carbondale, Carbondale, IL, USA

N. Guehlstorf (✉)
Southern Illinois University Edwardsville, Edwardsville, IL, USA
e-mail: nguehls@siue.edu

N. Guehlstorf (ed.), *Environmental Policy Science's Exploration for Innovative Data*, Natural Resource Management and Policy NA,
https://doi.org/10.1007/978-3-031-90889-7_5

Section 211 of the CAA requires gasoline, diesel fuel, and fuel additives produced and commercially distributed in the U.S. to be registered with the Environmental Protection Agency (EPA). In 2005, Section 1501 of EPAct05 amended CAA Section 211 to create a Renewable Fuel Program and directed the EPA Administrator to promulgate regulations within one year to ensure increasing amounts of renewable fuel volumes be blended into gasoline sold or dispensed to consumers. The original renewable fuel standard required 4 billion gallons of renewable fuels in 2006 with increasing volumes to reach 7.5 billion gallons in 2012 (*EPAct of 2005*).

Propelled by the rapid expansion of the ethanol industry under the original RFS with U.S. ethanol production climbing from 3.9 to 6.5 billion gallons between 2005 and 2007 (U.S. Department of Energy, 2023), the ongoing wars in Afghanistan and Iraq, and increasing public awareness around climate change and greenhouse gas emissions, the RFS was quickly expanded by the subsequent passage of RFS2 in 2007. RFS2 boasted lofty energy and environmental goals: greater energy independence and security; increased production of clean, renewable fuels; consumer protection; increased product, vehicle, and building efficiency; research and deployment of GHG capture and storage; and a more energy-efficient federal government. The legislation expanded renewable volume obligation (RVO) targets by nearly five times, from a maximum of 7.5 billion gallons in 2012 to 36 billion gallons by 2022.

The RFS initially enjoyed bipartisan legislative passage and coalitions of environmental and agriculture supporters, and attracted high-profile interest groups, with unusual alliances formed and disbanded as the law evolved over time. Advocates for renewable fuels have included organizations such as the Rossi, Growth Energy, National Biodiesel Board, National Corn Growers Association and state grower organizations, and the American Lung Association. Opposing coalitions include oil and gas organizations, primarily the American Petroleum Institute; environmental organizations such as the National Wildlife Federation, the Union of Concerned Scientists, and Sierra Club; small engine organizations representing marine and automobiles; and restaurant and grocery associations.

Nearly 20 years after the passage of the original RFS, the renewable fuels program faces shifting stakeholder alliances, complex scientific and technology questions, and an unclear consensus on the success of environmental and energy objectives. RFS advocates and opponents make their arguments in both the court of law and the court of public opinion, including on social media platforms such as those studied in this research. Phrases such as "food versus fuel," "RINSanity," and "the blend wall" are often used in opposition to biofuels, while supporters champion attributes such as "clean," "homegrown," "energy security," "jobs," "affordability," and "national security." These talking points simplify complex regulatory, scientific, and ethical questions and attempt to persuade lawmakers and citizens toward a favorable position. According to Ralston (2015), objective scientific information is unlikely to be a factor in support for a policy when uncertainty exists around scientists' findings. Political considerations, such as potential economic impacts and the role of subsidies and mandates, are more likely to be the subject of debate than technical concerns: "legislators can use this (technical) ambiguity to instead base their decisions off of their personal preferences and what is likely to benefit their electoral prospects most" (p. 351).

An Uncertain Future

While EISA07 outlines volumetric requirements through 2022, legislators chose not to specify volumes for 2023 and beyond, instead assigning responsibility for volume obligations post-2022 to the EPA Administrator in coordination with the Secretaries of Energy and Agriculture (Energy Independence and Security Act of 2007*)*. To be clear about a very cloudy environmental public policy, the RFS did not phase out or disappear with the end of Congressional volume standards in 2022. The EPA has listed new standards for cellulosic biofuel, biomass-based diesel, advanced biofuel, and total renewable fuel for 2023–2025, although trade organizations such as the American Fuel and Petrochemical Manufacturers and the Coalition for Renewable Natural Gas have filed requests for extensions on the finalization of the proposed standards, citing inadequate information to explain how the pathway would work moving forward. Whether the annual volumes are established by statute or directly set by the EPA, advocates and opponents continue to debate the RFS in formal comments, the judiciary, and in public discourse.

The Research Problem to be Investigated

Because of the ambiguity of the program's statutory requirements—renewable volume obligations (RVOs) are the decision of the President's appointed EPA administrator—the RFS presents an ideal case study to be viewed through the lens of Kingdon's (1995) Multiple Streams Framework (MSF) (Breckenridge & Guehlstorf, 2023). When examined within the context of framing and social media, the RFS poses interesting questions for researchers regarding how public and stakeholder opinions, industry lobbying, new technology, and shifting political dynamics have shaped the RFS in the past, present, and for its future directions. Previous examinations of this topic by Breckenridge and Guehlstorf used the Multiple Streams Framework to systematically analyze the events and variables that influence policy change and policy making through three streams: the problem stream, the politics stream, and the policy stream (Breckenridge & Guehlstorf, 2023). This work on multiple streams was largely theoretical and was not empirically rich at determining external factors and events in relation to both the initial passage and subsequent evolution of the RFS. Nonetheless, MSF is still used for policy context in this practical analysis. Twitter provides a data-rich research environment for examination of the policy stream—public opinion, sentiment, and advocacy on RFS-related issues such as climate change, air quality, and energy independence. As most federal elected officials, government agencies, and interest groups have a presence on

Twitter, the site provides a useful repository of conversation around the politics stream and the people and players who advocate for or against the RFS. Similarly, Twitter is a powerful tool for examination of policy debates and discussion, including issue framing. This study seeks to use machine learning and content analysis to systematically analyze RFS-related Twitter data to understand larger trends, patterns, sentiment, and sources associated with the discourse.

Multiple Streams Framework Literature

The Multiple Streams Framework as theorized by Kingdon illustrates the factors and events that drive the priority of a given issue or problem on the policy agenda through three streams: problem, politics, and policy. This chapter reviews the origin and evolution of the Renewable Fuel Standard throughout the policymaking cycle and seeks to develop a robust understanding of how each of Kingdon's three streams shape the landscape of the RFS debate in terms of both policymaking and public opinion. John Kingdon's (1995) problem stream describes how certain issues capture policymakers' attention and motivate them to prioritize the issue within their policy agenda: "Problem recognition is critical to agenda setting…some problems are seen as so pressing that they set agendas all by themselves" (p. 149). According to Kingdon, when problems that feature both significant magnitude in scale and a change in the current condition are coupled with a symbolic event or experience, the likelihood of problem recognition and subsequent action is increased. As it pertains to the passage of RFS, the problem stream relates to issues such as climate change, energy independence, and clean air.

Within the politics stream, factors such as national mood, elections and new administrations, and partisan or ideological beliefs further help establish an issue's prominence within policymakers' agendas. The politics stream also considers the goals of interest groups, building consensus across political caucuses and alliances, and how a given problem fits within the national mood and electorate. Although the relative salience of climate change, energy independence, and air quality has varied throughout the nearly two decades since passage of the RFS, these issues move up and down the public and policy agenda based on current events and the political party in office.

Described by Kingdon as a "policy primeval soup" with floating ideas that intersect into new combinations, the policy stream illustrates the process and criteria by which problems that have both risen within lawmakers' agendas and gained the necessary political attention are formed into policy solutions. From that initial soup, policy ideas are weighed against technical feasibility, community values, and budgetary restraints, going through a "softening up process" to refine public policy into passable public law. For the RFS, this included technological questions around feedstock and conversion processes, a complex system of Renewable Identification Numbers (RINS), and regulatory burdens or benefits to impacted industries such as agriculture producers and oil refiners.

Breetz (2013) details how interest groups played a non-typical role in the formulation of the RFS. Although largely welcomed by interest groups from agriculture and biofuels industries, special interests played a lagging role in the conceptualization of the RFS. According to Breetz, the RFS was formulated by the White House and Congress and was only brought to the table after the proposal was largely developed, at which time interest groups then "negotiated for favorable provisions" (p. 10), a reversal of interest groups' traditional leading role in policy formulation.

Media Framing, Agenda-Setting, and the RFS

While the RFS enjoyed modest public support after its passage, a lack of clear public understanding of the science, technology, and economics surrounding renewable fuels opened the door to strong interest group influence, which ultimately swayed public opinion away from support of the RFS. It is our assessment that this process was due to real and perceived issues such as food versus fuel, the environmental impacts of increased agricultural utilization, and questions regarding the net energy balance of ethanol (Russell & Guehlstorf, 2023). Delshad and Raymond's (2013) analysis of national media framing trends and public survey data found evidence that media framing impacts public opinion on biofuels. The researchers documented new negative frames in national media coverage to describe biofuels between 1998 and 2008, including high food prices, negative environmental impacts, and the economic costs of biofuels. Delshad and Raymond noted national survey data tracked weak support for biofuels generally, and corn ethanol specifically, during the same timeframe. The researchers assessed media framing can have a significant impact on public attitudes on a variety of technologies.

These implications extend beyond the realm of biofuels. Throughout the history of energy policy in the United States, the success of alternative sources of energy has relied in part on government backing of new technologies, which is affected by the level of public support for those technologies. In short, policymakers are more likely to subsidize or otherwise promote technologies favored by their constituents. In an era where concerns regarding climate change, energy security, energy costs, and the scarcity of energy supplies are higher on the national agenda, media framing of the costs and benefits of all energy technologies has an even greater salience (Delshad & Raymond, 2013, p. 208). In a series of focus groups of Indiana residents, Delshad et al. (2010) found participants to be narrowly in favor of biofuels generally, but more supportive about second generation and advanced biofuels. Despite living in Indiana, a corn producing state, participants were also generally unsupportive of corn-based ethanol technology, citing concerns regarding economic and environmental impacts rather than energy dependence. These trends reflect the negative media frames identified by Delshad and Raymond (2013), specifically environmental impacts and economic costs.

As a complimentary theoretical backdrop to the Multiple Streams Framework, Shafritz et al.'s (2016) policy-making process provides a helpful lens for understanding environmental policies such as the RFS. The process begins with agenda-setting, or how the problems the policy sets out to solve are perceived and defined by the public, stakeholders, and policymakers. The agenda-setting stage also considers how these issues are prioritized and framed by the media and discussed across public and policy conduits (Shafritz et al., 2016). When considering the agenda-setting of RFS2, several issues are immediately noteworthy. The law was propelled by the rapid expansion of the ethanol industry under RFS1, seen as an early program success, as well as the ongoing wars in Afghanistan and Iraq and the emergence of a public conscience around climate change and greenhouse gas emissions. In many ways, the agenda-setting of the RFS is a textbook illustration of the blurring line between environmental and energy policies, in large part due to early framing by policymakers and stakeholders presenting the program as both an environmental and energy solution.

This study specifically examines the agenda-setting power of speaker groups such as the public, elected officials, and U.S. government agencies. These groups set RFS policy agendas by focusing the preferred topic of debate on Twitter using frames such as energy, economics, environment, policy, and specialized subject frames such as food versus fuel and national security. In Rossiter's (2021) process study of agenda-setting dynamics in U.S. presidential debates, in-person deliberations, and online discussions, the author finds that "agenda setting is a form of power – participants who set the agenda get what they want out of the discussion (p. 349)." This power is created through interactive discussions, whether in debates, in-person, or online, through topic shifts and the defining of the topics of discussion. In the context of this Twitter study, the research has implications in understanding who is speaking, on what subject or frame they are using to contextualize the subject, the intensity with which the speaker is advocating, and the popularity of the opinion for which the speaker is advocating.

Rhetorical Intensity and Advocacy Literature

Grover et al. (2019) highlight the utility of Twitter for analyzing controversial issues, as it allows scientists to see "snapshots" of people's fundamental opinions, themes and patterns on a given issue. The researchers used Twitter data to compare rhetorical trends on social media between groups supportive or opposed to immigration issues such as the Trump administration's "Muslim Ban" and the repeal of Deferred Action for Childhood Arrivals (DACA). The study found that pro-immigration tweets emphasized themes such as harm, fairness, and loyalty, while anti-immigration tweets had themes of authority and cognitive rigidity. While Grover's work on international relations did not use three streams, it can be nicely synthesized with theoretical issue frames and "devils and angels" policy analysis identified by Pattison et al. (2022). The authors examined the "devil/angel shift" strategy to illustrate how rhetoric on Twitter is reframed following a significant political event. According to the authors, a devil shift is present when there is a bias that results from the belief that opponents are "evil," while the angel shift occurs when a bias results from the belief that allies are not evil. The study examined shifts in rhetoric shared online following the implementation of a state-wide moratorium on high-volume hydraulic fracturing in New York and found that tweets that used devil shift-associated emotions decreased substantially following the moratorium (Pattison et al., 2022). The authors hypothesize that people tend to utilize more positive angel shift messages when there is legislation in place that supports their beliefs, and that devil shift messages decrease when action is taken that supports those beliefs. In this case, the moratorium on high-volume hydraulic fracturing led people who supported the decision to change the messages they published following the implementation of that decision.

Issue Frames

While not directly studying social media discourse, Neville (2021) examines controversies over biofuels and fracking and how they compare between the northern and southern hemispheres by looking at case studies in the Canadian Yukon and Kenya. Neville argues that the contention over biofuels does not come from the perceived benefits or risks from the biofuels industry to the environment. Instead, other factors, such as the economic impacts of the biofuel industry, have a greater effect on individual's beliefs about the overall impact of biofuels. According to Neville, "organizers link issues, use salient symbols and slogans, deploy scientific uncertainty, and develop transnational alliances…through strategies of discourse, framing, and public performances, as they compete over problem definitions and project consequences" (p. 13). These issues clearly emerge in the social media debate over biofuels, particularly when considering emotionally charged themes such as the impact of renewable fuels on world hunger and national security. Neville's research also provides a foundation for analysis of the arguments used by supporters and opponents, such as economic impacts on jobs, taxes, and ripple effects on other industries.

Costie (2021) similarly focuses on issue frames, specifically how a message through a particular lens brings attention to different parts of the discussion, how coalitions use those issues, and how the issue frames change over time. According to Costie's analysis of the the issue frames used by oil and gas subsystems on Twitter, opposing speakers prioritize dominant risks and more actively participate in Twitter discourse while supporters emphasize dominant benefits of the policy. Costie also found that events and ideas easily translate to similar issues and subsystems, with lessons learned from the relative success or failure of an argument on public discourse translating to other areas. Like Costie, who would like to use machine learning for policy analysis, our work up to this point has used manual coding. While many of the same analyses can be conducted with manual coding methods, the time required makes the analysis of large datasets prohibitive. Alternatively, by harnessing machine learning to gather datasets and accelerate coding and interpretation of the data, we can leverage the benefits of larger samples in terms of reliability and replicability.

Study One Research Questions

Set against the backdrop of the Multiple Streams Framework and current literature, the first study in this chapter seeks to answer three related research questions:

- Research Question One (RQ1): What speaker groups and what topics generate the greatest interest based on the number of times a Tweet is retweeted?
- Research Question Two (RQ2): How is the advocacy level of the Tweet impacted by the topics used to describe the RFS and the speaker group posting the Tweet?
- Research Question Three (RQ3): How do the dominant frames used to describe the RFS vary across speaker groups?

Study One Results

An intercoder reliability analysis was performed to determine consistency among two coders using a random sample of 250 Tweets selected from the study sample. The intercoder reliability for the advocacy variable was found to be Kappa =0.7215 ($p < 0.001$), indicating good agreement between raters (1 indicates perfect agreement between coders). The total sample included 1000 units of analysis, evenly distributed across the three speaker groups: public (n = 334), U.S. government agency accounts (n = 333), and elected officials (n = 333). Across all speaker groups, the Tweet sample had an average advocacy score of 3.53, indicating a slightly above neutral score. Policy/Regulatory was the most frequently used frame (n = 456), followed by Environmental (n = 353), Technology/Feedstock (n = 347), Agriculture (n = 189), Economics (n = 181), Energy (n = 160), National Security (n = 53), and Food versus Fuel (n = 45).

To assess RQ1, *What speaker groups and what topics generate the greatest interest based on the number of times a Tweet is retweeted,* a mixed model analysis was performed. Because the retweet variable was highly skewed and followed a Poisson distribution, the natural logarithm (ln) was determined to be the appropriate transformation and the ln for the number of retweets was used for the analysis. An ANOVA was performed using PROC MIXED of SAS (version 9.4) to identify the most retweeted speaker groups and subject frames. Diagnostic measures indicated that a ln transformation was needed to satisfy the assumptions of the ANOVA. Therefore, the analysis was performed on the ln of the number of retweets, and back-transformed means were calculated for the levels of the main effects in Table 5.1.

Table 5.1. Least square means by statistically significant variable

Variable	Level	Estimate	Back-transformation
Economics	0	0.13	1.14
	1	0.58	1.79
Energy	0	0.27	1.31
	1	0.44	1.56
Agriculture	0	0.40	1.49
	1	0.87	2.38
Technology	0	0.19	1.21
	1	0.52	1.68
Speaker category			
1: Public	1	−0.76	0.47
2: Government	2	0.26	1.29
3: Elected officials	3	1.57	4.80

Table 5.2 Regression results

	Coefficients	Standard error	*t* Stat	*P*-value
Intercept	2.948	0.121	24.264	0.000
Economics	0.076	0.078	0.975	0.330
Environmental	−0.173	0.107	−1.620	0.106
Energy	0.368	0.083	4.436	0.000***
National Security	0.349	0.134	2.603	0.009***
Agriculture	0.127	0.076	1.665	0.096
Technology/feedstock	0.552	0.076	7.299	0.000***
Policy/regulatory	−0.114	0.068	−1.670	0.095
Food versus fuel	−0.142	0.062	−2.272	0.023***
Government agencies	0.360	0.116	3.111	0.002***
Elected officials	0.812	0.120	6.785	0.000***
N	1000			
R^2	0.19			

***P-value<0.05

For *Research Question Two (RQ2): How is the advocacy level of the Tweet impacted by the topics used to describe the RFS and the speaker group posting the Tweet,* a regression analysis was performed, utilizing advocacy score as the dependent variable with content frames and speaker type as the independent variables. Table 5.2 details the regression results, with the content frames of Energy, National Security, Technology/Feedstock, and Food versus Fuel showing a statistically significant effect on advocacy score. Speaker groups also had a statistically significant impact for both the Government and Elected Official categories. Among the statistically significant variables, Tweets referencing Energy, National Security, and Technology/Feedstock had a positive impact on the advocacy score, indicating higher levels of approval or advocacy. Conversely, Tweets referencing Food versus Fuel had a negative impact on the advocacy score, indicating the frame is more frequently used by opponents. Finally, Tweets posted by Government and Elected Official speaker groups both had a positive impact on the advocacy score associated with the Tweets.

To further examine the relationship between a Tweet's advocacy level and the frames used to describe the RFS, a logistic regression was performed, with an Advocacy level of 4 or 5 assigned as "Highly positive" (1) and other Advocacy levels assigned a value of 0. Explanatory variables with a p-value >0.20 were removed from the model, with the final model including highly significant ($P < 0.01$) variables of energy, national security, technology/feedstock, food vs. fuel, and speaker group. A logistic regression was performed using PROC GLIMMIX in SAS (Version 9.4; SAS Institute Inc., 2015). The purpose of this logistic regression was to identify the frames and speaker groups with a statistically significant impact on the Tweet's advocacy level and the results are contained in Table 5.3.

In analyzing *Research Question Three (RQ3): How do the dominant frames used to describe the RFS vary across speaker groups,* a logistic regression model was performed in PROC GLIMMIX of SAS (version 9.4) using the binomial distribution and the logit link function. The estimates and back-transformed means are presented in Table 5.4.

A final logistic regression was conducted within PROC GLIMMIX of SAS (version 9.4) using Speaker Group as an explanatory variable and each of the frames in Tables 5.3 and 5.4 as response variables in turn. As part of the logistic regression, a test of differences in Least Squares Means (LSMEANS) was conducted to determine if there were significant differences between Speaker Groups (Table 5.5). The Food versus Fuel frame is not included in the comparison because the overall model p-value was not significant.

Table 5.3 Least square means by variable impacting advocacy score

Variable	Present or absent	Estimate	Standard error	DF	*t* Value	Pr > |t|	Mean	Difference
Economics	0	1.2656	0.5853	991	2.16	0.0308	0.7800	4.34%
	1	1.5395	0.5976	991	2.58	0.0101	0.8234	
Energy	0	1.0165	0.5730	991	1.77	0.0764	0.7343	12.25%
	1	1.7887	0.6119	991	2.92	0.0035	0.8568	
National Security	0	0.4439	0.5132	991	0.87	0.3872	0.6092	30.46%
	1	2.3612	0.7521	991	3.14	0.0017	0.9138	
Food versus fuel	0	2.4238	0.3062	991	7.92	<0.0001	0.9186	−22.56%
	1	0.8141	0.5712	991	1.43	0.1544	0.6930	
Speaker category								
1: Public	1	0.4412	0.5941	991	0.74	0.4579	0.6085	
2: Government	2	1.1596	0.5894	991	1.97	0.0494	0.7613	
3: Elected officials	3	2.6068	0.6001	991	4.34	<0.0001	0.9313	

Table 5.4 Likelihood of frame use by speaker group (percentage)

Speaker group	Economics	Environment	Energy	National Security	Agriculture	Technology	Food vs. Fuel
Public	13.2	90.3	24.9	0.6	16.6	32.7	4.2
U.S. government	16.8	8.1	10.2	8.0	10.2	64.3	1.2
Elected officials	24.3	6.9	12.9	6.9	29.3	7.2	2.1

Table 5.5 Comparison of frame utilization by speaker group (p-values)

Speaker group	Economics	Environment	Energy	National Security	Agriculture	Technology
1 vs. 2	0.19	<0.01	<0.01	<0.01	0.02	<0.01
1 vs. 3	<0.01	<0.01	<0.01	<0.01	<0.01	<0.01
2 vs. 3	0.02	0.55	0.28	0.46	<0.01	<0.01

Study One Discussion

In response to *Research Question One (RQ1): What speaker groups and what topics generate the greatest interest based on the number of times a Tweet is retweeted,* all speaker groups were significantly different (Table 5.1), with Elected Officials having the most retweets (average of 4.8 retweets), followed by U.S. Government Agencies (average of 1.3 retweets), and posts from the Public speaker group (average of 0.5 retweets). The only subject frame to demonstrate a statistically significant impact on the number of retweets was the Agriculture frame, with 2.38 additional retweets predicted when the subject included themes reflective of farmers, rural communities, or general agricultural interests.

Regarding *Research Question Two (RQ2): How is the advocacy level of the Tweet impacted by the topics used to describe the RFS and the speaker group posting the Tweet,* several frames demonstrated a marked increase in the chance of a moderate to strong advocacy level (Table 5.3). Tweets referencing National Security had the greatest impact on the advocacy level, with a 30.46% higher chance of a positive advocacy score, followed by Energy (12.25%), and Economics (4.34%). Tweets referencing Food versus Fuel were the only frame to have a statistically significant negative impact on advocacy level, with a 22.56% lower chance of positive advocacy in Tweets that referenced Food versus Fuel. The relationship between the advocacy level of the Tweet and the speaker group posting the content is also statistically significant, with an increasingly higher probability of positive advocacy from the Public (60.9%) to U.S. Government Agencies (76.1%) to Elected Officials (93.1%). Given the nature of social media management among individuals posting on a U.S. Government Agencies, the increased likelihood of a positive advocacy core is somewhat expected—official agency accounts generally seek to avoid controversy and to highlight successes rather than failures. However, the high likelihood of positive for Elected Officials is somewhat surprising, given the highly polarized political environments in the years for which Tweets were examined (2009–2020).

For *Research Question Three (RQ3): How do the dominant frames used to describe the RFS vary across speaker groups,* all speaker groups showed statistically significant variation in frame utilization comparisons; however, the groups did have common trends, including consistent use of the Energy frame (third highest ranked across all speaker groups), and consistently low utilization of the National Security and Food versus Fuel frames. In the public speaker group, Table 5.4 shows Environment (90.3%) was the most highly used frame, followed by Technology (32.7%), and Energy (24.9%) with National Security (0.6%) as the least-used frame. In the U.S. Government Agency speaker group, Technology (64.3%) was the most-used frame, followed by Economics (16.8%), and Energy (10.2%), with Food versus Fuel (1.2%) as the least-used frame. Finally, Elected Officials were most likely to discuss Agriculture (29.3%), followed by Economics (24.3%) and Energy (12.9%), with Food versus Fuel (2.1%) as the least used frame.

Limitations to the current research include the use of retweets as a measure of the influence of Twitter. While retweets provide insight into the relative interest of other Twitter users in the opinions or information shared by the original poster, they are in no way a proxy for substantive policy advocacy, such as legislative voting records, stakeholder or voter policy engagement, or even voting amongst registered voters. An additional limitation is the methodology for determining a Tweet's relative advocacy score. The 5-point advocacy score scale utilized in this research (1 for strong opposition to 5 for strong support) does not reflect whether a Tweet which ranked highly on advocacy reflected the RFS's perceived benefits or risks or devil/angel shifts (Pattison et al., 2022). As such, we decided to use the same data set, but for Study Two we operationalized the research questions with machine learning methods to assess the correlation between the content frame, district characteristics, and advocacy position of elected officials.

Study Two Research Questions

Set again with backdrop of the Multiple Streams Framework and current literature but learning from the aforementioned regressions, this second study seeks to test two hypotheses:

- *Hypothesis One (H_1)*: Legislators' overall positions (advocate or opponent) are more strongly impacted by the characteristics of their districts than by their political parties. Therefore, legislators with significant corn acreage were more likely to be supporters of the RFS than those with large numbers of poultry producers or oil refineries.

- *Hypothesis Two (H_2)*: The frames legislators use to describe RFS reflect their overall positions, with supporters being more likely to frame their Tweets in terms of jobs, positive impacts on rural communities, and environmental benefits such as clean air. Conversely, opponents are more likely to discuss the negative environmental impacts such as intensified agriculture production and land use change, the negative impact of "mandates" on an open market and impacts on food supply (food versus fuel).

Study Two Research Design and Methods

To test these hypotheses, a content analysis of Tweets relating to the RFS posted by legislators in the 115th and 116th Congresses (n = 2784) was conducted. The research sample was generated using the TweetSet library from George Washington University (George Washington University Libraries, 2022). The TweetSets used includes the following libraries: 116th Congress, 115th Congress, 116th Senate, and 115th Senate. Within the selected libraries, all Tweets that included any of the following keywords were included in the initial sample: "ethanol, RFS, renewable fuel standard, biofuels, biodiesel, land use change, food versus fuel, growth energy, American petroleum institute, renewable fuels, renewable fuels association, biofuel, corn ethanol, cellulosic ethanol, advanced biofuels, renewable volume obligation, RVO, SREC, small refinery exemption credit, RIN, renewable identification number, RINs." Each library of Tweet IDs was downloaded in a text file, and then transformed to an Excel database using Hydrator (Version 0.3.0; Documenting the Now, 2021) to generate the full text of the tweet and accompanying metadata associated with the Tweet ID. Within the Excel database, Tweets where user location was not listed or was outside of the U.S. were manually deleted to limit the analysis to domestic policy discussion. All Tweets were made between 2009 and 2020.

While formal modelers consider everything an independent variable before research findings, our machine learning is a hybrid with two models. Tweets were given a combined sentiment analysis score using VADER (Hutto & Gilbert, 2014). Each tweet was paired with the corresponding corn yield, poultry production, and oil production value of the poster's legislative district, referenced by state and year. Corn yield and poultry production were pulled from USDA NASS Quick Stats (U.S. Department of Agriculture, National Agricultural Statistics Service, 2024). Oil production was pulled from the crude oil production by state and year from the Energy Information Administration's website (U.S. Energy Information Administration, 2024). Districts with no oil, corn, or poultry production were given a value of 0, representing minimal or 0 production. The combined sentiment analysis score, corn yield, crude oil production, and poultry production were then input as predictors into a linear discriminant analysis. A ten-fold cross-validation was used with three repeats. The classifier results were trained with manual coding for advocacy scores to assess accuracy.

The Study Two model is not just a sentiment analysis of advocacy scores but a classification of advocacy scores with sentiment analysis and framing. Taking the data from Study One, we classified the framing based on keywords used for manual coding (Breckenridge & Guehlstorf, 2023). We then took these additional categories and determined their individual frequency distributions. To avoid statistical bias, if less than 5% of the data fell into any one section, it was not included in the model. Categories included were Economics, Energy, Security, Agriculture, Policy and Regulation, and Corn Feedstock. Categories dropped were Environment, Technology, Food vs. Fuel, and Advanced Feedstocks. The combined sentiment analysis score, corn yield, crude oil production, poultry production, and framing categories were put into a linear discriminant analysis model. A ten-fold cross-validation was used with three repeats.

Study Two Results

The first model utilized the VADER-generated sentiment analysis score, crude oil production, corn yield, and poultry production as predictors into a linear discriminant analysis, with a final prediction accuracy calculated to be 73.1%. However, the accuracy of the classifier varied significantly on positive, negative, and neutral Tweets. Positive posts ($n = 1934$) were correctly identified 90.75% of the time, with negative posts ($n = 581$) only correctly identified for 47.5% of Tweets. The model was not able to identify neutral posts ($n = 269$). The second model involved the classification of advocacy scores with sentiment analysis and framing. While the final prediction accuracy was found to be 73.9%, the specificity of the second model was significantly improved from the first model. Positive Tweets were correctly identified 91.3% of the time, a slight increase from the original model, while negative Tweets were correctly identified 50.7% of the time. The algorithm was also able to parse through Tweets to detect a relative neutral element. Although the model only correctly classified two neutral Tweets, it is important to note that the categories are not absolute and therefore the algorithm detected neutral elements based on framing and diction.

Study Two Discussion

In studies using Ordinary Least Squares (OLS) regression, researchers typically find a data set, control for intervening variables, and invest significant time building an index for the dependent variable before running the regression. In this hybrid of inductive and deductive hypothesis testing, the research design is still built in a traditional way, with the hypothesis guiding the analysis, but the advent of larger datasets and artificial intelligence allows researchers to mine the process to look for relationships and confirm, add to, or even iteratively update hypotheses before moving into the predictive modeling portion of the machine learning pipeline. Early analysis of relationships leads to the exploration of potential causative variables, allowing researchers to start thinking about a causal relationship versus a correlation. This methodologically represents a significant change, as researchers are increasingly comfortable starting out with just correlations and then exploring if the variables are just predictive or causative.

Relative to the H_1, which considers the characteristics of a legislative district as a predictor of a legislator's position (advocate or opponent), the accuracy of the model's prediction provides strong evidence in support of the hypothesis. Particularly for positive Tweets (predicted to be associated with districts with high corn yield), the model was very effective at identifying supportive Tweets. The model's accuracy declined with negative Tweets, associated with crude oil and poultry production; however, the significant difference in the number of positive and negative Tweets (almost 4:1 positive to negative), likely impacts the ability to train the classifier. For H_2,which considered the frames legislators use to describe the RFS in addition to their overall advocacy or opposition, the second model improved significantly in its detection of both positive and negative Tweets, particularly negative posts. This provides strong evidence in support of the second hypothesis, as the words used by legislators in the content of their Tweet helped improve the models' ability to detect both positive and negative posts. Therefore, it can be deduced that the frames used by legislators and their overall opposition or support are correlated.

Significance and Conclusion

There is a growing population of scholars across the fields of political science, sociology, environmental sciences, and communications who study the impacts of "big data" on social science. This is important as researchers involved in natural resource administrative investigations and pollution control policy analysis must be entrepreneurial in finding and utilizing data sets to answer pressing policy questions. Successful researchers must go beyond publicly available federal programs assessments, original but local surveys, and collaborations or interviews with or about stakeholder groups to be relevant today.

While deductive hypothesis testing saves time and is better applied and situated toward literature reviews and theoretical designs, the environmental sciences discipline now has the ingenuity of positivist social scientists who use analytical chemistry, biological sampling, meteorological data, and agricultural statistics to test natural resource and pollution policy questions. Empirical environmental sciences research has reached new heights as scholars today are using huge data sets from Twitter, information from satellites, Tik Tok, Geographical Information Systems, and other previously unused sources to examine policy relevant questions. Examining new research activity in natural resource management and pollution control policy will help establish whether new inductive ways of doing policy analysis are an aberration or whether the use of untraditional data sources are in fact becoming the basis for a new generation of environmental political research.

Building off these emerging innovations, this research utilizes Kingdon's (1995) Multiple Streams Framework to analyze federal legislators' social media discourse on Twitter associated with the U.S. Renewable Fuels Standard. Much of the policy cycle associated with the passage, implementation, and legitimation of the RFS can be captured through Kingdon's three streams: problems, politics, and policies. From 2005 to 2008, these streams seemingly converged to enable the bipartisan passage of the EISA07 and the expansion of RFS into RFS2. Since 2007, debate around RFS has evolved, with increasing emphasis on controversial issues such as climate change, food versus fuel, questions of environmental impact, and the economic effects of the legislation on oil and agriculture industries. As the public and political debate has intensified, so, too, has the intensity of RFS advocates and opponents, with very little middle ground. This intensity can in part be attributed to complex scientific and technical questions without clear scientific consensus, and the tendency of proponents and opponents to utilize devil/angel shifts in their framing of issues (Pattison et al., 2022) to attempt to control the argument.

This research seeks to advance the work of previous scholars such as Cook (2018), who studied factors influencing policy outcomes through interviews with U.S. government agency staff and stakeholders to verify the MSF's utility in understanding policy formulation and outcomes, specifically a controversial rulemaking process by the U.S. EPA and National Highway Transportation Safety Agency (NHTSA). Cook's research found that the political and policy streams must converge early in the process to achieve successful outcomes. Within the context of the RFS, this convergence occurred early in the process but deteriorated as policy implementation progressed.

Similarly, Fowler (2020) examines the MSF policy process with policymaking and policy implementation as distinct but interconnected streams. Fowler's research emphasizes how "governance schemes evolve and become reliant on nongovernmental organizations and networks" (p. 635), reflecting the lagging role of interest groups in RFS policy formulation but increasingly prominent role in policy implementation. Fowler further suggests that for successful policy implementation, the initial policy architects' work must extend from formulation and passage through implementation and legitimation to avoid failed policies in practice. Given the initial impetus for the RFS and subsequent changes in political administrations and public discourse around issues surrounding climate change, energy independence, and national security, this need for continued policy and political champions is particularly relevant.

The results provide support for both the research hypotheses as well as the relevance of Multiple Streams as a theoretical framework, particularly as it relates to the politics stream. Legislators' advocacy or opposition is strongly correlated with the characteristics of their districts, which reflect the interests and livelihoods of the voters who elect them to office. Similarly, the problem stream is strongly reflected in the results. The "problems" the RFS is purported to solve—or the problems it creates—are directly reflected in legislators' framing of their position. Whether referring to energy supplies, the economy, or impacts on rural America, legislators appear to select the "problem" that most directly supports their position and frame their arguments accordingly.

Future research directions could expand beyond two sessions of Congress to capture changes to overall advocacy and opposition levels over time, providing an opportunity to better pinpoint the evolution and subsequent devolution of the RFS. Limitations to the current research include the size of the dataset, and changes to the availability of Tweets as a result of Elon Musk's purchase of the company (now known as X). This research also only relies on one machine learning method and could further test additional models to determine even more accurate predictive capabilities.

Acknowledgements We would like to offer a special thank you to Dr. Carolyn Butts-Wilmsmeyer, the Director of the Center for Predictive Analytics, for her assistance with the statistics. We would also like to thank the Southern Illinois University Edwardsville Graduate School for funding this research. Finally, we are grateful for the undergraduate researcher Jennifer Markfort from the Department of Environmental Sciences at Southern Illinois University Edwardsville who helped with an earlier version of this research project.

Appendices (Appendix 5.6 and 5.7)

Appendix 5.6 Operational definitions of coding categories

Category	Detailed definition	Sample tweet
Advocacy score	Extreme opposition (1): Strong negative opinion, shared with personal feeling or strong language	No real surprise here: Making ethanol from corn is a really bad idea. The US uses 40% of our corn harvest to produce less than 1% of our energy use. Lots of environmental problems with corn-ethanol system. Time to end this silly and needless subsidy. https://t.co/iiJuiSSkvT
	Moderate opposition (2): Negative view of the RFS but lacking strong personal feelings or language	The study "found that growing corn for biofuel is an inefficient use of land, and also that crop-based biofuels produce three times the emissions of gasoline or diesel. They also found that efficient agricultural practices are beneficial for climate change mitigation." https://t.co/WDUU6ZJVyl
	Neutral (3): Basic reporting of a fact or news without opinion	@Shell to spend $2bn on #WindPower, #biofuels and #EVs and sets new company #climate change target https://t.co/zztDRn34g9
	Moderate advocacy (4): Positive view of the RFS but not shared with strong personal feelings or language	Pleased to discuss the importance of biofuels and renewables today at the #IRFA2016 summit.@iowafuel https://t.co/7J1mW9vlx0
	Strong advocacy (5): Strong positive opinion, shared with personal feelings and/or strong language	Shameful if big oil & Carl Icahn are dictating trump's RFS policy. Either way, I'll fight for RFS & Iowa's farmers https://t.co/183qSRmoqp

(continued)

Appendix 5.6 (continued)

Category	Detailed definition	Sample tweet
Economics	Discussions of financial and employment impact of RFS: Taxes, tariffs, imports, trade, jobs	#China employs more people than the US in all #renewable sectors. The only American sector with higher employment is #biofuels
Environment	References to climate change, greenhouse gases, emissions, water quality, air quality, land use change	Plowing up native prairie habitat to grow corn for #ethanol is wrong for #wildlife like threatened grassland sparrows & wrong for our environment! New research shows the ethanol mandate is contributing to climate change: https://t.co/rjjbgjuSUW https://t.co/RCzmyxq5Yy
Energy	References to energy, energy usage, life cycle analysis, renewables, renewable energy, fossil fuels	From #windenergy to #ethanol, #Iowa has consistently been at the forefront of utilizing renewables while maintaining low costs for consumers and creating new jobs. https://t.co/7yqo2M7lwP
National Security	References to foreign oil, dictators, U.S. military apparatus	Ending the farm-to-Fleet program harms our farmers &amp, innovators in the biofuel industry. We need clean, homegrown energy, NOT oil bought from dictators. Our navy understands that climate change is a national security threat. Why doesn't @realDonaldTrump? https://t.co/O1AQMXgFzB
Agriculture	Tweets that discuss agriculture, farmers, rural communities	Poor farmers lose in the world of mass-produced biofuels. Read more: https://t.co/y2gmo7P1Jx #goodfoodmedia
Technology, feedstock	Tweets on new research, technological advancements, and biofuels feedstocks (corn, switchgrass, algae, second generation, cellulosic ethanol and advanced biofuels)	Medoff's inventive use of electron accelerators at his company Xyleco, breaks down plant biomass into environmentally- friendly biofuels which can be pumped right into car's fuel tank. His factory is expected to be operational this spring
Policy, regulatory	Discussions of policy or regulatory decisions, such as US EPA waivers, renewable volume obligations (RVOs), mandates, etc.	Announcement by @POTUS to lift restrictions on #E15 is great news for our ag community in #IL18. Ethanol helps drive demand for corn in #IL18 and this will expand opportunity for farmers looking to sell #E15YearRound while providing consumer choice and reducing emissions
Food versus fuel	Tweets that reference food prices, hunger, tradeoffs between biofuels and food production	Actually, #ClimateChange hits poor countries harder because in response to it we started turning tortillas/food/corn into fuel and made everything more expensive while producing garbage-fuel/#ethanol https://t.co/qXVO2BIcMO

Appendix 5.7 Least Squares Means provided but full SAS data output available by request

Least Squares Means										
Effect	Economics	Energy	Agriculture	technology	category	Estimate	Standard Error	DF	t Value	Pr > |t|
Economics	0					0.1280	0.5205	992	0.25	0.8058
Economics	1					0.5808	0.5326	992	1.09	0.2758
Energy		0				0.2671	0.5190	992	0.51	0.6069
Energy		1				0.4416	0.5349	992	0.83	0.4092
Agriculture			0			0.3961	0.08642	992	4.58	<.0001
Agriculture			1			0.8658	0.1330	992	6.51	<.0001
Agriculture			2			-0.1987	1.5468	992	-0.13	0.8978
technology				0		0.1924	0.5211	992	0.37	0.7121
technology				1		0.5164	0.5309	992	0.97	0.3310
category					1	-0.7630	0.5238	992	-1.46	0.1456
category					2	0.2583	0.5287	992	0.49	0.6252
category					3	1.5677	0.5316	992	2.95	0.0033

References

Breckenridge, C. & Guehlstorf, N. (2023, April 15). *Multiple streams framework and social media: An analysis of policy actor tweets on the U.S. renewable fuel standard* [paper presentation]. Midwest political science association conference.

Breetz, H. L. (2013). Fueled by crisis: U.S. alternative fuel policy, 1975–2007 (Doctoral dissertation, Massachusetts Institute of Technology). DSpace@MIT. https://dspace.mit.edu/handle/1721.1/83759

Cook, J. J. (2018). The EPA, NHTSA, and the multiple streams drive climate policy outcome. *Environmental Practice, 20*(1), 23–35. https://doi.org/10.1080/14660466.2018.1424489

Costie, D. P. (2021). "*Advocacy coalitions in the Twittersphere: Tracking variations in activity and discourse in unconventional oil and gas subsystems*" [paper].

Delshad, A., Raymond, L., Sawicki, V., & Wegener, D. (2010). Public attitudes toward political and technical options for biofuels. *Energy Policy, 38*, 3414–3425. https://doi.org/10.1016/j.enpol.2010.02.015

Delshad, A., & Raymond, L. (2013). Media framing and public attitudes toward biofuels. *Review of Policy Research, 30*(2), 190–210. https://doi.org/10.1111/ropr.12009

Documenting the Now. (2021). *Hydrator* (Version 0.3.0) [Software]. GitHub. https://github.com/DocNow/hydrator

Energy Independence and Security Act of 2007. *42 USC §17001* (2007). Retrieved from https://www.govinfo.gov/content/pkg/BILLS-110hr6enr/pdf/BILLS-110hr6enr.pdf

Favaretto, M., De Clercq, E., Schneble, C. O., & Elger, B. S. (2020). What is your definition of big data? Researchers' understanding of the phenomenon of the decade. *PLoS One, 15*(2), 1–20. https://doi.org/10.1371/journal.pone.0228987

Fowler, L. (2020). Using the multiple streams framework to connect policy adoption to implementation. *Policy Studies Journal, 50*(3), 615–639. https://doi.org/10.1111/psj.12381

George Washington University Libraries. (2022). *Tweetset: A tool for analyzing twitter datasets*. https://tweetset.org/.

Grover, T., Bayraktaroglu, E., Mark, G., & Ha Rim Rho, E. (2019). Moral and affective differences in U.S. immigration policy debate on twitter. *Computer Supported Cooperative Work: The Journal of Collaborative Computing., 28*(3/4), 317–355. https://doi.org/10.1007/s10606-019-09357-w

Hutto, C. J., & Gilbert, E. E. (2014). VADER: A parsimonious rule-based model for sentiment analysis of social media text. *Proceedings of the International AAAI Conference on Web and Social Media, 8*(1), 216–225. https://doi.org/10.1609/icwsm.v8i1.14550

Kingdon, J. W. (1995). *Agendas, alternatives, and public policies*. Longman.

Neville, K. J. (2021). *Fueling resistance: The contentious political economy of biofuels and fracking*. Oxford University Press.

Pattison, A., Cipolli, W., & Marichal, J. (2022). The devil we know and the angel that did not Fly: An examination of devil/angel shift in twitter fracking debates' in NY 2008–2018. *Review of Policy Research, 39*, 51–72. https://doi.org/10.1111/ropr.12452

Ralston, J. J. (2015). The unscientific determinants of voting on a controversial scientific issue: An evaluation of biofuels policy in the U.S. Congress. *Review of Policy Research, 32*, 323–344. https://doi.org/10.1111/ropr.12124

Rossiter, E. L. (2021). Measuring agenda setting in interactive political communication. *American Journal of Political Science, 66*, 337–351. https://doi.org/10.1111/ajps.12653

Russell, K., & Guehlstorf, N. (2023). Policy evaluations of the renewable fuel standard and agricultural land use changes in three Midwestern states for a decade: Variables that influence significant changes in crop decisions are not all about ethanol. *Biofuels, 14*(8), 825–833. https://doi.org/10.1080/17597269.2023.2184940

SAS Institute Inc. (2015). *SAS/STAT® 14.1 user's guide: The GLIMMIX procedure* (version 9.4). SAS Institute https://documentation.sas.com/doc/en/statug/14.1/statug_glimmix_gettingstarted.htm

Shafritz, J. M., Russell, E. W., Borick, C. P., & Hyde, A. C. (2016). *Introducing public Administration*. Routledge.

U. S. Department of Agriculture, National Agricultural Statistics Service. (2024). *Quick stats* [corn, poultry]. USDA. https://quickstats.nass.usda.gov/

U. S. Department. of Energy. (2023). Maps and data–global ethanol production by country or region. In *Alternative fuels data center: Maps and data*. Retrieved April 7, 2023, from https://afdc.energy.gov/data

U. S. Energy Information Administration. (2024). *Crude oil production* [Data set]. U.S. Department of Energy. https://www.eia.gov/dnav/pet/pet_crd_crpdn_adc_mbbl_m.htm

Chapter 6
Saving Little Swimmer, Jumper, and Digger: Three Survey Experiments Testing Kinship Appeals in Conservation Marketing

David S. Morris and Hector N. Qirko

As we wrestle with a variety of interrelated environmental problems, including climate change, deforestation, and environmental justice, the need for people to provide resources to pro-environmental causes and organizations has never been greater. The loss of species diversity is a particularly worrisome problem. The most current IUCN Red List shows 44,000 species, or over a quarter of those the organization has been able to assess to date, as threatened with extinction (IUCN, 2023). The current rate of extinction is estimated to be 1000 species per year (Brenna, 2020) and increasing (Johnson, 2021). Even after targeted conservation efforts, the status of many well-known endangered species has not improved (Rosen, 2022). Because governmental attention to this problem varies widely within and across nations (e.g., AZA Omnibus Survey, 2018; Bruder et al., 2022; Jarić et al., 2020), conservation organizations that address it increasingly make direct public appeals to obtain financial and other resources (Jacobson et al., 2015a). However, charitable and other contributions to environmental causes and organizations are typically very low (Anderson, 2018). For example, in 2020 less than 2% of total American charitable donations went to environmental nonprofits (Thomas, 2020). As environmental problems continue to increase in number and consequences, then, effective conservation-related marketing will likely be an increasingly necessary tool (Wright et al., 2015).

While there are many marketing strategies used by organizations in their attempts to elicit support from target populations, there remains a need for broad-based strategies that are effective for a wide spectrum of species and across audiences that differ demographically and culturally. In this chapter we describe one such marketing strategy that, while underexplored in the literature and rarely used in practice,

D. S. Morris (✉) · H. N. Qirko
College of Charleston, Charleston, SC, USA
e-mail: morrisds@cofc.edu; qirkoh@cofc.edu

N. Guehlstorf (ed.), *Environmental Policy Science's Exploration for Innovative Data*, Natural Resource Management and Policy NA,
https://doi.org/10.1007/978-3-031-90889-7_6

has the potential to be particularly effective: kinship appeals, or appeals to relatedness between target audiences and the species for which support is sought. We then discuss several survey experiments whose results suggest the likely effectiveness of kinship appeals as a marketing strategy.

Conservation Marketing

Conservation marketing is relatively new and still developing in terms of both organizational marketing knowledge and the means through which initiatives are evaluated by researchers (Robinson et al., 2019; Ryan et al., 2020). There are many different strategies in use, including appeals based on scientific data (e.g., Smith et al., 2010), moral/ethical precepts (Ghasemi & Kyle, 2021), social norms (Saracevic et al., 2022), and self-interest (De Dominicis et al., 2017). These appeals are often used in combination, resulting in many different initiatives whose effects are often difficult to tease apart (Veríssimo et al., 2019). There are also many variables that can lead to mixed results, even with the same strategy, depending on local contexts (for overviews, see Chen & Wu, 2023; Jacobson et al., 2015b). For example, depending on ecological and cultural factors, the same species can be viewed differently across and within communities (Camino et al., 2016; van Eeden et al., 2020); even repeated exposure to data can be ineffective where issues are large-scale and time-frames are long (Palomo-Vélez & Van Vugt, 2021; Rizzi et al., 2020); urgent appeals (i.e., "spectacles of extinction") can backfire when audience attention fades, especially on social media (Brandon, 2021); self-interest and ethical appeals vary in effectiveness depending on the degree to which contributions are made public (Green & Peloza, 2014); and levels of concern by audiences for environmental issues influence effects, as "preaching to the choir" tends to work equally well no matter what strategy is used (e.g., Balaskas et al., 2023; Schuhwerk & Lefkoff-Hagius, 1995). Thus, while there are many context-dependent strategies used to attempt to elicit financial and other contributions for threatened species, strategies that are effective for one species and one target population might not be for the next. And because we live in increasingly multicultural contexts and the problems we face transcend local and even national boundaries, the need for marketing strategies that appeal more broadly across cultural, demographic, and other contexts has increased.

In fact, two such broad-based strategies are commonly used, both based on presumed universal human psychological biases. One makes use of the "charisma," natural or manipulated, of specific threatened species, both for their sake and as "flagships" to generate support and funding for other species. Although what makes a species charismatic is hard to determine, there appear to be universal tendencies to favor large, exotic, terrestrial mammals (Albert et al., 2018) as well as those exhibiting neotenous features (e.g., Borgi et al., 2014; Estren, 2012). However, as a marketing strategy, appealing to charisma has problems, as the few species typically seen as "cute" or otherwise charismatic receive a disproportionally high percentage of attention and financial support, leaving many others unattended (e.g., Macdonald et al., 2015; Small, 2011, 2012). Further, factors that render species charismatic might not inspire conservation (e.g., Cermak, 2021), and the degree of direct exposure to species influences views of their charisma (de Pinho et al., 2014). In addition, the proliferation of images of charismatic species can backfire by causing target audiences to underestimate the degree to which they are threatened (Courchamp et al., 2018).

Another broad-based strategy is based on anthropomorphizing, or assigning human-like qualities to non-human species. Its effects can sometimes overlap those of strategies based on charisma in that similarity to humans may be what makes some species charismatic. However, anything, even an inanimate object, elicits empathy when anthropomorphized (e.g., Edwards & Shafer, 2022), suggesting that anthropomorphism is likely its own universal psychological tendency (Barrett, 2004; Urquiza-Haas & Kotrschal, 2015). But here too, researchers point out that while anthropomorphizing is often an effective marketing tool, the qualities we anthropomorphize, if human-like but negative, can lead to backfires. The marketing strategy can also lead to negative evaluations of species perceived by audiences to be competing with the anthropomorphized targets (Chan, 2012; Root-Bernstein et al., 2013; Williams et al., 2021).

In short, while there are many strategies currently in use, the need for additional effective appeals remains, even in the case of broad-based ones that can transcend local contexts and cultural boundaries. This chapter makes the case for an additional strategy that, while underexplored in the literature, has the potential to be particularly effective: kinship appeals, or appeals to relatedness between target audiences and the species for which support is sought.

Kinship Appeals

Kinship, a system of social and perceived biological relatedness, is the most important human organizing principle. In small-scale, traditional societies, it is the means through which virtually all aspects of life are regulated, not only reproductive and familial, but also as related to control of resources and political leadership. Although there is a great deal of cross-cultural variability in kinship systems, in all societies members have specific reciprocal roles and obligations associated with those they identify as their kin. And even in large-scale societies characterized by non-kin relations, kinship continues to shape and define important affiliations, with consequences continuing to play out even in the most impersonal of networks (Eggan, 2024; Fox, 1983; Holy, 1996).

Further, kinship, however locally defined and assigned, is associated with altruistic inclinations and behavior—that is, we have evolved tendencies to behave preferentially toward individuals identified via cues as genetic relatives (Mateo, 2015; Park et al., 2008). The explanation for the existence of these evolved preferences is inclusive fitness theory: copies of an individual's genes can spread even if carried by others who possess them, and genetic relatives carry more copies as a function of their genetic closeness. Thus, to help genetic relatives, even at a cost, is ultimately "selfish," and tendencies to do so can be passed on biologically (Bourke, 2011; Hamilton, 1964). In humans, some relatedness cues are contextual, as in association during development (e.g., Lieberman et al., 2007); others are phenotypic, as in facial and other forms of physical similarity (DeBruine et al., 2009); and, most relevantly for this discussion, kin terms serve as important cues. Many studies have established that kinship terminology, notwithstanding variability in kinship systems, is similarly structured cross-culturally, reflecting patterns of interdependence and suggesting innate associated cognitive features (Cronk et al., 2019; Daly et al., 1997; Jones, 2004).

There is a great deal of evidence that we are prone to sacrifice time, energy, and financial and other resources to help those we identify as kin (e.g., Leonetti, 2008; Madsen et al., 2007; Neyer & Lang, 2003; Schriver et al., 2019), and that kin terms are a primary means through which we identify them. Further, kinship terms so reliably occasion positive emotional and behavioral responses that in a variety of contexts non-kin are categorized as "fictive" kin. Here, kinship labels are used to assign kinship roles and obligations among non-relatives (Atkinson, 2023; Bloch, 1971; Johnson et al., 1991; Qirko, 2011), motivating helping and support among non-kin not only in daily life (e.g. Rakopoulos, 2017) but also in political and conflict situations, even when they demand terminal sacrifice (Abou-Abdallah et al., 2016; Miller, 2018; Pawłowski & Chmielińska, 2023; Qirko, 2013; Salmon, 1998).

Fictive kinship is also often assigned to non-human species. Pets seen and described as family members is a well-known example (Brown, 2023; Charles & Davies, 2008; Podberscek et al., 2000), but many traditional societies also recognize both predator and prey non-human species as kin, with responsibilities towards them defined accordingly. There is some debate as to whether hunter-gatherers and other small-scale indigenous groups are explicitly conservationist or simply too small to seriously deplete resources or otherwise cause environmental damage (Alvard, 1998; McLeod et al., 2024). However, what is uncontestable is that many of these groups conceptualize at least some non-human species as their kin (e.g., Cormier, 2003; Harrod, 2000; Salmón, 2000), and that this practice tends to be accompanied by beneficial behavioral obligations towards them (Qirko, 2017; Thompson, 2024).

Why kin terms are so effective in promoting positive evaluations and behavior is ultimately a complicated question. The answer is likely a combination of enculturation, social patterning (as kin are typically the people we are closest to spatially, and thus emotionally), and evolved predispositions that operate irrespective of these kinds of contextual factors (Curry et al., 2013). But the point is that they *are* effective: identifying and labeling others as kin is a reliable way to stimulate effort—commitment, aid, sacrifice, and so forth—on their behalf. For all these reasons, kinship appeals should be effective as a broad-based, conservation marketing strategy. However, the strategy appears to be only infrequently used. Certainly appeals to help "mother earth" (e.g. United Nations, 2022) and "mother nature" (e.g. Apple, n.d.) are common in advertising campaigns, but aside from the occasional characterization of primates as "cousins" to humans (e.g., Orangutan Outreach, 2021), examples regarding specific species are hard to come by. Further, kinship appeals do not appear to have figured prominently in the work of researchers—one exception is experimental work by Palomo-Vélez et al. (2020), wherein appeals to their children's welfare increased participants' intentions to provide time and money to pro-environmental causes.

For these reasons, we have conducted research on the effectiveness of kinship labels in eliciting potential support of conservation efforts, while also exploring the potential effects of anthropomorphism, species charisma, and degree of interest in environmental causes. We began by developing the underlying theory as summarized above (Qirko, 2017) and then created an experimental scenario in which a fictional salamander species was described as threatened, with survey respondents asked about their willingness to come to its aid (Morris & Qirko, 2019). A salamander was selected because the seeming lack of current popular culture associations suggests it is unlikely to produce either strongly positive or strongly negative emotions from most respondents—i.e., to be charismatically neutral. This initial work indicated that fictive kinship appeals can influence public support of the salamander, and we then extended our research by replicating our survey experiment using different species of animals. In these additional survey experiments, we examined a likely charismatically negative fictive spider species (e.g., Zvaríková et al., 2021) and an imaginary species of pocket gopher we felt likely to be charismatically positive based on the gopher's common portrayal in popular culture as friendly and cute (e.g., "The Goofy Gophers" cartoon characters; also Firman, 2024).

Survey Experiments and Testing Fictive Kinship Appeals

Our research tests the ability of fictive kinship terms to increase support for a hypothetical conservation effort as compared to neutral or anthropomorphic terminology. Because our research is aimed at showing causal relationships rather than simple correlational association, we wanted to rely on research techniques designed to reveal cause and effect relationships. Survey experiments are such a research methodology (Mutz, 2011). "Survey experiments" is a broad umbrella term for a variety of research approaches that meld elements of large-scale surveys with experimental methods, such as split-ballot surveys, conjoint survey experiments, factorial survey experiments, population-based survey experiments, and vignette survey experiments (Alexander & Becker, 1978; Hainmueller et al., 2015; Mutz, 2011; Wallander, 2009).

Our study approach is best described as population-based vignette survey experiments. Population-based survey experiments are experiments administered to a representative sample of the population of interest through the use of survey sampling methods. Sample members are then randomly assigned to treatment or control conditions. The advent of computer platforms that allow for online data collection for human subjects, such as CloudResearch and Amazon's Mechanical Turk (MTurk), have made contacting large pools of potential participants more efficient and less expensive, although potentially at the cost of representativeness (Berinsky et al., 2012; Hauser et al., 2022; Keith & McKay, 2024). Vignette survey experiments are surveys that include a detailed description of a social situation—a vignette—that contains precise references to factors that are thought to be key in the decision-making process (Alexander & Becker, 1978; Mutz, 2011). In our case, the vignettes focus on the effort to protect an endangered species, and depict the species in kin, anthropomorphic, or neutral terms. Different versions of the vignette are then randomly administered to portions of the sample in the survey, as in a classical experimental design. We combine the population-based approach with the vignette approach by gathering a representative sample of the adult population of the United States and providing that sample with a questionnaire that includes randomly assigned vignettes describing a hypothetical conservation effort taking place in the United States. In classical experimental design terminology, our survey experiment fits the description of a post-test only control group design with two treatment groups (Campbell & Stanley, 1963).

Although survey experiments are not as widely known as other foundational data collection strategies typically found in research methods courses (Mutz, 2011; Wallander, 2009), they are growing in popularity and have often been used to examine public attitudes on conservation and environmental issues (Bakaki & Bernauer, 2016; Busch et al., 2020; Coley et al., 2021; Leavitt et al., 2021; Marquina et al., 2022; Morris & Qirko, 2019). For example, Bakaki and Bernauer (2016) used quota sampling and randomly allocated vignettes whose descriptions varied regarding the positive benefits of forest conservation to test how those factors affect people's willingness to pay for conservation efforts in Brazil. Similarly, Marquina et al. (2022) used large-scale surveys and randomly allocated vignettes that emphasized either an instrumental, intrinsic, relational, or information-based values approach to identify salient factors that shape preferences on watershed protection in the United States. It is our aim to extend the use of population-based vignette survey experiments to test the ability of fictive kin terms—a novel theoretical perspective developed by Qirko (2017)—to affect attitudes toward conservation efforts in the United States. To the best of our knowledge, we are the first researchers to combine such a methodological approach with a fictive kinship perspective to examine conservation marketing.

Methods

Data Collection

We developed three studies and administered them at three different points in time: 2017, 2018, and 2024. The three survey instruments used to collect data for each study were constructed using Qualtrics survey platform. The samples were gathered using CloudResearch, previously known as TurkPrime, which is a survey research platform that connects researchers and their surveys to various pools of potential survey respondents—in our case, to Mechanical Turk (MTurk) Workers. MTurk is a crowdsourcing Internet marketplace that provides a pool of "Workers" who complete online tasks, like responding to surveys or completing games for experimental studies, usually for a monetary award.

CloudResearch was founded in 2015 by academics and survey researchers and is a tool designed for online data collection of human subjects (Litman et al., 2017; Moss, 2023). CloudResearch originally relied solely on pulling survey participants from MTurk, and so our first study conducted in 2017 relied on MTurk Workers via CloudResearch. CloudResearch now offers access to several opt-in online participant pools. However, to maintain consistency across all three of our studies, we continued to rely on CloudResearch's MTurk Toolkit to only draw survey participants from MTurk in our second and third studies.

Conducting academic research online using opt-in internet-based samples for human subjects has become one of the primary methods of gathering data (Chmielewski & Kucker, 2020; Lu et al., 2022; Smith et al., 2016). However, as the reliance on opt-in online samples has increased over the last 10 years, so has scrutiny of the respondents drawn from such sample pools, as well as of the quality of the data gathered from such platforms that specialize in providing online samples (Chmielewski & Kucker, 2020). Using the MTurk platform and gathering samples from the MTurk Worker pool was originally seen as an effective strategy for data collection (Berinsky et al., 2012; Goodman et al., 2013; Kees et al., 2017). However, concerns arose in the late 2010s that MTurk Worker pools were filled with inattentive participants, participants providing fraudulent data, and software applications that mimic humans programmed to repeatedly complete surveys, commonly referred to as bots (Chmielewski & Kucker, 2020). Using simple measures like attention checks—questionnaire items checking to see if respondents are thoughtfully answering each question—were recommended as the key strategy to filter out these problems. However, at the end of the 2010s it became clear that the quality of MTurk data gathered using MTurk's platform was weakening and that additional data quality measures were necessary. CloudResearch's built-in data quality measures as well as relying on Qualtrics metadata helps to alleviate many of the data quality concerns for samples drawn from the MTurk Worker pool (Douglas et al., 2023; Hauser et al., 2022). Recent research finds that using CloudResearch to draw samples from the MTurk Worker pool provides high-quality data, and now CloudResearch is viewed as one of the better options for obtaining reliable data from opt-in online participant pools, especially when making use of participant screening tools offered on CloudResearch and within Qualtrics (Douglas et al., 2023; Hauser et al., 2022; Keith & McKay, 2024; Lu et al., 2022; Peer et al., 2021).

Study Designs

In each study we randomly provided respondents with a description of the plight of a fictitious species to convey one of three message elements: kinship (Little Sister, Little Brother), anthropomorphism (Little Woman, Little Man), and neutral (Little Swimmer, Little Jumper, Little Digger). The neutral vignette was designed to appeal to neither kinship nor anthropomorphism. Each vignette differed in only one keyword. We wanted to change only one keyword in each scenario in order to provide the most stringent test possible in the evaluation of differences among appeals. In experimental design terms, our two treatment conditions are the kinship and anthropomorphic message elements, and our control condition is the neutral message element.

Study 1: The Effort to Save Little Swimmer. The survey was administered on June 3, 2017, and restricted to people living in the United States who were 18 or older. Six respondents were dropped from the analysis for failing attention checks and three respondents were dropped for not providing responses for all 3 dependent variables, resulting in a sample size of 1418 people. Respondents were each paid 50 cents upon submission of their survey.

We provided respondents with one of three presentations of the plight of a fictitious salamander species, with vignettes differing only in the key words communicating message elements:

> High in the mountains of Southern Appalachia lives a small salamander, Desmognathus ficta, commonly referred to as "Little [Swimmer, Woman, Sister] under the Stones," a name given to the salamander by the Native peoples of the area. Extensive logging and other human activity in the 1930s and 1940s nearly eradicated Little [Swimmer, Woman, Sister]. However, conditions have changed, and there is presently an effort underway to repopulate the salamander in its original home range. There will be no adverse environmental impacts associated with this reintroduction, but repopulation will require financial support to be successful.

Study 2: The Effort to Save Little Jumper. The survey was administered on June 18, 2018, and restricted to people living in the United States who were 18 or older. Nine respondents were dropped from the analysis for failing attention checks and 44 respondents were dropped for not providing responses for all 3 dependent variables, resulting in a sample size of 1044 people. Respondents were each paid 50 cents upon submission of their survey. Again we provided respondents with one of three presentations, this time of the plight of a fictitious spider species, with the vignettes differing only in the message elements' key words: kinship (Little Sister), anthropomorphic (Little Woman), and neutral (Little Jumper). Otherwise, the presentation was identical to that used in Study 1.

> High in the mountains of Southern Appalachia lives a spider, Salticidae ficta, commonly referred to as "Little [Jumper, Woman, Sister] on the Stones," a name given to the spider by the Native peoples of the area. Extensive logging and other human activity in the 1930s and 1940s nearly eradicated Little [Jumper, Woman, Sister]. However, conditions have changed, and there is presently an effort underway to reintroduce the spider in its original home

range. There will be no adverse environmental impacts associated with this reintroduction, but it will require financial support to be successful.

Study 3: The Effort to Save Little Digger. The survey was administered between May 29 and June 3, 2024, and restricted to people living in the United States who were 18 or older. In an attempt to address recent concerns about data quality and respondent attentiveness that have arisen since 2019, responses were screened for fraudulent data, the presence of bots, and duplicates in addition to the attention check item within the survey. CloudResearch protocols prevented MTurk Workers shown to provide fraudulent data or MTurk workers with suspicious geocode locations from taking the survey. Seventy-nine respondents were dropped from the analysis since Qualtrics indicated that the MTurk Worker was providing fraudulent data, was a bot, was a duplicate respondent, or failed attention checks while taking the survey. Another 15 respondents were dropped for not providing responses on all 3 dependent variables. This resulted in a sample size of 976 people. Respondents were each paid 1 dollar upon submission of their survey.

We provided respondents with one of three presentations of the plight of a fictitious gopher species, with vignettes differing in only one keyword, to convey one of three message elements: kinship (Little Brother), anthropomorphic (Little Man), and neutral (Little Digger). Again, we changed only one keyword in each vignette, and otherwise the presentations are identical in all three studies:

High in the mountains of Southern Appalachia lives a pocket gopher, Geomyidae ficta, commonly referred to as "Little [Digger, Man, Brother] Under the Ground," a name given to the gopher by the Native peoples of the area. Extensive logging and other human activity in the 1930s and 1940s nearly eradicated Little [Digger, Man, Brother]. However, conditions have changed, and there is presently an effort underway to reintroduce the gopher in its original home range. There will be no adverse environmental impacts associated with this reintroduction, but it will require financial support to be successful.

Independent and Dependent Variables

Our three dependent variables are based on three survey items presented to respondents after the vignettes: "After hearing this request for support of the salamander/spider/gopher, would you be willing to donate money to contribute to the effort to save Little Sister/Little Brother/Little Woman/Little Man/Little Swimmer/Little Jumper/Little Digger?" (1) yes, (0) no; "Would you encourage a friend or family member to donate to this effort?" (1) yes, (0) no; "Would you be willing to participate in political activities—like signing a petition, contacting policymakers, or attending a demonstration—to support this cause?" (1) yes, (0) no.

To measure the likely charisma of each animal, we relied on feeling thermometers. Feeling thermometers range from 0 degrees, representing the coldest and most negative feelings, to 100 degrees, representing the warmest and most positive feelings toward a person or thing. They are often used in survey research to measure people's attitudes toward subject matter (Masci, 2019). Feeling thermometer scores for salamander and spider were collected only from Study 2 and Study 3 and feeling thermometer scores for gopher were collected from Study 3 only.

In addition to these questions, we included a set of items to act as control variables in our multivariate logistic regression models: level of concern about the environment (1 = not at all concerned, 5 = extremely concerned), liberalness (1 = very conservative, 5 = very liberal), age, educational attainment (bachelor's or more = 1, no bachelor's = 0), income, gender (male = 1, not male = 0), and race/ethnicity (racial/ethnic minority = 1, white = 0). Multiple imputation (MI), which uses all variables in the models to create regression equations to estimate missing values, was used to impute missing data on each of the independent variables so that all cases and their data could be included in our analyses rather than relying on listwise deletion (Enders, 2022; White et al., 2011). Cases that did not provide responses on all three dependent variables were dropped from the analysis.

Results

Table 6.1 displays means, proportions, minimums, and maximums for the sample from each study completed. Table 6.1 also provides means and proportions for salient U.S. population demographic data to compare our samples to the U.S. population. Our samples appear to be whiter, more educated, and less well-off financially

Table 6.1 Means and proportions

	Study 1		Study 2		Study 3		U.S.		
Condition	M/P	SD	M/P	SD	M/P	SD	M/P	Min	Max
Kin	0.334	0.472	0.333	0.472	0.334	0.472	–	0	1
Anthropomorphic	0.334	0.472	0.331	0.471	0.321	0.474	–	0	1
Neutral	0.332	0.471	0.335	0.472	0.325	0.469	–	0	1
Independent variables									
Male	0.517	0.500	0.520	0.500	0.533	0.499	0.491	0	1
Racial-ethnic minority	0.276	0.447	0.277	0.448	0.256	0.436	0.411	0	1
Bachelor's or more	0.522	0.500	0.566	0.496	0.604	0.489	0.343	0	1
Family income (in 1000)	56.9	42.3	63.7	44.7	74.4	54.8	125	5	250
Age	36.4	12.7	37.5	11.8	44.1	13.3	38.5	18	77
Liberalness	3.50	1.10	3.26	1.19	3.37	1.19	–	1	5
Environmental concern	3.59	1.05	3.59	1.06	3.51	1.13	–	1	5
Dependent variables									
Donate	0.615	0.487	0.489	0.500	0.609	0.488	–	0	1
Tell a friend	0.572	0.495	0.471	0.499	0.568	0.496	–	0	1
Participate politically	0.425	0.495	0.463	0.499	0.528	0.499	–	0	1
Sample size	1418		1044		976				

Note: M/P = Means and proportions. SD = Standard deviation. U.S. population data comes from the 2022 American Community Survey 5-Year Estimates

than the U.S. population but appear to be fairly representative in terms of gender and age.

The proportions for each of the three dependent variables in our analyses show that people are least likely to report that they are willing to donate money, tell a friend, or participate politically to support the conservation of a spider compared to the conservation of a salamander or gopher. It also appears that people are more likely to participate politically on behalf of saving a gopher compared to a salamander or a spider. These differences align with the literature suggesting that charisma plays a part in influencing popular support for conservation efforts.

The feeling thermometer scores we obtained, presented in Table 6.2, provide further support for this idea. Respondents reported colder feelings toward the spider than the other two species and reported warmer feelings toward the gopher. The salamander scores landed between the spider and gopher but closer to the gopher, indicating a clear dislike for spiders among the sample, on average, compared to the other two animals.

The multivariate logistic regression analyses examining how different marketing appeals (i.e., kinship, anthropomorphic, neutral) are related to the willingness of respondents to contribute to the conservation of endangered species tend to support our predictions about kinship appeals for the salamander and gopher, but not the spider. Table 6.3 presents the results from Study 1 that focused on saving a salamander. Kinship appeals are more likely to result in willingness to tell a friend about the conservation effort compared to the anthropomorphic appeal as those respondents who received the anthropomorphic condition of "woman" were statistically less likely to say they would tell a friend (log odds = −0.325, $p < 0.05$). However, no other outcome variable shows statistically significant differences among the three conditions. These findings indicate that in the context of a salamander, kinship appeals have a small but statistically significant effect on audience reception of the conservation effort compared to anthropomorphic appeals.

Table 6.4 presents the results from Study 2 that focused on saving a spider. In this analysis, kinship appeals are no more or less likely to result in willingness to support the conservation effort of the spider as no outcome variable indicates statistical significance. One possible explanation for these results is that generalized dislike of

Table 6.2 Animal feeling thermometer scores

Animal	Mean temp	SD
Salamander	55.8	28.7
Spider	38.7	31.3
Gopher	63.1	26.5

Note: Scores range from 0 very cold to 100 very warm. Feeling thermometer scores come only from Study 2 and Study 3 for salamander and spider and from Study 3 for gopher

Table 6.3 Study 1 with Salamander: fictive kinship appeals compared to other appeals on the willingness to support a conservation effort

	Donate		Tell a friend		Participate politically	
	Log odds	SE	Log odds	SE	Log odds	SE
Condition						
Woman	−0.194	(0.142)	−0.325*	(0.142)	−0.052	(0.145)
Swimmer	0.014	(0.144)	−0.092	(0.143)	0.122	(0.144)
Controls						
Environmental concern	0.661***	(0.064)	0.717***	(0.065)	0.764***	(0.068)
Male	−0.306**	(0.118)	−0.379**	(0.117)	−0.246*	(0.120)
Racial-ethnic minority	0.150	(0.133)	0.009	(0.131)	−0.195	(0.133)
Bachelor's or more	−0.165	(0.122)	0.001	(0.121)	−0.127	(0.124)
Family income (in 1000)	−0.000	(0.001)	−0.002	(0.001)	−0.000	(0.001)
Age	0.001	(0.005)	−0.005	(0.005)	−0.017**	(0.005)
Liberalness	0.065	(0.060)	0.015	(0.061)	0.217***	(0.062)
Intercept	−1.851***	(0.355)	−1.668***	(0.351)	−3.043***	(0.371)

*$p < 0.05$, **$p < 0.01$, ***$p < 0.001$ (one-tailed). Sample size = 1418. SE = standard error

Table 6.4 Study 2 with Spider: fictive kinship appeals compared to other appeals on the willingness to support a conservation effort

	Donate		Tell a friend		Participate politically	
	Log odds	SE	Log odds	SE	Log odds	SE
Condition						
Woman	0.148	(0.166)	−0.125	(0.169)	0.019	(0.167)
Jumper	0.160	(0.167)	−0.073	(0.169)	−0.060	(0.168)
Controls						
Environmental concern	0.810***	(0.077)	0.910***	(0.080)	0.866***	(0.079)
Male	0.241	(0.139)	−0.041	(0.141)	0.299*	(0.140)
Racial-ethnic minority	0.679***	(0.158)	0.736***	(0.160)	0.502**	(0.158)
Bachelor's or more	0.044	(0.143)	0.140	(0.145)	0.115	(0.145)
Family income (in 1000)	−0.002	(0.002)	−0.003	(0.002)	−0.003*	(0.002)
Age	−0.013*	(0.006)	−0.014*	(0.006)	−0.010	(0.006)
Liberalness	−0.108	(0.064)	−0.196**	(0.065)	−0.052	(0.063)
Intercept	−2.440***	(0.423)	−2.286***	(0.428)	−2.908***	(0.434)

*$p < 0.05$, **$p < 0.01$, ***$p < 0.001$ (one-tailed). Sample size = 1044. SE = standard error

spiders leads to little latitude on respondents' willingness to make any effort to help such a species, no matter how that effort is presented to audiences.

Table 6.5 presents the results from Study 3 that focused on saving a gopher. When asked if they were willing to donate to the conservation effort, respondents reported greater willingness to support the effort when provided with the kinship condition compared to the other conditions, as the coefficients for the anthropomorphic (log odds = −0.388, $p < 0.05$) and neutral (log odds = −0.381, $p < 0.05$)

Table 6.5 Study 3 with Gopher: fictive kinship appeals compared to other appeals on the willingness to support a conservation effort

	Donate		Tell a friend		Participate politically	
	Log odds	SE	Log odds	SE	Log odds	SE
Condition						
Man	−0.388*	(0.174)	−0.224	(0.172)	−0.125	(0.172)
Digger	−0.381*	(0.176)	−0.297*	(0.174)	−0.028	(0.173)
Controls						
Environmental concern	0.770***	(0.077)	0.831***	(0.078)	0.785***	(0.077)
Male	−0.237	(0.145)	−0.324*	(0.144)	−0.155	(0.144)
Racial-ethnic minority	0.387*	(0.173)	0.118	(0.168)	0.095	(0.167)
Bachelor's or more	−0.015	(0.156)	−0.004	(0.155)	0.287	(0.155)
Family income (in 1000)	0.001	(0.001)	−0.000	(0.001)	−0.002	(0.001)
Age	−0.008	(0.006)	−0.011	(0.006)	−0.017**	(0.006)
Liberalness	−0.131	(0.070)	−0.180**	(0.070)	0.005	(0.068)
Intercept	−1.187**	(0.417)	−1.199**	(0.413)	−1.811***	(0.416)

*$p < 0.05$, **$p < 0.01$, ***$p < 0.001$ (one-tailed). Sample size = 976. SE = standard error

conditions were statistically significant. When asked if they were willing to tell a friend about this effort, the point estimates for both the anthropomorphic (log odds = −0.224, $p > 0.05$) and neutral (log odds = −0.297, $p < 0.05$) conditions are negative, indicating a greater ability of the kinship appeal to encourage people to tell friend about the effort, although it is important to emphasize that only the neutral appeal is statistically different from the kinship appeal. It does not appear that kinship appeals impact political support for the conservation effort of the gopher, as our results show no statistically significant differences among the three conditions when it comes to participating politically to help save the mammal. Perhaps this is the result of greater effort being required to participate politically compared to simply donating money or telling another person about the conservation effort.

Discussion

This chapter attempts to explore the possible effectiveness of kinship appeals in conservation marketing by means of three population-based vignette survey experiments. To the best of our knowledge, we are the first researchers to combine this emerging methodological approach with a fictive kinship perspective to examine support for conservation efforts. Each survey experiment measured the willingness of respondents to aid a different imaginary species alternatively described by means of kin, anthropomorphic, or neutral terms. Overall, our results are that kinship appeals have a small but statistically significant positive impact on survey participants' willingness to support conservation efforts. Specifically, in the context of an effort to save a salamander, respondents given the kinship appeal are statistically more likely to say they would be willing to tell a friend about the conservation effort compared to respondents given the anthropomorphic appeal. In the context of an effort to save a gopher, respondents given the kinship appeal are statistically more likely to say they would be willing to donate to the conservation effort compared to respondents given the anthropomorphic or neutral appeal; and respondents given the kinship appeal are statistically more likely say they would be willing to tell a friend about the conservation effort of the gopher compared to respondents given the neutral appeal.

Although the effects are limited, the results of our survey experiments provide compelling evidence that labeling a species in kin terms, as opposed to anthropomorphic or neutral ones, can significantly affect the degree of resources people would at least hypothetically be willing to commit to the non-humans' survival. These findings are promising, given that the experimental treatments vary only in the use of one word (which is stated two times in each vignette and once more in one of the subsequent questions). A reasonable prediction is that developing scenarios that more fully highlight differences in appeals should produce more powerful results, and is a logical next step in pursuing this line of research. Importantly, while significant results were obtained for the kin appeal, they were not for the anthropomorphic alternative. Given that the latter is highly touted in the literature as a broad-based and effective marketing tool (e.g., Chan, 2012; Root-Bernstein et al., 2013; Williams et al., 2021), these findings too suggests that kinship appeals merit a close look by conservation marketers.

In terms of which specific outcomes were statistically related to kinship appeals, we found it interesting that effects were present for willingness to donate or to tell a friend about the conservation effort, but not for political participation. Our data do not allow us to discern exactly why respondents given the kinship appeal are more likely to report a willingness to tell a friend about and to donate to the effort, but do not show a willingness to participate politically. One potential explanation, though, rests in the effort and commitment required to tell a friend or to donate money compared to becoming politically involved with a conservation effort. Sending a message to a friend or cutting a check, so to speak, is much easier than contacting public officials, petitioning, or protesting, for example. Consequently, we have to consider the possibility that kinship appeals are more effective when requesting undemanding support for a conservation effort opposed to requests that require more time, effort, commitment, or resources on the part of the audience.

The findings also suggest that cultural views of different species (or groups or classes of species) are an important variable influencing the power of appeals. Based on what we could learn of public (American) perceptions, we predicted that spiders would be viewed in a less favorable light than salamanders and, particularly, gophers, and this was supported by survey findings as well as the feeling thermometer results. It appears that the impact of kinship appeals is affected by the perceptions of the species at the center of the conservation effort. This too requires additional research, and while it is tempting to continue to describe perceptions of different species in terms of the concept of charisma, this may require further consideration. Species charisma is a complicated and multifactorial concept, hard to identify and measure (Ducarme et al., 2013). Perhaps of more relevance for this research is *the degree to which we feel related* to different species and groups of species and how such views correspond to commitment and resource contributions to their survival (for a start on how to explore this possibility, see Harrison & Hall, 2010).

There are other issues that require further exploration as well. Words can carry not only several meanings but different connotations, even in reference to species and their study, which can have unintended effects (e.g., Qirko, 2021), and for this experiment we did not attempt to tease these connotations apart. Calling the animals "little," for example, may help elicit positive feelings in its own right, as size does appear to be linked to perceptions of cuteness (e.g., Li & Eastman, 2023), which in turn is often associated with responses to neoteny (e.g., Shin & Mattila, 2021). Our using the word "little" across all treatments and studies should control for any associated effects. However, the potential effect of gender could not be similarly controlled, as in the experiments the animals were either consistently female or male ("man" and "brother" for gopher, "woman" and "sister" for spider and salamander). It may well be that manipulating gender would influence results for different species independent of the kinship factor, given that gender designations have been shown to influence how even inanimate objects are conceptualized (e.g., Boroditsky et al., 2003). However, to test that possibility, we would have needed six treatments in each experiment, three male and three female for all conditions. There may be a less clumsy way to further explore that variable in future experiments.

Another consideration is that we used U.S. population samples only. While the emotional appeal of at least close kinship terms is likely to be similar across cultures (e.g., Jones, 2004; Madsen et al., 2007), research suggests that species will be looked at differently by different groups, not only within societies as a consequence of degree of direct exposure (de Pinho et al., 2014) but across cultures even when direct exposure is not an issue (Bruder et al., 2022). Thus, different cultural groups may feel different levels of sympathy for different species, and the degree to which species may be viewed differently by different samples may influence the strength of kinship appeals.

Finally, although these results are based on hypothetical conservation efforts and people are not actually required to act, recent research shows that vignette survey experiments are remarkably predictive of actual behavior in the real-world (Hainmueller et al., 2015). Our studies are yet another example of the usefulness of population-based vignette survey experiments to gauge individual attitudes on a complex social issue. It is difficult to bring a representative sample of thousands of people to a lab to participate in experiments examining potential support of a conservation effort, traditional surveys measuring support for conservation only allow for correlational analysis and lack the ability to expose cause and effect relationships, and it is challenging to find circumstances in the field where conditions allow for a natural experiment to test kinship appeals in conservation marketing. Survey experiments are a unique and powerful approach that combines the best of what experimental design and survey research have to offer to address the pressing issues related to conservation and the environment.

In sum, although the findings are preliminary and the methods still in the exploratory stage, we feel there is reason to expect that future work on kinship appeals as a broad-based marketing strategy to elicit support for species conservation should show them to be effective and worth trying out in the field.

References

Abou-Abdallah, M., Kashima, Y., & Harb, C. (2016). "Brothers" in arms: Does metaphorizing kinship increase approval of parochial altruism? *Journal of Cognition and Culture, 16*(1–2), 37–49. https://doi.org/10.1163/15685373-12342167

Albert, C., Luque, G. M., & Courchamp, F. (2018). The twenty most charismatic species. *PLoS One, 13*(7), e0199149. https://doi.org/10.1371/journal.pone.0199149

Alexander, C. S., & Becker, H. J. (1978). The use of vignettes in survey research. *Public Opinion Quarterly, 42*(1), 93–104. https://www.jstor.org/stable/2748094

Alvard, M. S. (1998). Evolutionary ecology and resource conservation. *Evolutionary Anthropology, 7*(2), 62–74. https://doi.org/10.1002/(SICI)1520-6505(1998)7:2<62::AID-EVAN3>3.0.CO;2-I

Anderson, J. (2018, October). *Donation preferences and attitudes among people who donate to animal causes*. Faunalytics.org. https://faunalytics.org/wp-content/uploads/2018/10/Faunalytics-Blackbaud-Data-Report.pdf

Apple. (n.d.). *Environment/mother nature* [video]. Apple. https://www.apple.com/environment/mother-nature/

Atkinson, A. R. (2023). Could religions augment cooperation by recruiting Hamilton's rule through the use of fictive kinship language? *Journal of Cognition and Culture, 23*(3–4), 265–288. https://doi.org/10.1163/15685373-12340163

AZA. (2018). *AZA omnibus survey: Consumer engagement around wildlife conservation*. https://assets.speakcdn.com/assets/2332/aza_endangered_species_survey_summary.pdf

Bakaki, Z., & Bernauer, T. (2016). Measuring and explaining the willingness to pay for forest conservation: Evidence from a survey experiment in Brazil. *Environmental Research Letters, 11*(11), 114001. https://doi.org/10.1088/1748-9326/11/11/114001

Balaskas, S., Panagiotarou, A., & Rigou, M. (2023). Impact of environmental concern, emotional appeals, and attitude toward the advertisement on the intention to buy green products: The case of younger consumer audiences. Sustainability, 15(17), 13204. https://doi.org/10.3390/su151713204

Barrett, H. C. (2004). Cognitive development and the understanding of animal behavior. In B. Ellis & D. Bjorklund (Eds.), *Origins of the social mind* (pp. 438–467). Guilford.

Berinsky, A. J., Huber, G. A., & Lenz, G. S. (2012). Evaluating online labor markets for experimental research: Amazon.com's mechanical Turk. *Political Analysis, 20*(3), 351–368. https://doi.org/10.1093/pan/mpr057

Bloch, M. (1971). The moral and tactical meaning of kinship terms. *Man, 6*, 79–87. https://doi.org/10.2307/2798429

Borgi, M., Cogliati-Dezza, I., Brelsford, V., Meints, K., & Cirulli, F. (2014). Baby schema in human and animal faces induces cuteness perception and gaze allocation in children. *Frontiers in Psychology, 5*, 411. https://doi.org/10.3389/fpsyg.2014.00411

Boroditsky, L., Schmidt, L. A., & Phillips, W. (2003). Sex, syntax and semantics. In D. Gentner & S. Goldin-Meadow (Eds.), *Language in mind: Advances in the study of language and thought* (pp. 61–79). Boston Review.

Bourke, A. F. G. (2011). The validity and value of inclusive fitness theory. *Proceedings of the Royal Society B: Biological Sciences, 278*(1723), 3313–3320. https://doi.org/10.1098/rspb.2011.1465

Brandon, S. (2021). Selling extinction: The social media(tion) of global cheetah conservation. *Geoforum, 127*, 189–197. https://doi.org/10.1016/j.geoforum.2021.10.016

Brenna, L. (2020, 11 February). Animal and plant species declared extinct between 2010 and 2019, the full list. *Lifegate Daily*. https://www.lifegate.com/extinct-species-list-decade-2010-2019

Brown, A. (2023). *About half of U.S. pet owners say their pets are as much a part of their family as a human member*. Pew Research Center. https://pewrsr.ch/3JPtwoR

Bruder, J., Burakowski, L. M., Park, T., Al-Haddad, R., Al-Hemaidi, S., Al-Korbi, A., & Al-Naimi, A. (2022). Cross-cultural awareness and attitudes toward threatened animal species. *Frontiers in Psychology, 13*, 898503. https://doi.org/10.3389/fpsyg.2022.898503

Busch, J. T. A., Watson-Jones, R. E., & Legare, C. H. (2020). Cultural variation in the development of beliefs about conservation. *Cognitive Science, 44*(10), e12909. https://doi.org/10.1111/cogs.12909

Camino, M., Cortez, S., Cerezo, A., & Altrichter, M. (2016). Wildlife conservation, perceptions of different co-existing cultures. *International Journal of Conservation Science, 7*(1), 109–122.

Campbell, D. T., & Stanley, J. C. (1963). *Experimental and quasi-experimental designs for research*. Houghton Mifflin.

Cermak, I. (2021). Jumping the shark: White shark representations in 'great white serial killer' lives–the fear and the (pseudo-)science. *Journalism and Media, 2*(4), 584–604. https://doi.org/10.3390/journalmedia2040035

Chan, A. A. Y.-H. (2012). Anthropomorphism as a conservation tool. *Biodiversity and Conservation, 21*, 1889–1892. https://doi.org/10.1007/s10531-012-0274-6

Charles, N., & Davies, C. A. (2008). My family and other animals: Pets as kin. *Sociological Research Online, 13*(5), 13–26. https://doi.org/10.5153/sro.1798

Chen, T., & Wu, P. (2023). Framing effectiveness of nature conservation ads: the influence of environmental value orientation and mental imagery. *Current Psychology, 42*, 2565–2575. https://doi.org/10.1007/s12144-022-03677-9

Chmielewski, M., & Kucker, S. C. (2020). An MTurk crisis? Shifts in data quality and the impact on study results. *Social Psychological and Personality Science, 11*(4), 464–473. https://doi.org/10.1177/1948550619875149

Coley, J. D., Betz, N., Helmuth, B., Ellenbogen, K., Scyphers, S. B., & Adams, D. (2021). Beliefs about human-nature relationships and implications for investment and stewardship surrounding land-water system conservation. *Land, 10*(12), 1293. https://doi.org/10.3390/land10121293

Cormier, L. A. (2003). *Kinship with monkeys: The Guaja foragers of eastern Amazonia*. Columbia University Press.

Courchamp, F., Jaric, I., Albert, C., Meinard, Y., Ripple, W. J., & Chapron, G. (2018). The paradoxical extinction of the most charismatic animals. *PLoS Biology, 16*(4), e2003997. https://doi.org/10.1371/journal.pbio.2003997

Cronk, L., Steklis, D., Steklis, N., van den Akker, O., & Aktipis, C. A. (2019). Kin terms and fitness interdependence. *Evolution and Human Behavior, 40*(3), 281–291. https://doi.org/10.1016/j.evolhumbehav.2018.12.004

Curry, O., Roberts, S. G., & Dunbar, R. I. (2013). Altruism in social networks: Evidence for a 'kinship premium'. *British Journal of Psychology, 104*(2), 283–295. https://doi.org/10.1111/j.2044-8295.2012.02119.x

Daly, M., Salmon, C., & Wilson, M. (1997). Kinship: The conceptual hole in psychological studies of social cognition and close relationships. In J. A. Simpson & D. T. Kenrick (Eds.), *Evolutionary social psychology* (pp. 265–296). Lawrence Erlbaum Associates, Inc.

De Dominicis, S., Schultz, P. W., & Bonaiuto, M. (2017). Protecting the environment for self-interested reasons: Altruism is not the only pathway to sustainability. *Frontiers in Psychology, 8*, 1065. https://doi.org/10.3389/fpsyg.2017.01065

de Pinho, J. R., Grilo, C., Boone, R. B., Galvin, K. A., & Snodgrass, J. G. (2014). Influence of aesthetic appreciation of wildlife species on attitudes towards their conservation in Kenyan agropastoralist communities. *PLoS One, 9*(2), e88842. https://doi.org/10.1371/journal.pone.0088842

DeBruine, L. M., Smith, F. G., Jones, B. C., Roberts, S. C., Petrie, M., & Spector, T. D. (2009). Kin recognition signals in adult faces. *Vision Research, 49*(1), 38–43. https://doi.org/10.1016/j.visres.2008.09.025

Douglas, B. D., Ewell, P. J., & Brauer, M. (2023). Data quality in online human-subjects research: Comparisons between Mturk, prolific, Cloudresearch, Qualtrics, and Sona. *PLoS One, 18*(3), e0279720. https://doi.org/10.1371/journal.pone.0279720

Ducarme, F., Luque, G., & Courchamp, F. (2013). What are "charismatic species" for conservation biologists? *BioSciences Master Reviews, 1*, 1–8.

Edwards, A. D., & Shafer, D. M. (2022). When lamps have feelings: Empathy and anthropomorphism toward inanimate objects in animated films. *Projections, 16*(2), 27–52. https://doi.org/10.3167/proj.2022.160202

Eggan, F. (2024). *Introduction to kinship*. International Encyclopedia of the Social Sciences. https://www.encyclopedia.com/social-sciences/applied-and-social-sciences-magazines/kinship

Enders, C.K. (2022). *Applied missing data analysis*. Guilford Publications.

Estren, M. J. (2012). The neoteny barrier: Seeking respect for the non-cute. *Journal of Animal Ethics, 2*(1), 6–11. https://doi.org/10.5406/janimalethics.2.1.0006

Firman, J. (2024). *Beyond Minnesota's Golden gophers: How the animal is seen in pop culture*. Gopherhole.com. https://gopherhole.com/beyond-minnesotas-golden-gophers-how-the-animal-is-seen-in-pop-culture/

Fox, R. (1983). *Kinship and marriage: An anthropological perspective*. Cambridge University Press.

Ghasemi, B., & Kyle, G. T. (2021). Toward moral pathways to motivate wildlife conservation. *Biological Conservation, 259*, 109170. https://doi.org/10.1016/j.biocon.2021.109170

Goodman, J. K., Cryder, C. E., & Cheema, A. (2013). Data collection in a flat world: The strengths and weaknesses of mechanical Turk samples. *Journal of Behavioral Decision Making, 26*(3), 213–224. https://doi.org/10.1002/bdm.1753

Green, T., & Peloza, J. (2014). Finding the right shade of green: The effect of advertising appeal type on environmentally friendly consumption. *Journal of Advertising, 43*(2), 128–141. https://doi.org/10.1080/00913367.2013.834805

Hainmueller, J., Hangartner, D., & Yamamoto, T. (2015). Validating vignette and conjoint survey experiments against real-world behavior. *Proceedings of the National Academy of Sciences, 112*(8), 2395–2400. https://doi.org/10.1073/pnas.1416587112

Hamilton, W. D. (1964). The genetical evolution of social behaviour, I. *Journal of Theoretical Biology, 7*, 1–16. https://doi.org/10.1016/0022-5193(64)90038-4

Harrison, M. A., & Hall, A. E. (2010). Anthropomorphism, empathy, and perceived communicative ability vary with phylogenetic relatedness to humans. *Journal of Social, Evolutionary, and Cultural Psychology, 4*(1), 34–48. https://doi.org/10.1037/h0099303

Harrod, H. I. (2000). *The animals came dancing: Native American sacred ecology and animal kinship*. University of Arizona Press. https://doi.org/10.2307/j.ctv1mssswz8

Hauser, D. J., Moss, A. J., Rosenzweig, C., Jaffe, S. N., Robinson, J., & Litman, L. (2022). Evaluating CloudResearch's approved group as a solution for problematic data quality on MTurk. *Behavior Research Methods, 55*(8), 3953–3964. https://doi.org/10.3758/s13428-022-01999-x

Holy, L. (1996). *Anthropological perspectives on kinship*. Pluto Press. https://doi.org/10.2307/j.ctt18mvnwk

IUCN. (2023). *The IUCN red list of threatened species*. Version 2023–1. https://www.iucnredlist.org

Jacobson, S. K., McDuff, M., & Monroe, M. (2015a). *Conservation education and outreach techniques* (2nd ed.). Oxford University Press. https://doi.org/10.1093/acprof:oso/9780198716686.001.0001

Jacobson, S. K., McDuff, M., & Monroe, M. (2015b). Marketing conservation. In S. K. Jacobson, M. McDuff, & M. Monroe (Eds.), *Conservation education and outreach techniques* (2nd ed., pp. 263–293). Oxford University Press. https://doi.org/10.1093/acprof:oso/9780198716686.001.0001

Jarić, I., Bellard, C., Courchamp, F., Kalinkat, G., Meinard, Y., Roberts, D. L., & Correia, R. A. (2020). Societal attention toward extinction threats: A comparison between climate change and biological invasions. *Scientific Reports, 10*, 11085. https://doi.org/10.1038/s41598-020-67931-5

Johnson, C. N. (2021). *Past and future decline and extinction of species*. The Royal Society. https://royalsociety.org/news-resources/projects/biodiversity/decline-and-extinction/

Johnson, J. L., McAndrew, F. T., & Harris, P. B. (1991). Sociobiology and the naming of adopted and natural children. *Ethology and Sociobiology, 12*(5), 365–375. https://doi.org/10.1016/0162-3095(91)90031-K

Jones, D. (2004). The universal psychology of kinship: Evidence from language. *Trends in Cognitive Sciences, 8*(5), 211–215. https://doi.org/10.1016/j.tics.2004.03.001

Kees, J., Berry, C., Burton, S., & Sheehan, K. (2017). An analysis of data quality: Professional panels, student subject pools, and Amazon's mechanical Turk. *Journal of Advertising, 46*(1), 141–155. https://doi.org/10.1080/00913367.2016.1269304

Keith, M. G., & McKay, A. S. (2024). Too anecdotal to be true? Mechanical Turk is not all bots and bad data: Response to Webb and Tangney (2022). *Perspectives on Psychological Science., 19*, 900. https://doi.org/10.1177/17456916241234328

Leavitt, K., Wodahl, E. J., & Schweitzer, K. (2021). Citizen willingness to report wildlife crime. *Deviant Behavior, 42*(10), 1256–1272. https://doi.org/10.1080/01639625.2020.1738643

Leonetti, D. L. (2008). Cultural dimensions of kin investment: An introduction. *Human Nature, 19*, 227–230. https://doi.org/10.1007/s12110-008-9040-6

Li, Y., & Eastman, J. (2023). As cute as a button: The effect of size on online product cuteness perception. *Journal of Product & Brand Management, 32*(8), 1306–1318. https://doi.org/10.1108/JPBM-11-2022-4212

Lieberman, D., Tooby, J., & Cosmides, L. (2007). The architecture of human kin detection. *Nature, 445*, 727–731. https://doi.org/10.1038/nature05510

Litman, L., Robinson, J., & Abberbock, T. (2017). Turkprime.com: A versatile crowdsourcing data acquisition platform for the behavioral sciences. *Behavior Research Methods, 49*, 433–442. https://doi.org/10.3758/s13428-016-0727-z

Lu, L., Neale, N., Line, N. D., & Bonn, M. (2022). Improving data quality using Amazon mechanical Turk through platform setup. *Cornell Hospitality Quarterly, 63*(2), 231–246. https://doi.org/10.1177/19389655211025475

Macdonald, E. A., Burnham, D., Hinks, A. E., Dickman, A. J., Malhi, Y., & Macdonald, D. W. (2015). Conservation inequality and the charismatic cat: Felis felicis. *Global Ecology and Conservation, 3*, 851–866. https://doi.org/10.1016/j.gecco.2015.04.006

Madsen, E. A., Tunney, R. J., Fieldman, G., Plotkin, H. C., Dunbar, R. I., Richardson, J. M., & McFarland, D. (2007). Kinship and altruism: A cross-cultural experimental study. *British Journal of Psychology, 98*(Pt 2), 339–359. https://doi.org/10.1348/000712606X129213

Marquina, T., Hackenburg, D., Duray, H., Fisher, B., & Gould, R. K. (2022). Lessons from an experiment with values-based messaging to support watershed conservation. *Conservation Biology, 36*(5), e13910. https://doi.org/10.1111/cobi.13910

Masci, D. (2019). *In U.S., familiarity with religious groups is associated with warmer feelings toward them*. Pew Research Center. https://www.pewresearch.org/short-reads/2019/10/31/in-u-s-familiarity-with-religious-groups-is-associated-with-warmer-feelings-toward-them/

Mateo, J. M. (2015). Perspectives: Hamilton's legacy: Mechanisms of kin recognition in humans. *Ethology, 121*(5), 419–427. https://doi.org/10.1111/eth.12358

McLeod, L. J., Kitson, J. C., Dorner, Z., Tassell-Matamua, N. A., Stahlmann-Brown, P., Milfont, T. L., & Hine, D. W. (2024). Environmental stewardship: A systematic scoping review. *PLoS One, 19*(5), e0284255. https://doi.org/10.1371/journal.pone.0284255

Miller, A. (2018). Kin-work in a time of jihad: Sustaining bonds of filiation and care for Tunisian foreign combatants. *Cultural Anthropology, 33*(4), 596–620. https://doi.org/10.14506/ca33.4.07

Morris, D. S., & Qirko, H. N. (2019). Saving 'little sister': A test of the effectiveness of kinship appeals in conservation marketing. *Environmental Communication, 14*(4), 481–491. https://doi.org/10.1080/17524032.2019.1687102

Moss, A. (2023). *What is CloudResearch? A rundown of CloudResearch's products and the best use-case for each one*. https://www.cloudresearch.com/resources/blog/cloudresearch-products-and-use-cases/

Mutz, D. C. (2011). *Population-based survey experiments*. Princeton University Press.

Neyer, F. J., & Lang, F. R. (2003). Blood is thicker than water: Kinship orientation across adulthood. *Journal of Personality and Social Psychology, 84*(2), 310–321. https://doi.org/10.1037/0022-3514.84.2.310

Orangutan Outreach. (2021). *Meet our cousins: Orangutan conservation around the globe* [video]. redapes.org. https://redapes.org/international-orangutan-day-2021/

Palomo-Vélez, G., Buczny, J., & Van Vugt, M. (2020). Encouraging pro-environmental behaviors through children-based appeals: A kin selection perspective. *Sustainability, 12*(2), 748. https://doi.org/10.3390/su12020748

Palomo-Vélez, G., & Van Vugt, M. (2021). The evolutionary psychology of climate change behaviors: Insights and applications. *Current Opinion in Psychology, 42*, 54–59. https://doi.org/10.1016/j.copsyc.2021.03.006

Park, J. H., Schaller, M., & Van Vugt, M. (2008). Psychology of human kin recognition: Heuristic cues, erroneous inferences, and their implications. *Review of General Psychology, 12*(3), 215–235. https://doi.org/10.1037/1089-2680.12.3.215

Pawłowski, B., & Chmielińska, A. (2023). Kin term mimicry hypothesis. *Theory in Biosciences, 142*(3), 199–203. https://doi.org/10.1007/s12064-023-00393-1

Peer, E., Rothschild, D., Gordon, A., Evernden, Z., & Damer, E. (2021). Data quality of platforms and panels for online behavioral research. *Behavior Research Methods, 54*(4), 1643–1662. https://doi.org/10.3758/s13428-021-01694-3

Podberscek, A.L., Paul, E.S., & Serpell, J.A. (Eds.) (2000). *Companion animals and us: Exploring the relationships between people and pets*. Cambridge University Press.

Qirko, H. N. (2011). Fictive kinship and induced altruism. In C. Salmon & T. Shackelford (Eds.), *The Oxford handbook of evolutionary family psychology* (pp. 310–328). Oxford University Press.

Qirko, H. N. (2013). Induced altruism in religious, military, and terrorist organizations. *Cross-Cultural Research, 47*(2), 131–161. https://doi.org/10.1177/1069397112471804

Qirko, H. N. (2017). Kinship appeals and conservation social marketing. *Biodiversity and Conservation, 26*(5), 1009–1026. https://doi.org/10.1007/s10531-017-1297-9

Qirko, H.N. (2021). What is a 'critter'? Potential problems with the scientific community's use of informal language to describe non-human species *Language & Ecology*, http://ecolinguistics-association.org/journal.

Rakopoulos, T. (2017). Antimafia families: Cooperative work and flexible kinship in Sicily. *Critique of Anthropology, 37*(2), 115–131. https://doi.org/10.1177/0308275X17694942

Rizzi, F., Annunziata, E., Contini, M., & Frey, M. (2020). On the effect of exposure to information and self-benefit appeals on consumer's intention to perform pro-environmental behaviours: A focus on energy conservation behaviours. *Journal of Cleaner Production, 270*, 122039. https://doi.org/10.1016/j.jclepro.2020.122039

Robinson, B. S., Creasey, M. J. S., Skeats, A., Coverdale, I., & Barlow, A. (2019). Global survey reveals a lack of social marketing skills in the conservation sector and shows supply of training doesn't meet demand. *Social Marketing Quarterly, 25*(1), 9–25. https://doi.org/10.1177/1524500418813542

Rosen, T. (2022). Protecting endangered species. *IISD Earth Negotiations Bulletin, Policy Brief, #33*, 1–10. https://www.iisd.org/system/files/2022-02/still-one-earth-endangered-species_0.pdf

Root-Bernstein, M., Douglas, L., Smith, A., & Veríssimo, D. (2013) Anthropomorphized species as tools for conservation: Utility beyond prosocial, intelligent and suffering species. *Biodiversity and Conservation, 22*, 1577–1589. https://doi.org/10.1007/s10531-013-0494-4

Ryan, J., Mellish, S., Dorrian, J., Winefield, T., & Litchfield, C. (2020). Effectiveness of biodiversity-conservation marketing. *Conservation Biology, 34*(2), 354–367. https://doi.org/10.1111/cobi.13386

Salmon, C. A. (1998). The evocative nature of kin terminology in political rhetoric. *Politics and the Life Sciences, 17*(1), 51–57. https://doi.org/10.1017/S0730938400025351

Salmón, E. (2000). Kincentric ecology: Indigenous perceptions of the human–nature relationship. *Ecological Applications, 10*(5), 1327–1332. https://doi.org/10.1890/1051-0761(2000)010[1327:KEIPOT]2.0.CO;2

Saracevic, S., Schlegelmilch, B. B., & Wu, T. (2022). How normative appeals influence pro-environmental behavior: The role of individualism and collectivism. *Journal of Cleaner Production, 344*, 131086. https://doi.org/10.1016/j.jclepro.2022.131086

Schriver, J., Perunovic, W. Q. E., Brymer, K., & Hachey, T. (2019). Do relatives with greater reproductive potential get help first? A test of the inclusive fitness explanation of kin altruism. *Evolutionary Psychology, 17*(3). https://doi.org/10.1177/1474704919867094

Schuhwerk, M. E., & Lefkoff-Hagius, R. (1995). Green or non-green? Does type of appeal matter when advertising a green product? *Journal of Advertising, 24*(2), 45–54. https://doi.org/10.1080/00913367.1995.10673475

Shin, J., & Mattila, A. S. (2021). Aww effect: Engaging consumers in "non-cute" prosocial initiatives with cuteness. *Journal of Business Research, 126*, 209–220. https://doi.org/10.1016/j.jbusres.2020.11.046

Small, E. (2011). The new Noah's ark: Beautiful and useful species only. Part 1. Biodiversity conservation issues and priorities. *Biodiversity, 12*(4), 232–247. https://doi.org/10.1080/14888386.2011.642663

Small, E. (2012). The new Noah's ark: Beautiful and useful species only. Part 2. The chosen species. *Biodiversity, 13*(1), 37–53. https://doi.org/10.1080/14888386.2012.659443

Smith, R. J., Veríssimo, D., & MacMillan, D. C. (2010). Conservation and marketing: How to lose friends and influence people. In N. Leader-Williams, W. M. Adams, & R. J. Smith (Eds.), *Trade-offs in conservation: Deciding what to save* (pp. 215–232). Wiley-Blackwell.

Smith, S. M., Roster, C. A., Golden, L. L., & Albaum, G. S. (2016). A multi-group analysis of online survey respondent data quality: Comparing a regular USA consumer panel to Mturk samples. *Journal of Business Research, 69*(8), 3139–3148. https://doi.org/10.1016/j.jbusres.2015.12.002

Thomas, M. (2020). Environmental nonprofits receive less than 2% of charitable donations. *Carbonswitch.com*. https://carbonswitch.com/analysis-of-environmental-giving/#:~:text=Highlights%20from%20this%20report&text=Here's%20what%20we%20discovered%3A,billion%20went%20to%20environmental%20nonprofits

Thompson, B. A. (2024). Concern for animals among hunter-gatherers. *Cross-Cultural Research, 0*(0). https://doi.org/10.1177/10693971241234109

United Nations Regional Information Center for Western Europe (2022). *Mother earth day 2022* [video]. YouTube. https://www.youtube.com/watch?v=6qszQnrjsoo

Urquiza-Haas, E. G., & Kotrschal, K. (2015). The mind behind anthropomorphic thinking: Attribution of mental states to other species. *Animal Behaviour, 109*, 167–176. https://doi.org/10.1016/j.anbehav.2015.08.011

van Eeden, L. M., Newsome, T. M., Crowther, M. S., Dickman, C. R., & Bruskotter, J. (2020). Diverse public perceptions of species' status and management align with conflicting conservation frameworks. *Biological Conservation, 242*, 108416. https://doi.org/10.1016/j.biocon.2020.108416

Veríssimo, D., Tully, B., & Douglas, L. R. (2019). Conservation marketing as a tool to promote human-wildlife coexistence. In B. Frank, J. A. Glikman, & S. Marchini (Eds.), *Human-wildlife interactions: Turning conflict into coexistence* (pp. 335–358). Cambridge University Press.

Wallander, L. (2009). 25 years of factorial surveys in sociology: A review. *Social Science Research, 38*(3), 505–520. https://doi.org/10.1016/j.ssresearch.2009.03.004

White, I. R., Royston, P., & Wood, A. M. (2011). Multiple imputation using chained equations: Issues and guidance for practice. *Statistics in Medicine, 30*(4), 377–399. https://doi.org/10.1002/sim.4067

Williams, M., Whitmarsh, L., & Chríost, D. M. G. (2021). The association between anthropomorphism of nature and pro-environmental variables: A systematic review. *Biological Conservation, 255*, 109022. https://doi.org/10.1016/j.biocon.2021.109022

Wright, A. J., Veríssimo, D., Pilfold, K., Parsons, E. C. M., Ventre, K., Cousins, J., et al. (2015). Competitive outreach in the 21st century: Why we need conservation marketing. *Ocean & Coastal Management, 115*, 41–48. https://doi.org/10.1016/j.ocecoaman.2015.06.029

Zvaríková, M., Prokop, P., Zvarík, M., Ježová, Z., Medina-Jerez, W., & Fedor, P. J. (2021). What Makes Spiders Frightening and disgusting to People? *Frontiers in Ecology and Evolution, 9*. https://doi.org/10.3389/fevo.2021.694569

Chapter 7
Climate Change and Food Security: The Role of Natural Language Processing and Machine Learning in Automating the Analysis of Social Media Data to Discern Public Opinion of Agriculture's Impact on the Environment

Carrie J. Butts-Wilmsmeyer

Climate change is one of the greatest threats currently facing the world. Shifting climatic patterns have created extreme weather patterns, as highlighted by intense heatwaves, prolonged droughts, increased frequency of hurricanes and violent storms, and devastating wildfires (AghaKouchak et al., 2020). While damaging in and of themselves, the extreme weather patterns and natural disasters indicative of climate change also are associated with significant downstream consequences. In a 2023 report, the Intergovernmental Panel on Climate Change (IPCC) summarized observed widespread and substantial impacts, losses, and damages attributed to climate change. Among these challenges were increased risk of inland flooding and damage to infrastructure in cities near bodies of water, diminished agricultural production, and reduced access to clean drinking water (IPCC, 2023). These climate and weather extremes were found to be increasingly driving displacement in Africa, Asia, North America, Central America, and South America, as people seek refuge from harsh weather extremes and food insecurity. Concerningly, displacement, food insecurity, and other pressures from climate change are often intertwined with increased risk of conflict, prompting the United States' Intelligence Community to highlight climate change as one of the leading challenges in its 2024 Annual Threat Assessment report (Office of the Director of National Intelligence, 2024).

Supplementary Information The online version contains supplementary material available at https://doi.org/10.1007/978-3-031-90889-7_7.

C. J. Butts-Wilmsmeyer (✉)
Southern Illinois University Edwardsville, Edwardsville, IL, USA
e-mail: cbuttsw@siue.edu

N. Guehlstorf (ed.), *Environmental Policy Science's Exploration for Innovative Data*, Natural Resource Management and Policy NA,
https://doi.org/10.1007/978-3-031-90889-7_7

As the impact of climate change on people worldwide grows, the level of interest in climate change has also increased. According to the PEW Research Center's Global Attitudes Surveys from 2022, 72.9% of respondents indicated that they believed climate change was a major threat (PEW Research Center, 2022) (Fig. 7.1). This is a marked increase from 61.1% of respondents in 2017 (PEW Research Center, 2017) and 52.5% of respondents in 2013 (PEW Research Center, 2013) (Fig. 7.1). In a massive survey undertaken by the Yale Program on Climate Change Communication in partnership with Data for Good at Meta, a majority of respondents in 72.7% of countries and territories surveyed indicated that climate change was extremely or very important to them on a personal level. Furthermore, out of the 110 countries and territories surveyed, the majority of participants in 109 countries indicated that they believed climate change posed a serious threat to their country or territory, with the majority of respondents from 104 of these surveyed areas indicating that climate change should be a high priority for their government (Leiserowitz et al., 2022) (Fig. 7.2). Similar patterns were observed across the United States between 2008 and 2020 (Marlon et al., 2023) (Fig. 7.3), demonstrating that interest in climate change is increasing among the public even within countries that have a lower percentage of individuals that believe that climate change is a major threat.

While there appears to be broad consensus worldwide that policies are needed to address and mitigate climate change, there is also concern regarding how these policies may be implemented effectively. As an example, it is widely accepted that the commitments outlined in the Paris Agreement will not be achieved without transitioning to renewable energy sources worldwide (Zhao et al., 2022; Murshed, 2020). This represents a significant challenge, as the cost of producing renewable energy represents a considerable burden for many nations. For the purposes of this

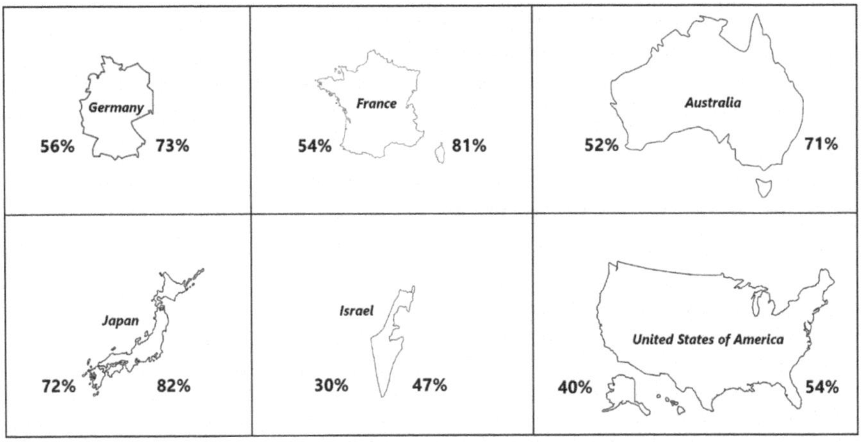

Fig. 7.1 Change in percentage of individuals who believe that climate change is a major threat. The percentages for 2013 are shown to the left, and the percentages for 2022 are shown to the right of each respective country. Not all countries included in the referenced PEW Research Center studies are included above. Source: PEW Research Center's Global Attitudes Survey, 2013 and 2022

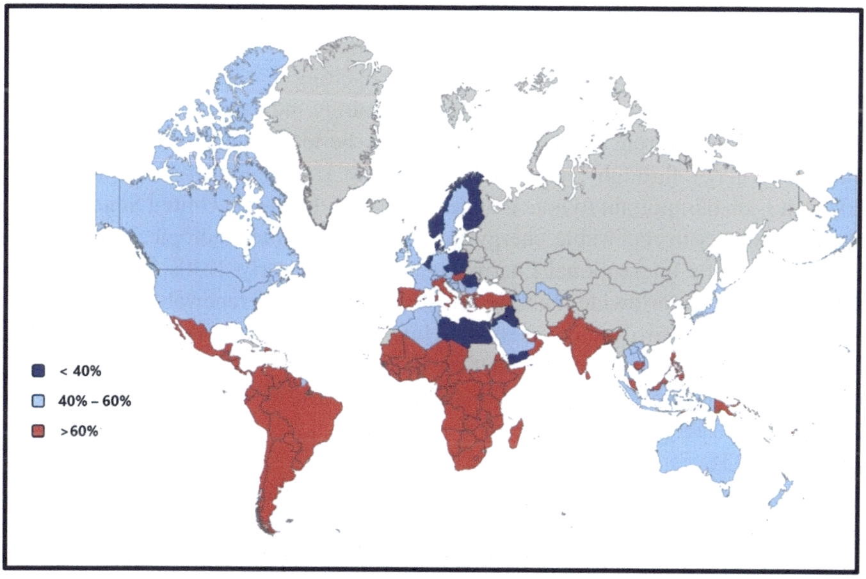

Fig. 7.2 Perception of whether climate change is personally important by country. The percentages shown are the percentage of respondents who indicated that the issue of climate change is "extremely" or "very" important to them personally. Source: Yale Program on Climate Change/Data for Good at Meta. International Public Opinion on Climate Change, 2022

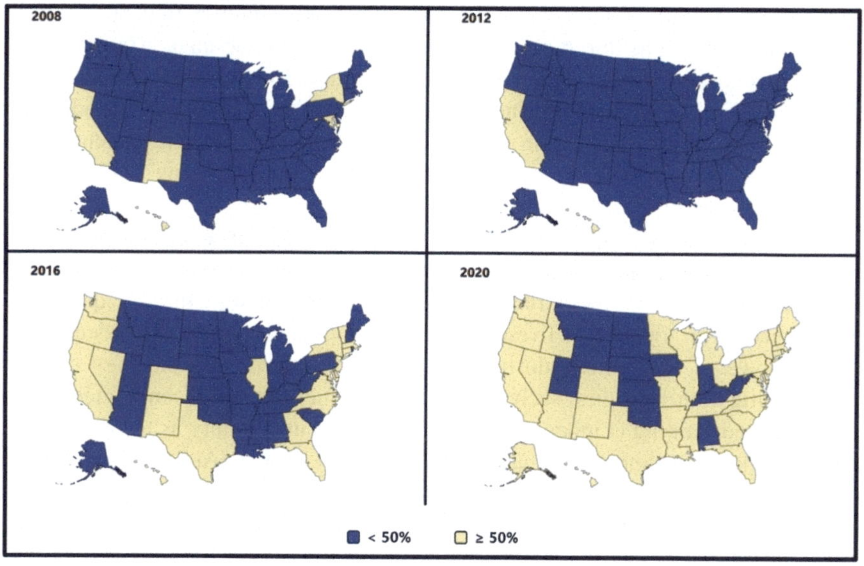

Fig. 7.3 Change in public perception of climate change in the U.S. over time. Individuals were asked whether they believed global warming is already harming or will harm the USA. The percentage of adults responding yes to that question by state is shown above. Source: Yale Program on Climate Change Communication. Change in U.S. state-level public opinion about climate change: 2008–2020

discussion, the term production includes both the operational tasks that lead to the generation of clean energy, as well as the investment in infrastructure and necessary research and development costs. Although it is exciting that the most recent studies released by Energy Innovation Policy & Technology indicate that the cost of producing electricity through renewables may now be less expensive than producing the same energy through coal production in the United States (Solomon et al., 2023), it is also important to note that this is largely due to the United States' previous investments in renewable energy infrastructure and technological innovation. According to the International Energy Agency, by the early 2030s, approximately 4.5 trillion USD worldwide must be invested per year into renewable energy if we are to achieve net-zero carbon emissions (International Energy Agency, 2023). This cost may be prohibitive for some nations with limited resources, highlighting the need for international support and for effective domestic policies that are tailored to the needs of each geographical region (Osman et al., 2023; International Energy Agency, 2023).

The transition to clean energy also requires significant upfront investment by private citizens and businesses. Therefore, although the public often perceives a great need for mitigative climate change strategies, including lessening reliance on fossil fuel energy sources, adoption of renewable energy sources is likely to be limited without first addressing public concerns. Thus, many nations have begun to offer incentives to help promote the adoption of renewable energy technologies, such as through the Rural Energy for America Program (REAP) offered in the United States (United States Department of Agriculture, 2024), the Residential Clean Energy Credit for homeowners in the United States (Internal Revenue Service, 2024), tax deductions for home energy renovations in Germany (International Energy Agency, 2021), and the Small-scale Renewable Energy Scheme in Australia (Australian Government Clean Energy Regulator, 2024). The successful adoption of renewable energy sources through incentivized programs is a testament to the need to understand public perception and concerns when crafting public policy (Energy Information Administration, 2023).

One sector that is particularly vulnerable to both the impacts of climate change as well as the potentially negative impacts of poorly implemented public policy is the agriculture industry. As extreme weather conditions become more frequent and widespread, crop yields and livestock health are likely to suffer (Howden et al., 2007). However, this same industry must contend with the challenges of climate change mitigation strategies, such as upfront investment in new technologies, infrastructure, and training (Lipper et al., 2014); risk and uncertainty as to whether the newly proposed technologies may be economically viable (Arslan et al., 2014); inconsistent policies, weak support systems, and lack of coordination among government agencies, nongovernmental organizations (NGOs), and private sector stakeholders that hinder the scaling up of successful practices (FAO, 2017); and misalignment of proposed policies with socio-cultural norms, traditions, and labor constraints within farming communities that impact the adoption of climate change mitigative practices (Scheelbeek et al., 2018). Furthermore, with a growing world population, the transition entirely from intensive farming practices to practices that reduce food production is not feasible without threatening food security. Complicating matters, farmers ultimately are responsible for producing the agricultural products that consumers desire, and they must do so within a price range that consumers will accept. Therefore, it is essential that policies promoting the adoption of climate change mitigative strategies within agriculture not only address the challenges facing agriculturists, but also the perspectives of the general public.

The complexities of the challenges and perspectives surrounding climate change and agricultural production cannot be fully captured in responses to Likert scale survey questions, such as those surveys that have been applied worldwide in the past. This is not a dismissal of Likert scale data, as these and other survey questions can provide very insightful information. Each research approach, including the novel approach presented in this chapter, has its limitations. In the case of Likert scale data and close-ended survey questions, while these tools are excellent for capturing general sentiment and sentiment across pre-identified demographics of interest, these tools also do not allow for exploration of the nuances that drive differences in sentiment between potential stakeholder groups. Consideration of these nuances is likely to determine whether a policy is effective or not. To explore these nuances, rich qualitative data that describe the perspectives, experiences, and sentiment of the public are required. These data have historically been nearly impossible to collect, as their collection required interviews, focus groups, and other intensive qualitative research efforts. However, with the advent and widespread use of social media platforms, it has become possible to collect the written, qualitative perspectives of individuals worldwide. In 2022, the Reddit Climate Change Dataset was released publicly to foster research aimed at addressing climate change challenges (Kaggle, 2022). This dataset consists of 620,000 Reddit posts and 4.6 million comments that mentioned both "climate" and "change" and were posted prior to September 1, 2022. These data offer a rich repository to understand not only sentiment and perspective surrounding climate change, but also how viewpoints change across communities (Treen et al., 2022) and within the context of different topics.

Furthermore, because of the density of the Reddit Climate Change Dataset, there is sufficient data to enable the use of natural language processing (NLP) and machine learning (ML) techniques. NLP and ML techniques have been used extensively in other disciplines to mine information from Reddit and other social media platforms. Examples of the use of NLP and ML in conjunction with Reddit data include the detection of depression-related posts (Tadesse et al., 2019), the evaluation of patient experiences to improve healthcare outcomes (Okon et al., 2020), and detection of suicidality among opioid users (Yao et al., 2020). Interestingly, while NLP and ML have been used extensively to study health outcomes using Reddit datasets, the use of these techniques as applied to Reddit data has been limited within policy contexts. Given that Reddit's platform architecture is more conducive to fostering constructive deliberative debate, as opposed to the more frequent polarization, echo chambers, and misinformation characteristic of X (formerly Twitter) (Treen et al., 2022), this presents an opportunity to delve into both the positive viewpoints and constructive criticisms surrounding climate change mitigative strategies within agriculture, as well as the debates surrounding other policies.

The overall goal of this study is to use NLP and ML techniques applied to social media data to understand the perspectives and concerns surrounding climate change mitigative strategies and agricultural production. The perspectives and concerns will be classified into common themes, as well as common themes by stakeholder group. Specifically, NLP and ML will be applied to the Reddit Climate Change Dataset to identify core themes and public sentiment surrounding those themes within this dataset. Unsupervised ML techniques, such as K-Means analysis, offer the ability to automatically identify themes without prior coding of data when used in conjunction with NLP techniques. It is anticipated that different themes will emerge over time and across agricultural, environmental, political, and general public subreddit stakeholder groups. Subsequently, the themes that are of most importance or are of greatest concern for each stakeholder group will be identified. This information provides not only insightful information that will enable the development of efficacious climate change mitigation policies, but also generalizable techniques that can be employed to address stakeholder concerns across a variety of public policy issues.

Methods

Data

The Reddit Climate Change Dataset was downloaded from Kaggle (Kaggle, 2022). Preliminary examination of the dataset indicated that original posts were often links or questions as opposed to discussion. Therefore, the data was filtered to include only comments. Strings were cleaned by turning all letters lowercase to ensure proper string parsing. Comments containing the strings “agri,” “food,” “hunger,” or “hungry” were retained in the dataset. This resulted in a dataset with 232,575 comments, spanning the years 2010 through 2022. Strings were further cleaned to remove stop words and punctuation. The matrix of TF-IDF (short for term frequency-inverse document frequency) values was retrieved using the TfidfVectorizer function in the sci-kit learn library of Python (version 3.11). The TF-IDF values matrix was then used to conduct the thematic analysis using ML as described below. Additionally, the Reddit Climate Dataset contains the sentiment analysis scores, as calculated by the Valence Aware Dictionary and sEntiment Reasoner (VADER) algorithm. These scores range from −1 (extremely negative) to +1 (extremely positive).

```
#This code imports the dataset, identifies the strings of interest,
#and creates a new dataset, af.
import os
os.chdir("C:\\Users\\...")

import pandas as pd
reddit = pd.read_csv("the-reddit-climate-change-dataset-comments.csv")

from datetime import timezone
import datetime

reddit.body = reddit.body.str.lower()
ag = reddit[reddit.body.str.contains("agri")]
food = reddit[reddit.body.str.contains("food")]
hunger = reddit[reddit.body.str.contains("hunger")]
hungry = reddit[reddit.body.str.contains("hungry")]
af = pd.concat([ag, food, hunger, hungry])
af = af.drop_duplicates()

af.created_utc = pd.to_datetime(af.created_utc, unit="s")
```

```
#This code completes the TF-IDF step.
from sklearn.feature_extraction.text import TfidfVectorizer
def vectorize(text, maxx_features):
    vectorizer = TfidfVectorizer(max_features = maxx_features, stop_words="english")
    X = vectorizer.fit_transform(text)
    return X

af.body = af.body.astype(str)
af.body = af.body.str.replace('[^\w\s]','')
af.body = af.body.str.lower()

text = af.body.values
X = vectorize(text, 2**12)

#This completes the PCA step.
from sklearn.decomposition import PCA
pca = PCA(n_components = .95, random_state=42)
X_reduced = pca.fit_transform(X.toarray())
X_reduced.shape
```

Thematic Analysis with Unsupervised Machine Learning

The TF-IDF matrix contains information indicating the relative importance of each word in the collection of all comments. However, the cooccurrence of some word pairs is more likely than others. Therefore, the correlation structure among all words and their occurrence lends itself to Principal Component Analysis

(PCA), a dimension reduction technique. PCA scores were calculated using the PCA function from within the sci-kit learn library. The scores were then used to conduct the K-Means cluster analysis using the KMeans function, also from the sci-kit learn library within Python. The ideal number of clusters (k) was identified by using the "Elbow Method," or a method that seeks to identify the number of clusters after which the distortion plateaus. Distortion is defined as the sum of the squared distances from the cluster centers to each data point within the respective clusters.

```
#This performs the preliminary K-Means analysis and allows for selection
#of the optimal number of clusters.
from sklearn.cluster import KMeans
import numpy as np
from scipy.spatial.distance import cdist

distortions = []
K = range(2, 20)

for k in K:
    k_means = KMeans(n_clusters=k, random_state=42).fit(X_reduced)
    k_means.fit(X_reduced)
    distortions.append(sum(np.min(cdist(X_reduced, k_means.cluster_centers_,"euclidean"),axis=1))/X.shape[0])
X.shape[0]
```

The clusters identified represent the major themes present in the dataset. Following the K-Means analysis, TF-IDF vectorizers as previously described were again fit to the word corpus from each specific cluster. TF-IDF, as opposed to similar measures, provides a measure of the relative importance of a word instead of simply the word count. Keywords were identified from each cluster based on calculated level of importance. The context in which these keywords were used was explored manually by taking a random subsample of 1400 comments, or 200 comments per cluster. Special consideration was taken to select comments from across all years and all key stakeholder groups. Emergent themes were noted for each cluster based on the context in which these keywords were used.

```
#This performs the K-Means analysis with the optimal number of clusters.
#Additionally, a new variable "y" is added to the dataset that contains
#the assigned cluster number.
k=7
kmeans = KMeans(n_clusters=k, random_state=42)
y_pred = kmeans.fit_predict(X_reduced)
af["y"] = y_pred.tolist()
```

```
#This performs the topic analysis.
#Note that Python stores the first item as 0, the second item as 1, etc.
#Therefore, k0 contains the observations for Theme 1.
#The final output are each comment and the most important words associated
#with each theme, as identified through TF-IDF.
#The code below shows the analytical steps for Theme 1.
k0 = af.loc[af.y==0]

k0list = k0.body.tolist()
vec0 = CountVectorizer(stop_words="english").fit(k0list)
bow0 = vec0.transform(k0list)
sw0 = bow0.sum(axis=0)

wf0 = [(word, sw0[0,idx]) for word, idx in vec0.vocabulary_.items()]
wf0 = sorted(wf0, key = lambda x: x[1], reverse=True)
wf0[0:49]

vec0idf = TfidfVectorizer(max_features = 2**12, stop_words="english").fit(k0list)
bow0idf = vec0idf.transform(k0list)
sw0idf = bow0idf.sum(axis=0)

wf0idf = [(word, sw0idf[0,idx]) for word, idx in vec0idf.vocabulary_.items()]
wf0idf = sorted(wf0idf, key = lambda x: x[1], reverse=True)
wf0idf[0:49]
```

Analysis of Thematic Changes Over Time and by Stakeholder Group

Following the K-Means analysis, each comment was assigned to a primary thematic cluster. The percentage of comments that were assigned to each thematic cluster was calculated for each year from 2010 to 2022. Key stakeholder groups were identified by subreddit group. Two general public subreddits, two agriculture-oriented subreddits, two environmentalist-oriented subreddits, and two political subreddits were selected. Subreddit selection was made based on alignment within each of these stakeholder areas and number of comments, the latter consideration being in place to avoid small-sample bias. The subreddits selected were *worldnews* and *askreddit* (general public), *agriculture* and *farming* (agriculture-oriented), *environment* and *climatechange* (environmentalist-oriented), and *politics* [left-leaning] and *conservative* [right-leaning] (political). This created a sub-dataset consisting of 47,911 observations. Selection of subreddits is an absolutely crucial step, as this is the step that ensures the perspectives of and most important topics to key stakeholder groups are correctly identified. Although the K-Means analysis will identify clusters of topics regardless of the number of comments that fall into each of those clusters (i.e., the K-Means analysis can adjust for unbalanced datasets), the number of comments that fall into each identified cluster is likely to vary by stakeholder group. One key concern when approaching this study was that Reddit users do not typically disclose demographic information within each of their comments. However, stakeholder demographics are likely to vary across different subreddits, as users typically subscribe to and participate in subreddits that are of most interest to them. Therefore, although Reddit users do not provide self-identifying information to questions such as, "Do you classify yourself as an agriculturist?" or, "Do you consider yourself more liberal or conservative?" participation in subreddits based on interests and shared belief systems can provide insight to these demographic questions. Frequencies of thematic occurrence were calculated for each subreddit selected for examination in this study. Lastly, the average sentiment and distribution of sentiment scores surrounding each of these themes was calculated by year and by subreddit.

Results and Discussion

Frequency of Comments Across Time and Across Stakeholder Group: Is Public Discourse of Climate Change Growing on Reddit?

The final dataset of comments consisted of a total of 232,575 Reddit comments that included both words "climate" and "change" as well as one of the following words or character strings: "agri," "food," "hunger," or "hungry." All years from 2010 to 2022 were represented. The earliest recorded comment was from January 2, 2010, while the latest comment recorded was from August 31, 2022. The distribution of comments by year can be found in Fig. 7.4. Additionally, across the selected subreddits of *farming*, *agriculture*, *worldnews*, *askreddit*, *environment*, *climatechange*,

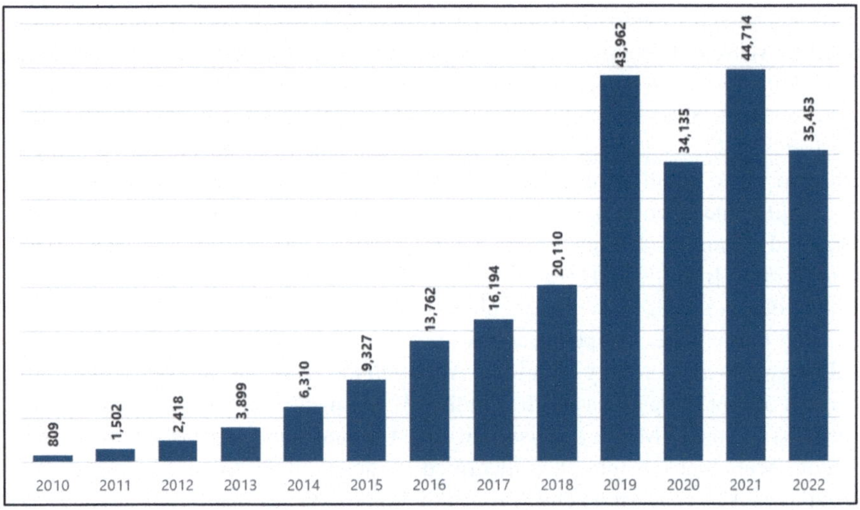

Fig. 7.4 Number of comments discussing climate change within the context of agriculture and food security by year. *Note*: Only a partial year of data is available for 2022, as data collection in the Reddit Climate Change dataset ended on September 1, 2022

politics, and *conservative*, there were a total of 47,911 observations. Furthermore, after a subreddit became live, it was represented in the dataset each year.

An overarching assumption of this research is that growing public interest in climate change is reflected on social media websites, such as Reddit, and that this information can be used to mine information that can inform effective public policy. Therefore, a pivotal question that was essential to answer before any additional analyses were conducted was whether this assumption was true, and whether it was true across multiple stakeholder groups. If the discourse surrounding climate change did not mirror the increase in public interest seen in the PEW Research Center's Global Attitudes Surveys (Fig. 7.1) and the Yale Program on Climate Change Communication (Fig. 7.3), this would call into question the validity of using Reddit data to examine public opinion surrounding climate change. Overall, public discourse on climate change across Reddit is growing. Given that the total number of posts and comments remained relatively stable across all topics (not just limited to climate change) in all but the politically oriented subreddits (Subreddit Stats, 2023c), where decreases were seen in both *politics* and *conservative* after November 2020, the increase in comments related to climate change (Figs. 7.4 and 7.5) is unlikely due to simply an overall increase in the number of Reddit posts (Ceci, 2024c). Said another way, the proportion of total posts across these subreddits during the timeframe of this study that addressed climate change increased. This phenomenon appears to be at least partially attributable to an increasing willingness to engage in meaningful discourse surrounding climate change on social media platforms. Overall and across seven of the eight subreddits examined, discourse surrounding climate change grew beginning in 2019 and has remained higher than levels prior to 2019. This provides confirmation that the growing interest in climate change and its impacts on people worldwide is being captured in Reddit data.

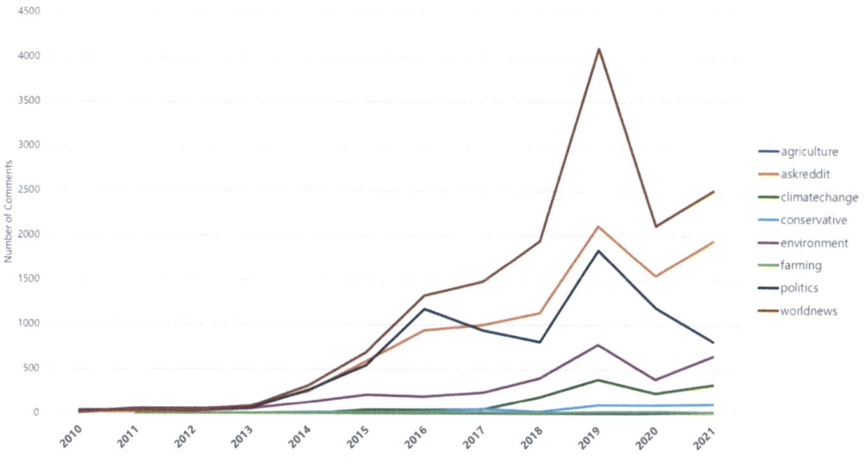

Fig. 7.5 Number of comments by selected subreddit over time. *Note*: 2022 data is not shown because data was not collected for all of 2022

Giving further evidence that Reddit is capturing public discourse and sentiment surrounding climate change, there was a sharp increase in the number of comments overall and across all selected subreddits in 2019, highlighting an increase in public discourse surrounding climate change in that year (Figs. 7.4 and 7.5). At the time, 2019 was the second warmest year on record since the National Oceanic and Atmospheric Administration (NOAA) began keeping records in 1880 (NOAA, 2020). Interestingly, although 2020 was hotter on record than 2019 (NOAA, 2023), there was an overall decrease in the number of comments related to climate change that year. This trend was also reflected in the overall dataset and not only in the smaller subreddit dataset, with a marked decrease of 40,988 comments related to climate change in 2019 to 31,512 comments in 2020. There was again a spike in the number of comments regarding climate change in 2021 overall (40,640 comments) and across six of the eight subreddits specifically selected for study, with *farming* and *politics* being important but different exceptions. In all subreddits except *politics*, the number of comments related to climate change in 2021 exceeded the number of comments prior to 2019. It is also important to note that data collection did not take place for the entirety of 2022, only until September 1 of that year. With this in mind, the number of comments related to climate change on the *agriculture* and *climatechange* subreddits were on track to meet 2021 levels of activity, while the number of comments regarding climate change on the *conservative*, *environment*, and *farming* subreddits were projected to exceed the number of comments seen in 2019 and 2021 by significant margins. Similarly, the overall number of comments related in climate change in 2022 had already surpassed all years except 2019 and 2021 and was on track to surpass both years. By contrast, the number of comments regarding climate change dropped significantly on the *politics* subreddit from its peak in 2019.

The trends in the observed number of comments offer key insights regarding the public's perception of climate change and its impact on their lives. One question that arises with these trends is whether the increase in the public's interest in climate change in 2019 was a momentary spike, or if there is sustained interest. To answer this question, the deviations witnessed in 2020 and across subreddits must be explored. Given the impact of the Covid-19 pandemic in 2020 and the associated public discourse surrounding that life-altering event, a decrease in the number of comments surrounding climate change in 2020 is not unexpected. In the case of *farming*, the number of comments regarding climate change remained relatively and consistently high from 2019 to 2022, without the decrease witnessed in 2020 that was seen across other subreddits. This also stands to reason, as the Covid-19 pandemic placed strains on food security and the logistics of food production. Thus, the stresses of logistical hurdles and changing climatic conditions on food production were both significant priorities for farmers and the agricultural industry.

Likewise, deviations from the peak number of comments seen in 2019 across some subreddits offer insight into the priorities facing each stakeholder group. The drop in the number of comments related to climate change in the *politics* subreddit is expected, since the number of comments per day across that subreddit dropped by approximately half or more from 2019 to 2022 (Subreddit Stats, 2023a). Additionally, as indicated by the top keywords in Reddit *politics*, the focus of the subreddit shifted to concern over U.S. right-wing governmental officials and policies, including calls for impeachment (Subreddit Stats, 2023a). Thus, the decreases seen in 2020 and within the *politics* subreddit are reflective of external factors that are not indicative of the public's long-term interest in climate change.

Furthermore, the drop in the number of comments related to climate change in the *worldnews* subreddit must also be addressed if we are to answer the question as to whether climate change remains important to the general public. While the number of comments in this subreddit again increased in 2021 and this number was higher than in 2020, it still remained lower than that seen in 2019. Unlike *politics*, this subreddit maintained a relatively consistent number of comments from 2019 through 2022, with the exception of a major spike following the Russian invasion of Ukraine in February of 2022 (Subreddit Stats, 2023b). This reduction in the number of comments in *worldnews* may stem from media coverage and desensitization. The five hottest years on record from 1880 to 2022 were 2016, 2020, 2019, 2015, and 2017, with 2016 being the hottest year on record until 2023 (NOAA, 2023). Media coverage of climate change and global warming rose sharply in August 2019 and persisted into January 2020. With the exception of the Covid-19 pandemic and the Russian invasion of Ukraine, media coverage of global climate change remained relatively high through 2022 (Boykoff et al., 2024). The greatest number of Reddit comments surrounding climate change in 2019 occurred in August and September of that year, when media coverage of climate change was first increasing (Fig. 7.6).

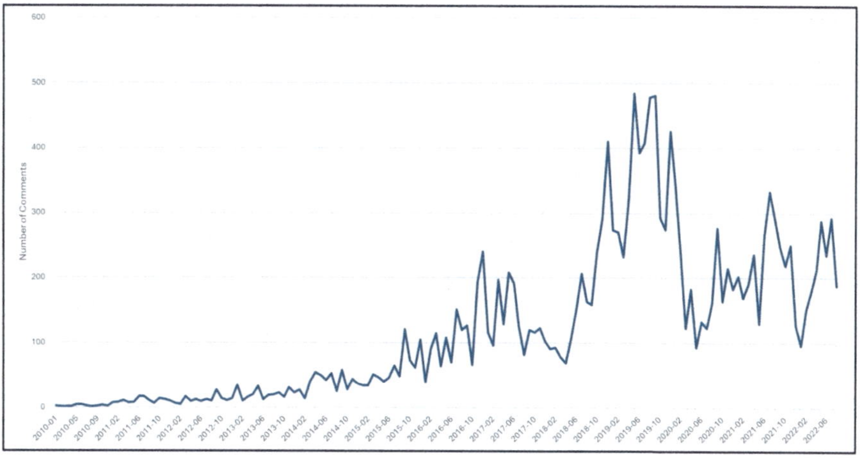

Fig. 7.6 Number of comments on the *worldnews* subreddit over time

K-Means Analysis: How Many Themes Emerge in the Reddit Climate Change Dataset when Focusing on Agriculture and Food Security?

A total of seven clusters, corresponding to seven themes, were identified following the calculation of distortion and the deviation in distortion from the straight line connecting ($k = 2, D_2$) and ($k = 19, D_{19}$) where D_i is the distortion value when $k = 2$ and when $k = 19$, respectively (Fig. 7.7). Table 7.1 indicates the number of Reddit comments that fell into each cluster theme.

Thematic Analysis Continued: What Are the Seven Themes?

Thematic analysis can be described as two stages: determination of the number of themes and grouping texts sharing a predominant theme together and characterizing the themes. K-Means clustering analysis is a powerful unsupervised ML method that enables textual information to be classified into common themes without prior knowledge or prior manual coding. Together with NLP to preprocess and clean data prior to clustering, K-Means offers a computationally efficient method for accomplishing the first step of thematic analysis. Following cluster assignment, a number of possible NLP techniques may be used to characterize the themes.

One of the secondary goals of this chapter is to provide readers with access to accessible tools that they can use to process their own data. As such, one of the most powerful computational tools, latent Dirichlet allocation (LDA), was overruled in favor of less computationally intensive methods. However, it is anticipated that computational power will continue to increase, and a brief discussion of LDA is imperative. LDA is a Bayesian network approach that automatically identifies and extracts themes from texts. When used following K-Means clustering analysis,

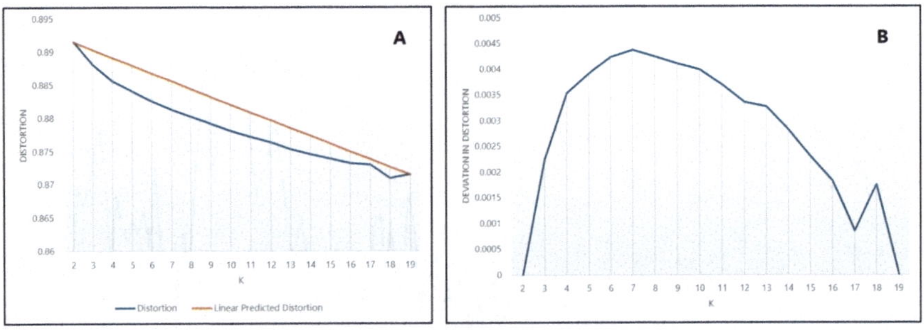

Fig. 7.7 Identification of optimal number of clusters (k) based on distortion. A: Plot of calculated distortion and the straight line between the points ($k = 2, D_2$) and ($k = 19, D_{19}$), also known as the linear predicted distortion. B: Plot of the deviation between the linear predicted distortion and the calculated distortion at each possible level of k

Table 7.1 Thematic analysis of climate change discourse on Reddit as it pertains to agriculture and food security

Theme number	Theme description	Keywords	Number of comments
1	Transition to new technology and solutions	People, energy, resources	50,738
2	Extent of climate change impacts	Water, carbon, warming, emissions, earth, land, science	37,580
3	Social responsibility	People, live, eat, help, human, planet	22,123
4	Reciprocal impacts of agribusiness and climate change	Emissions, carbon, water, greenhouse, impact, land, environmental, CO_2, gas, tax	12,060
5	Animal agriculture and plant-based diets	Meat, animal, vegan, food, eat, livestock, plant-based, methane	18,907
6	Governmental regulation and policies	Government, money, human, power, state, economy	34,384
7	Challenges	Food, people, hunger, water, shortages, production, energy, time, land, problem, supply, weather	56,783

topics describing the overarching theme of each cluster can be identified automatically. This is a powerful tool, as it enables thematic clusters to be characterized automatically and with no human involvement other than validation.

In light of computational constraints, the TF-IDF matrix can be used to identify the most important keywords. Unlike LDA, the use of TF-IDF to characterize cluster themes is only partially automated. The most important terms for each cluster, based on TF-IDF importance metrics, can be automatically extracted. However, the context in which those keywords are used is still unknown. Furthermore, some keywords are nonsensical (e.g., "www" often appeared as a keyword because of the use of web URLs in comments). Therefore, keywords must be filtered manually. Then, to ensure correct coding, random subsamples of comments must be examined to understand the context in which the keywords are being used. The keywords associated with each cluster are summarized in Table 7.1.

Upon completion of these steps, seven clear themes emerged. The variation in comments and their assigned predominant themes are shown in Fig. 7.8.

The themes and example comments for each cluster are:

Theme 1: Transition to New Technology and Solutions. Comments falling in this cluster largely focused on conversations surrounding transition to new technologies and new climate change mitigative strategies. Discussion extended to include the benefits and disadvantages of potential solutions.

> *[Comment 1]: It isn't that simple for farmers to change their ways, to be fair. Working out what is effective in your region via regenerative farming is trial and error, and therefore a huge risk. Realistically, the government should be offering subsidies for carbon storage, and help poorer farmers upgrade their machinery to no-till. Same with chemicals - there are no eco-friendly alternatives; I wish people would start to fund science that looks into this.* From Reddit *worldnews*.

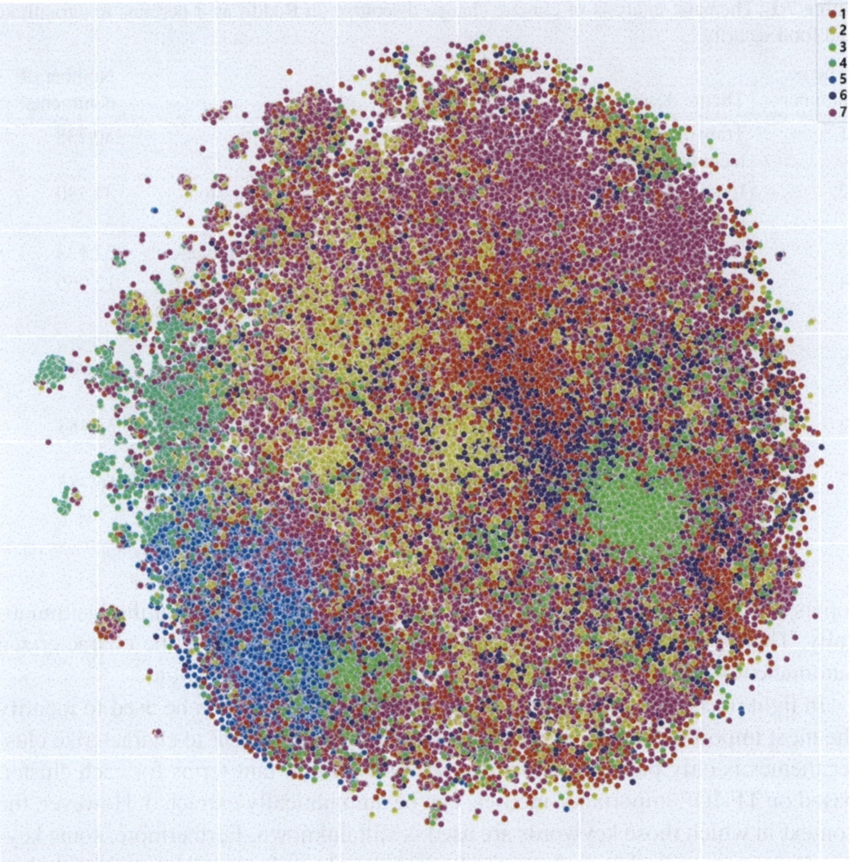

Fig. 7.8 Variation and distribution of Reddit comments by theme. Distinct regions emerge for Themes 3, 4, 5, and 6, and to some degree for Theme 2. Themes 1 and 7 are much more dispersed, indicating the shared overlap in topics between Themes 1 and 7 and the other themes

> *[Comment 2]: I think energy saving battery systems are something that can both earn money and help to reduce it's* [sic] *consumption/production. There are some interesting emerging technologies like iron-air batteries or pressurised air systems. Obviously this would need software to operate (eg., buy and store cheap energy at night, sell during peak hours). Especially in Europe there are big problems with energy shortages and prices spikes, so it's probably a very profitable opportunity as well.*
>
> …
>
> *Also, I've got another one - there's a Chinese study saying that intercropping can improve yeld* [sic] *by 20~30%, which has amazing carbon sequestration potential. I guess GPS software for this type of agricultural works would be useful. Also soil management can stop climate change on its own (check 4 per 1000 initiative). Any app helping to achieve this goal would be golden.* From Reddit *climatechange*.

Theme 2: Extent of Climate Change Impacts. Comments focused on natural disasters and the extent of climate change impacts. Related to this conversation, some comments falling in this cluster communicated a perceived disconnect between science and policy, and an uncertainty as to whether policy was addressing climate change proportional to its predicted impacts. Comments communicating a perceived underservice and comments communicating a perceived overreaction to climate change impacts through policy measures were present.

[Comment 3]: The argument isn't over whether climate change is happening. It is. The argument is over to what extent, and why. Is it an existential threat, or are we simply going to see warmer temperatures that are more conducive to agriculture? Is it entirely or mostly anthropogenic in nature, or is it naturally occurring as we continue our [exit from the little ice age](https://en.wikipedia.org/wiki/little_ice_age) and perhaps return to a temperature state similar to the [mid-holocene warm period] (https://www.ncdc.noaa.gov/global--warming/mid-holocene-warm-period)? From Reddit *conservative*.

[Comment 4]: Part of the issue is a fundamental disagreement on what government policy should do. The government stepping in to force a change will cause many unforeseen trade offs [sic] *in other industries. The alternative is transitioning away from oil, but on the market's own time.*

...

Of course money is also an issue. Oil is not simply for transportation either. Plastic products and a litany of chemical inputs are all derived from petroleum. Heavily regulating the petroleum market makes fertilizer more expensive causing food prices to go up. Any product containing plastics would be effected [sic].

imho, there's a conservative case for being a responsible steward of the planet. At the same time, we shouldn't panic and cause millions to go out of work to fulfill an ideal via governmental involvement. From Reddit *conservative*.

Theme 3: Social Responsibility. Comments centered on both individual and collective social responsibility. Discussions included actions and efforts that could be undertaken to slow climate change.

[Comment 5]: About 50% of greenhouse gas emissions worldwide emissions [sic] *come from electricity generation and transportation. As an individual, you have some ability to impact these sectors. You can buy an electric car, install solar panels, carpool, and simply endeavor to use less electricity in your home. Another 25% comes from agriculture (mostly through beef/dairy farming, as cattle grazing produces large amounts of methane.) The best way to impact this part of emissions is not eating beef.*

...

It's important to do your part as an individual, and if we all do our part we can make great strides toward achieving true sustainability. From Reddit *environment*.

[Comment 6]: Individual actions matter. Even the smallest action has consequences. They aren't enough to do all the work, but they do matter. From Reddit *climatechange*.

Theme 4: Reciprocal Impacts of Agribusiness and Climate Change. These comments focused on the impacts of agriculture on the environment and climate change, as well as the impact of climate change on agribusiness. Financial or industrial considerations were typically key to these conversations. The impact of agriculture on the environment and climate change often mentioned emissions and loss of biodiversity, particularly insect biodiversity. Conversely, the impact of climate change mitigative strategies and policies on economic sustainability of farms and agribusiness entities were often cited.

[Comment 7]: This is really interesting. Not only do we have to consider how to make crop yields better as the climate changes, we also have to consider how our farming techniques contribute to climate change. From Reddit *climatechange.*

[Comment 8]: It seems to me politicians avoid ag and food policy like the plague because its fraught with the potential for them to lose massive amounts of financial backing (for every candidate regardless of affiliation), particularly with the increased influence that special interests have had post [citizens united](http://www.ncbi.nlm.nih.gov/pmc/articles/pmc3110222/).

…

I don't care what your politics are, or what you grow, or how you grow it- food matters in a big way and the fact that these politicians aren't even talking about it just shows how broken our system is. From Reddit *farming.*

Theme 5: Animal Agriculture and Plant-Based Diets: Many of the comments in this cluster focused on the sustainability of animal agriculture. Discussion and deliberation contrasted the environmental impact of diets rooted in animal agriculture in comparison to those relying on plant-based protein sources. Topics tended to focus on emissions, land and water usage, and the feasibility of plant-based diets.

[Comment 9]: Going vegan reduces one's carbon footprint nearly as much as not driving. Animal agriculture contributes 14.5% of GHG emissions globally - the 3rd largest contributor behind industry and transportation according to the UN. From Reddit *askreddit.*

[Comment 10]: There's actually a lot the average person can do. Animal agriculture is a huge driver of climate change, water use, and land erosion. We could quit eating meat, it isn't good for us anyway ...The list goes on and on, there really is a lot the average person can do. From Reddit *environment.*

Theme 6: Government Regulation and Policies: Two nearly polar themes emerged. Left-leaning comments communicated a concern that the government was doing too little in its regulatory measures and climate change policies. There were expressed concerns that governments' efforts would address climate change too slowly, and that innocent individuals would suffer. Subsequently, the comments also expressed a concern that lack of regulation and more progressive policies were synonymous with a lack of humanity. Conversely, right-leaning comments perceived that regulations and policies were too extensive or debilitating. Furthermore, these comments also typically expressed a concern that government regulations and policies do not adequately capture and address bottlenecks to implementing climate change mitigative strategies. As such, there was a persistent concern that climate change regulation and policies, when they do not address these bottlenecks or other societal concerns, may create more issues than they address.

[Comment 11]: We are not prepared. The governments of the world have completely failed to do anything meaningful or significant to halt the progress of disastrous climate change, and have even encouraged and profited off of virulent disinformation sown across the people of the world.

Climate change is not a problem that can be solved, like a viral outbreak. Once the climate tips, that's it. It will happen. It will plunge the world into ever greater levels of destabilization.

Third-world countries will be hit first. It will render crops and ecosystems unsustainable to life, and thus render all civilization in that nation or region unsustainable. That will create mass migration fleeing from uninhabitable areas on a scale we have never witnessed before. From Reddit *politics*.

[Comment 12]: ...First off no administration GOP or dem has ever really given a [expletive] outside of subsides [sic] *for farmers...And all the while both parties just sort of ignore us. Also while this happens the rest of the world is also developing their own agricultural output. If tomorrow Hillary Clinton came out with a milk quota system like Canada? I might seriously consider voting for her...all I want to do is milk my cows, plant my corn, and raise my kids like my dad did.* From Reddit *farming*.

Theme 7: Challenges. Theme 7 was the most variable theme, as shown in Fig. 7.8. Theme 7 can largely be described as the challenges facing the agriculture industry and food production in the context of climate change. Interestingly, part of the variability in this cluster is due to the fact that these challenges do not exist in a vacuum. Rather, the challenges presented are discussed within the context of their interactions with science and policy. Seen in this light, Theme 7 is a natural extension of many of the other themes previously presented, but with a special focus on challenges and how to address them.

[Comment 13]: Humans only started seriously advancing our technological knowledge once we settled down and started forming agricultural cities, which we only did because climate change (the ice age ended and a lot of our favorite prey like mammoths went extinct) made our old ways of hunting and gathering unsustainable. It's a very fine line to walk between having to innovate to survive, and simply going extinct because your environment changed in a way you're no longer suited to. From Reddit *askreddit*.

[Comment 14]: Yes! Farming is hard work, and no solution to climate change is going to be a one size fits all band-aid. Rather than looking down on farmers as yokels that are ruining the environment, they'd be better off learning from farmers. If agriculture is such a big problem for climate change, you need farmers on your side helping to develop solutions. And exactly like you said, they know what will and won't work on their land! From Reddit *agriculture*.

Reddit is, or at least through 2022 was, being used for thoughtful public discourse regarding the adoption of new technology and the challenges facing agriculture. This indicates the general population's willingness to work toward real solutions. Indeed, the largest proportion of comments fell into Theme 1: Transition and Solutions (23.5%) and Theme 7: Challenges (28.1%). Furthermore, as seen in Fig. 7.9, these two themes are the fastest growing themes. In comparison, Theme 2: Extent and Theme 6: Government Regulation and Policies saw the greatest decrease, providing further evidence that dialog has shifted from discussions of climate change's impact and concerns surrounding policy, to constructive deliberations focused on identifying solutions.

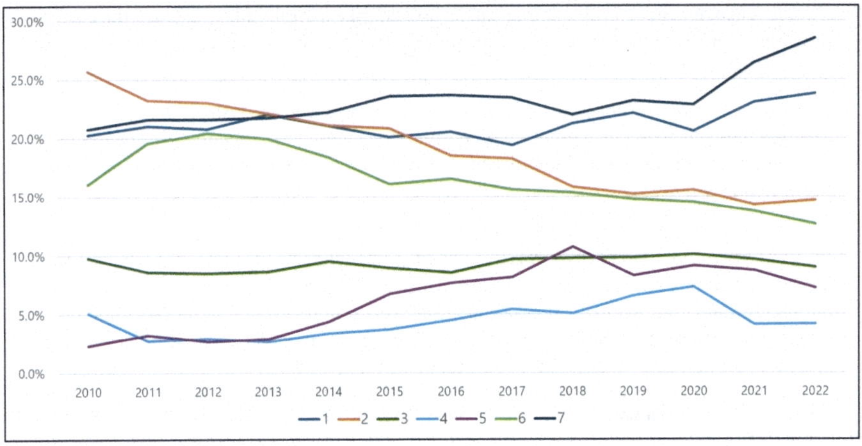

Fig. 7.9 Relative frequency of Reddit comments by Theme over time

Table 7.2 Relative importance of Theme by subreddit stakeholder group

	Theme						
Subreddit	1	2	3	4	5	6	7
Farming	23.4%	14.4%	7.2%	4.8%	3.6%	17.4%	29.3%
Agriculture	21.6%	17.6%	6.8%	8.1%	5.4%	9.5%	31.1%
Worldnews	25.2%	15.7%	7.6%	7.1%	7.5%	11.3%	25.5%
Askreddit	23.7%	10.5%	7.5%	2.7%	10.2%	10.2%	35.3%
Environment	19.8%	16.1%	9.0%	7.0%	16.5%	10.9%	20.7%
Climatechange	24.8%	24.8%	9.0%	6.9%	2.0%	14.2%	18.3%
Politics	22.2%	19.0%	7.2%	6.6%	1.7%	15.2%	28.1%
Conservative	21.0%	23.1%	8.2%	4.0%	1.7%	16.1%	25.8%
Overall	23.5%	15.4%	7.7%	5.7%	7.7%	11.9%	28.1%

Themes of Importance by Stakeholder Group and Public Sentiment

The themes that are of most importance or of greatest concern for agricultural, environmental, political, and general public subreddit stakeholder groups were anticipated to vary across stakeholder groups. Although this was found to be accurate, several common trends also emerged. For example, Themes 1 (Transition and Solutions) and 7 (Challenges) were typically the most common across all subreddits, with only two close exceptions. Notably, Themes 1 and 2 (Extent) tied for most common themes for the *climatechange* subreddit, and Theme 7 was ranked as the third most important. Similarly, Themes 2 and 7 were the most commonly identified themes on the *conservative* subreddit, with Theme 1 being ranked as a close third. The frequency of comments by theme across the eight subreddits included in this study are shown in Table 7.2.

Somewhat surprisingly, the *farming* and *agriculture* subreddits explored different themes and topics related to agricultural production. The common theme between the two agriculture-oriented subreddits was the challenges facing agricultural production, as both had disproportionately high frequencies of comments in Theme 7 (Challenges). The *farming* subreddit had a much higher frequency of comments that explored the theme of government regulation and policies (Theme 6), whereas the *agriculture* subreddit had a high percentage of comments that discussed the reciprocal impacts of agribusiness and climate change policies on one another (Theme 4). Interestingly, the average sentiment scores (Fig. 7.10) across *farming* and *agriculture* were typically the highest of any subreddit, with the exception of Theme 5: Animal Agriculture and Plant-Based Diets. Even these sentiment scores, however, were neutral. The *farming* and *agriculture* subreddits are very narrow-focused subreddits. Only those individuals with an interest in agricultural production are likely to frequent these subreddits. As such, it appears that Reddit has offered these stakeholders a platform for communicating and seeking constructive discourse, if not outright solutions, in a supportive environment. The relatively high sentiment scores suggest that farmers may be in agreement on the perceived challenges they face. Secondly, to create effective climate change mitigation policies, policy makers must be mindful that agriculture stakeholders are interested in seeking solutions that address challenges and the logistics of implementation.

Moving to the environmentalist-oriented subreddits, both *environment* and *climatechange* had a relatively high frequency of comments that were categorized under Theme 3: Social Responsibility. Much as with the agriculture-oriented subreddits, the environmentalist-oriented subreddits addressed different aspects of the green movement. The shared high frequency of comments classified under Theme 3: Social Responsibility provides insight into the motivation behind individuals engaging in the green movement and environmentalist strategies. Likewise, both subreddits shared a low frequency of comments that were classified under Theme 7: Challenges. This indicates that many individuals posting within these forums may

Subreddit	**1**	**2**	**3**	**4**	**5**	**6**	**7**
farming	0.32	0.36	-0.09	0.35	-0.01	0.38	0.13
agriculture	0.55	0.54	0.75	0.40	-0.04	0.40	0.15
worldnews	-0.18	-0.10	-0.08	0.18	0.04	-0.08	-0.15
askreddit	-0.14	-0.06	0.01	-0.08	-0.01	-0.01	-0.14
environment	-0.09	0.05	-0.09	0.04	0.11	0.00	-0.05
climatechange	0.02	0.00	0.21	0.08	0.42	0.08	0.01
politics	-0.12	0.00	-0.05	-0.17	0.12	-0.01	-0.15
conservative	-0.08	0.03	0.09	-0.08	-0.04	0.17	-0.01

Fig. 7.10 Heat map of average VADER sentiment analysis scores by Theme and subreddit. Relatively negative average sentiment values by theme are shown in red, whereas relatively positive average sentiment values by theme are shown in green. Sentiment values greater than 0.3 are considered to be positive, sentiment values less than −0.3 are considered to be negative, and sentiment values between −0.3 and 0.3 are considered to be neutral. Sentiment values can range between −1 (highly negative) to +1 (highly positive)

find the social responsibility of implementing climate change mitigative strategies absolutely imperative, and that the humanitarian benefit of implementing climate change mitigative strategies outweighs the challenges associated with implementation.

Within the *climatechange* subreddit, a high frequency of comments fell into Themes 1 (Transition and Solutions) and 2 (Extent), both with a neutral average sentiment score. Many of the comments made use of scientific evidence or other facts as part of their discussion, as one might expect given these two thematic areas. Interestingly, the *conservative* subreddit also had a high frequency of comments that fell under Theme 2 because of the reference to the scientific literature and climatic events. As with the *climatechange* subreddit, the *conservative* subreddit also had an overall average neutral sentiment score. However, an average VADER score may be neutral for many reasons. The VADER sentiment score measures both polarity and intensity of comments. VADER sentiment scores range from −1 to +1, with comments receiving a score of −1 being very negative, comments receiving a score of 0 being neutral, and comments receiving a score of +1 being very positive. Therefore, when an average neutral score is observed, it is possible that the comments all tend to be neutral, or that positive and negative comments have balanced one another out. It should also be noted that positive and negative sentiment do not necessarily imply appropriate and derogatory, as might be surmised. Rather, positive and negative sentiment capture the degree of agreement or disagreement, as well as a discussion of benefits versus concerns. Example comments from this dataset and corresponding VADER scores are shown below.

Positive

> [Comment 15] This would require a much more prolonged conversation to talk about it, but I'll try to summarize.
>
> *The theory of climate change purports that fossil fuels are responsible for c02 flooding our atmosphere, thereby causing a greenhouse effect and drastically altering the temperature* [sic] *our biosphere. The best way to solve this problem is to reduce c02 emissions by a considerable amount, hopefully within the next decade, so that we could prevent what would undoubtedly be an extinction level in it's* [sic] *own right.*
>
> Unfortunately, because humanity doesn't exist in a global egalitarian state, we can't ask everyone to play nice and simply stop using fossil fuels. in fact, fossil fuels are the only way humanity has managed to maintain our current population level. They are integral to our ability to maintain heavy industry and agriculture. If we ask people to stop using coal, oil etc., then we're basically asking them to starve.
>
> The "plan" so to speak is to let the situation play itself out. Because barring a real extinction level event, or winning a global conflict by which we could force everyone to comply with heavily restrictive standards on energy usage, there's no real way to lower c02 emissions. The technology and infrastructure required to do what is necessary while meeting our energy needs simply doesn't exist. and even assuming that it did, we don't have the time required to scrap everything and start anew. Everything else is just meaningless party politics.
>
> *tl;dr damned if we do, damned if we don't. we're [expletive], and I'm drinking heavily.*

From Reddit *conservative*. VADER compound sentiment score = 0.9043.

*[Comment 16] Very interesting, thanks for this! After looking through the 3 degrees section, it seems like a lot of what I've read before. although I've seen some papers saying some conflicting things (such as the permafrost may actually be a net sink, food production up way more, slr a bit higher, and vegetation "releasing more co2 than absorbing" not being the case for numerous reasons, *edit: oh, and the 3rd of species extinction thing. It's actually mainly because of pesticides and deforestation* [sic], *climate change has little to do with extinction besides lowering the climactic range of species)*, but overall this seems to be a pretty good overview. that stuff is likely due to new research.*

From Reddit *climatechange*. VADER compound sentiment score = 0.9491.

Neutral

[Comment 17] "I partly agree. I think factory farming which doesn't allow animals to be on grazing on land limits the lands ability to absorb carbon. This is a mistake as the emissions don't match the absorption.

In any case, I still think agriculture gets a bad wrap [sic].

It sounds like we can both agree that there are meaningful changes people can make in their own lives. These are the same people that blame cows for climate change and yet drive their car to work (alone) everyday [sic] *because biking or walking is too hard or its* [sic] *too cold outside. or people that buy a house 1hr away from their job and have to commute long distances everyday* [sic]."From Reddit *conservative*. VADER compound sentiment score = −0.1429.

[Comment 18] Why does it matter whether climate change is man made [sic] *or not? Even if it is occurring naturally, we don't want the climate to change because it is disrupting our way of life by causing intense storms, droughts, and eventually the loss of food chains that we depend on. We still need to do things, the planet is most liveable* [sic] *for humans in the stable climate it has been in for the last several thousand years.*

From Reddit *climatechange*. VADER compound sentiment score = 0.0201.

Negative

[Comment 19] "I'm going to level with you here. If what climate activists are saying is true, then the primary cause of climate change is the use of fossil fuels, and we only have a short amount of time before we reach an irreconcilable tipping point.

The problem is that we can't sustain our current population, supply chains or energy requirements without them. It would be an impossible task to retool our entire energy sector, transportation sector, agricultural sector and manufacturing sector around renewable energy in that period of time. we literally do not have the resources, manpower or technology to make it happen.

If we decided to pull the plug anyways, and fossil fuels disappeared from the face of the earth tomorrow, hundreds of millions of people in the us alone would be dead from a lack of food and water within the span of two weeks. there wouldn't be any 'rich' or 'poor', it would simply be a matter of who stockpiled the most food before the collapse of civilization."

From Reddit *conservative*. VADER compound sentiment score = -0.9205.

[Comment 20] "No we're not. Some of the main problems that will be caused by climate change are sea level rise and more extreme and unpredictable weather events and patterns.

Sea level rise is bad because a lot of big cities are on coastlines and their flooding will obviously be very expensive and will force inhabitants to move. another big problem is places like Bangladesh; highly populated areas that are close to sea level. Dealing with the millions of refugees fleeing from the sea is likely to be very complex, expensive, and deadly.

Extreme weather patterns such as drought are bad because they affect freshwater supply and agriculture. according to the IPCC, 2 ° C+ of warming above late c20 levels could result in anything from 10% increase in crop yields (10% of models) to a 25% decrease in yields (10% of models).

So, climate change will be an expensive and, for some, a deadly challenge. However, we can reduce the impact by reducing our carbon output by shifting from fossil fuels to renewable and nuclear energy, and preparing and planning for the problems that we know we will face in the decades to come.

I have not seen any serious scientist suggest in a peer reviewed paper that humans will be extinct in a century. we're looking at, realistically, 4 ° C warming by 2100 *if we do nothing to reduce our carbon emissions*. Make no mistake, that's catastrophic, but it's not enough to make the whole planet inhospitable to human life. the only possible way I can see climate change posing an existential threat to the human race within a century is if conflicts over food and water were to cause a nuclear conflict, but again, the severity of these future impacts depends on how much we reduce our carbon emissions over the next 3-5 decades, and how well we prepare for the impacts that we know will be coming."

From Reddit *climatechange*. VADER compound sentiment score = -0.9290.

In examining the distribution of sentiment analysis scores, thresholds were established as follows: a score less than or equal to −0.7 was considered highly negative, a score between −0.7 and − 0.4 was considered negative, a score between −0.4 and 0.4 was considered neutral, a score between 0.4 and 0.7 was considered positive, and a score greater than or equal to 0.7 was considered highly positive. The distribution of VADER compound sentiment analysis scores by theme and stakeholder group is presented in Table 3.

Notably, both *climatechange* and *conservative* had very polar sentiment analysis scores, with 36.6% and 32.0% of all comments being rated highly positive and 31.7% and 31.9% of all comments on these subreddits being rated highly negative, respectively. This is to be expected in online settings where healthy open discussion is taking place, as counterpoints and challenges will be raised (resulting in highly negative scores), and acknowledgement of others' positions and discussion of potential benefits will also be present (resulting in highly positive scores). This is in contrast to subreddits like *agriculture* and *farming*, where the comments were overall highly positive. These communities typically have shared interests, and users are less likely to disagree with one another. Likewise, *politics* and *worldnews* were overall relatively negative, which stems from these communities' tendency to discuss challenges. Interestingly, comments in the *conservative* subreddit were much more likely to have a positive or neutral rating than were comments in the *politics* subreddit. However, given that both the *climatechange* and *conservative* subreddits were much more likely to be associated with Theme 2: Extent, as opposed to opinions surrounding regulations in the case of the *politics* subreddit, it makes sense that conversations surrounding facts and scientific evidence are more likely to be overall more neutral than conversations surrounding regulatory challenges (Theme 6). Therefore, distributions of sentiment analysis scores can also prove informational to policy makers because these distributions can provide an indicator of the level of agreement or disagreement within a stakeholder group.

Unlike *climatechange*, the *environment* subreddit had a high frequency of comments that fell under Theme 5: Animal Agriculture and Plant-Based Diets. Therefore, unlike *climatechange*, the *environment* subreddit was focused more on the individual personal actions that could be taken to mitigate climate change's impact on the environment, as opposed to a broad discussion of the scientific evidence supporting the impact of climate change on the environment. Both, however, show that there is a sense of moral obligation to mitigate humanity's impact on the environment. Although stakeholders with a strong sense of obligation to support climate change mitigative strategies are likely to be generally supportive of climate change policy, policies will ideally align with humanitarian need, scientific evidence, and support of infrastructure that enables individuals to contribute toward climate change mitigative strategies on a personal level.

Political stakeholders had similar frequencies across all thematic clusters. Both *politics* and *conservative* had a relatively high frequency of comments that were assigned to Theme 2: Extent. Both subreddits had neutral average sentiment scores for the comments that fell under this theme and had a relatively high frequency of both highly positive and highly negative comments, again indicating that Reddit provides opportunity for deliberation. Both subreddits also had a relatively high frequency of comments that were assigned to Theme 6: Government Regulation and Policies. This is expected given that both subreddits are political in nature. Upon closer examination, it was found that left-leaning commenters tended to desire more government regulation, and right-leaning commenters feared that more government regulation may do more harm than good, as described above. Therefore, effective policies must clearly articulate the positive impact of climate mitigative strategies on the human condition, without overexaggeration or being sensationalized. Likewise, logistical hurdles to the implementation of policies must be considered and articulated; potential solutions that work within the context of existing systems must be developed, or investments in infrastructure to incentivize adoption of climate change mitigative measures must be made. This finding is in close alignment with the existing literature (FAO, 2017; Arslan et al., 2014; Lipper et al., 2014). It is also worth noting that comments that were assigned to Theme 6 were much more likely to have an overall negative sentiment analysis score relative to other themes (Table 7.3), and this stands to reason as discussion of regulation and policies involves the discussion of differing viewpoints.

Lastly, two subreddits that are open to the general public, *worldnews* and *askreddit*, were studied to understand how the general public may view climate change, and whether this may be different than the findings when considering the overall number of comments. The distribution of comments from *worldnews* that fell into each theme closely mirrored that of the distribution of all comments. The frequency of comments from *askreddit* was also relatively similar, with one key exception. Relative to the distribution of all comments, *askreddit* had a higher ratio of comments that fell into Theme 7: Challenges relative to Theme 2: Extent. This stands to reason, as this subreddit attracts discussions that seek to understand challenges and opposing viewpoints. Therefore, overall, it can be said that much of the public discourse surrounding climate change, agriculture, and food security within the general public focuses on Themes 1 (Transition and Solutions) and 7 (Challenges), and the search for logical solutions to minimize the impact of climate change. This is a finding of extreme importance, as it indicates a willingness to collaborate that otherwise might be absent on other social media platforms because of the reduced likelihood that users with differing viewpoints would interact (De Francisci Morales et al., 2021; Treen et al., 2022).

One potential limitation of using social media platforms, including but not limited to Reddit, for the identification of topics of interest or concern to stakeholder groups is that data scraped from social media sites constitute an observational study, as opposed to a highly controlled experiment. Although the K-Means analysis can adjust for unbalanced representation of stakeholder groups and even unbalanced stakeholder demographics, the study in the variation of topics of most importance to each stakeholder group can provide misleading information if data are not queried so that stakeholders are accurately represented. For the purposes of this study, the key stakeholders of interest were based on interests (agriculture and the environment) and political-orientation (liberal or conservative) relative to the general population of comments. The approach presented in this study satisfactorily captures these groups of stakeholders because Reddit users tend to subscribe to and comment on subreddits of interest to them. As an example, users that are involved in agricultural production or who are interested in the agriculture industry are much more likely to subscribe to *agriculture* or *farming* than are users who are not involved in or who do not have an interest in these topics.

Special care was also taken to select subreddits that were most likely to be representative of the general public's opinions. When selecting the "general public" subreddits, the criteria that were used were number of subscribers during the study period, tone of the subreddit and known significant biases, and whether the subreddit allowed for open discussion of topics from multiple perspectives and potential viewpoints. Specifically, *askreddit* is the second largest subreddit, with 45 million subscribers as of February 2024 (Ceci, 2024b). When making selections, it was noted that the tone of this subreddit community is such that its primary purpose is to foster discussion of topics from multiple perspectives, whereas another large subreddit like *science* might only focus on discussion of the same topics from a scientific-only perspective. While not an inherently negative quality, the *science* subreddit is not likely to capture the sentiment of the general public or economic, social, or emotional considerations. The subreddit *worldnews* was also a very popular subreddit, with 34.9 million subscribers as of February 2024 (Ceci, 2024b). Whereas *askreddit* was selected based on its likelihood of comments that explored questions relating to climate change, agriculture, and food security, *worldnews* was selected based on its likelihood of providing insight into the topics related to this area that were frequently appearing in other media sources and that were generating conversation among the public. Furthermore, relative to other subreddits, such as the subreddit *news*, *worldnews* had a relatively high number of comments while also maintaining a similar distribution of positive, negative, and neutral comments as the overall dataset.

Of additional note is that while this study focused on stakeholder groups based on interests and political affiliation, other studies may instead focus on demographics such as gender identity, age group, or other identifying characteristics. Overall, Reddit users tend to be young, male, and liberal (Barthel et al., 2016; Buchholz, 2023; Ceci, 2024a; Ceci, 2024d), and identifying gender or age demographics may not be as simple as focusing on particular subreddits. In these instances, the data science approaches demonstrated in this chapter can be modified to include additional NLP and ML tools to predict gender identity, age groups, or even personality characteristics (Gjurković & Šnajder, 2018; Chew et al., 2021; Fabian et al., 2015). Furthermore, the approaches demonstrated in this chapter are not limited to only Reddit social media data. NLP and ML tools can be employed using posts and comments from other social media platforms, or even open-ended survey responses. It is also important to note that the data used in this study were collected prior to the implementation of stricter moderator policies on Reddit, and that the quality of information collected from some subreddits may shift over time. Therefore, while NLP and ML techniques can be used, a caution is that researchers must always first verify the quality of data that are being fed into the algorithms.

Conclusion

This study presents a comprehensive example of the use of NLP and ML to automate or mostly automate thematic analysis as applied to social media data. Specifically, we have shown that within the Reddit Climate Change dataset, seven clear themes emerge that lie at the intersection of climate change, agriculture, and food security. Furthermore, we demonstrated that the themes of greatest importance have changed over time, and that Reddit has fostered an online environment where there is an increased willingness of members of the general public to exchange viewpoints, address challenges, and work together to arrive at real solutions. Additionally, the themes of greatest importance vary across stakeholder groups, and it is important that policymakers understand the viewpoints of multiple stakeholders simultaneously if they are to develop effective climate change mitigative policy. Thanks to the advent of social media, and the computational ability to mine the themes of importance from these data using NLP and ML, the ability to understand the viewpoints of multiple stakeholder groups is now a reality. This chapter provides the foundation for future research in this area of automated qualitative analysis as additional social media datasets become publicly available.

References

AghaKouchak, A., Chiang, F., Huning, L. S., Love, C. A., Mallakpour, I., Mazdiyasni, O., Moftakhari, H., Papalexiou, S. M., Ragno, E., & Sadegh, M. (2020). Climate extremes and compound hazards in a warming world. *Annual Review of Earth and Planetary Sciences, 48*, 519–548. https://doi.org/10.1146/annurev-earth-071719-055228

Arslan, A., McCarthy, N., Lipper, L., Asfaw, S., & Cattaneo, A. (2014). Adoption and intensity of adoption of conservation farming practices in Zambia. *Agriculture, Ecosystems & Environment, 187*, 72–86. https://doi.org/10.1016/j.agee.2013.08.017

Australian Government Clean Energy Regulator. (2024). *Small-scale renewable energy scheme*. Canberra. https://cer.gov.au/schemes/renewable-energy-target/small-scale-renewable-energy-scheme

Barthel, M., Stocking, G., Holcomb, J. & Mitchell, A. (2016). *Nearly eight-in-ten Reddit users get news on the site*. PEW Research Center. https://www.pewresearch.org/journalism/2016/02/25/seven-in-ten-reddit-users-get-news-on-the-site/

Boykoff, M., Fernández-Reyes, R., Katzung, J., Nacu-Schmidt, A. & Pearman, O. (2024*). A review of media coverage of climate change and global warming in 2023*. Media and Climate Change Observatory, Cooperative Institute for Research in Environmental Sciences. http://sciencepolicy.colorado.edu/icecaps/research/media_coverage/summaries/special_issue_2023.html

Buchholz, K. (2023, February 28). How politically divided are social media networks? *Statista*. https://www.statista.com/chart/29395/political-preference-social-media/

Ceci, L. (2024a, August 24). Distribution of Reddit users worldwide as of 1st quarter 2024, by gender. *Statista*. https://www.statista.com/statistics/1255182/distribution-of-users-on-reddit-worldwide-gender

Ceci, L. (2024b. April 11). *Most popular communities on Reddit Worldwide as of* February 2024, By number of subscribers. Statista. https://www.statista.com/statistics/1396267/subreddits-with-the-most-subscribers/

Ceci, L. (2024c, February 27). Number of monthly active Reddit users worldwide from 2018 to 2026. *Statista*. https://www.statista.com/forecasts/1309791/reddit-mau-worldwide

Ceci, L. (2024d, February 28). Percentage of U.S. adults who use Reddit as of September 2023, by age group. *Statista*. https://www.statista.com/statistics/261766/share-of-us-internet-users-who-use-reddit-by-age-group/

Chew, R., Kery, C., Baum, L., Bukowski, T., Kim, A. Y., & Navarro, M. (2021). Predicting age groups of Reddit users based on posting behavior and metadata: Classification model development and validation. *JMIR Public Health and Surveillance, 7*, e25807. https://doi.org/10.2196/25807

De Francisci Morales, G., Monti, C., & Starnini, M. (2021). No Echo in the chambers of political interactions on Reddit. *Scientific Reports, 11*, 2818. https://doi.org/10.1038/s41598-021-81531-x

Energy Information Administration. (2023). *2022 annual solar photovoltaic module shipments report*. United States Department of Energy. https://www.eia.gov/renewable/annual/solar_photo/pdf/pv_full_2022.pdf

Fabian, B., Baumann, A. & Keil, M. (2015, May). Privacy on Reddit? *Towards large-scale user classification* [Conference Paper]. 23rd European Conference on Information Systems (ECIS 2015). https://aisel.aisnet.org/ecis2015_cr/43

FAO. (2017). *Climate-smart agriculture sourcebook*. Food and agriculture organization of the United Nations. https://www.fao.org/climate-smart-agriculture-sourcebook/en/

Gjurković, M. & Šnajder, J. (2018). *Reddit: A gold mine for personality prediction*. Proceedings of the Second Workshop on Computational Modeling of People's Opinions, Personality, and Emotions in Social Media, 87–97. https://doi.org/10.18653/v1/W18-1112.

Howden, S. M., Soussana, J. F., Tubiello, F. N., Chhetri, N., Dunlop, M., & Meinke, H. (2007). Adapting agriculture to climate change. *PNAS, 104*(50), 19691–19696. https://doi.org/10.1073/pnas.0701890104

Internal Revenue Service. (2024). *Residential clean energy credit*. IRS. https://www.irs.gov/credits-deductions/residential-clean-energy-credit

International Energy Agency. (2021, July 15). *Tax deductions for building renovations* [Online]. IEA. Accessed Aug 29, 2024, from https://www.iea.org/policies/11633-tax-deductions-for-building-renovations

International Energy Agency. (2023). *Net zero roadmap. A global pathway to keep the 1.5°C Goal in reach. 2023 Update*. [Online]. IEA. Accessed Aug 27, 2024, from https://iea.blob.core.windows.net/assets/9a698da4-4002-4e53-8ef3-631d8971bf84/NetZeroRoadmap_AGlobalPathwaytoKeepthe1.5CGoalinReach-2023Update.pdf

Kaggle. (2022). *The Reddit climate change dataset* [Online]. Accessed July 01, 2024, from https://www.kaggle.com/datasets/pavellexyr/the-reddit-climate-change-dataset

IPCC, 2023: Sections. In: *Climate change 2023: Synthesis report. Contribution of working groups I, II and III to the sixth assessment report of the intergovernmental panel on climate change* [Core Writing Team, H. Lee and J. Romero (eds.)]. IPCC, pp. 35-115, https://doi.org/10.59327/IPCC/AR6-9789291691647.

Leiserowitz, A., Carman, J., Buttermore, N., Neyens, L., Rosenthal, S., Marlon, J., Schneider, J., & Mulcahy, K. (2022). *International public opinion on climate change, 2022*. Yale Program on Climate Change Communication and Data for Good at Meta. https://climatecommunication.yale.edu/publications/international-public-opinion-on-climate-change-2022/

Lipper, L., Thornton, P., Campbell, B., et al. (2014). Climate-smart agriculture for food security. *Nature Climate Change, 4*, 1068–1072. https://doi.org/10.1038/nclimate2437

Marlon, J., Wang, X., Bergquist, P., Howe, P., Leiserowitz, A., Maibach, E., Mildenberger, M., & Rosenthal, S. (2023). Change in US state-level public opinion about climate change: 2008-2020. *Environmental Research Letters, 17*, 124046. https://doi.org/10.1088/1748-9326/aca702

Murshed, M. (2020). An empirical analysis of the non-linear impacts of ICT-trade openness on renewable energy transition, energy efficiency, clean cooking fuel access and environmental sustainability in South Asia. *Environmental Science and Pollution Research, 27*, 36254–36281. https://doi.org/10.1007/s11356-020-09497-3

NOAA. (2020). *Annual 2019 global climate report*. NOAA National Centers for Environmental Information. https://www.ncei.noaa.gov/access/monitoring/monthly-report/global/201913

NOAA. (2023). *Annual 2022 global climate report*. NOAA National Centers for Environmental Information. https://www.ncei.noaa.gov/access/monitoring/monthlyreport/global/202213/supplemental/page-1

Office Of The Director Of National Intelligence (2024, February 25). Annual threat assessment of the U.*S. Intelligence Community*. DNI.gov. https://www.dni.gov/files/ODNI/documents/assessments/ATA-2024-Unclassified-Report.pdf

Okon, E., Rachakonda, V., Hong, H. J., Callison-Burch, C., & Lipoff, J. B. (2020). Natural language processing of Reddit data to evaluate dermatology patient experiences and therapeutics. *Journal of the American Academy of Dermatology, 83*(3), 803–808. https://doi.org/10.1016/j.jaad.2019.07.014

Osman, A., Chen, L., Yang, M., Msigwa, G., Farghali, M., Fawzy, S., Rooney, D., & Yap, P. (2023). Cost, environmental impact, and resilience of renewable energy under a changing climate: A review. *Environmental Chemistry Letters, 21*, 741–764. https://doi.org/10.1007/s10311-022-01532-8

Pew Research Center. (2013). *Spring 2013 global attitudes survey* [Online]. Accessed July 03, 2024, from https://www.pewresearch.org/dataset/spring-2013-survey-data/

Pew Research Center. (2017). *Spring 2017 global attitudes survey* [Online]. Accessed July 03, 2024, from https://www.pewresearch.org/dataset/spring-2017-survey-data/

Pew Research Center. (2022). *Spring 2022 global attitudes survey* [Online]. Accessed July 03, 2024, from https://www.pewresearch.org/dataset/spring-2022-survey-data/

Scheelbeek, P. F., Bird, F. A., Tuomisto, H. L., Green, R., Harris, F. B., Joy, E. J. M., Chalabi, Z., Allen, E., Haines, A., & Dangour, A. D. (2018). The effect of environmental changes on vegetable and legume yields and nutritional quality. *PNAS, 115*(26), 6804–6809. https://doi.org/10.1073/pnas.1800442115

Solomon, M., Gimon, E., O'Boyle, M., Paliwal, U. & Phadke, A. (2023). *The coal cost crossover 3.0. Local renewables plus storage create new opportunities for customer savings and community reinvestment*. EnergyInnovation.org. https://energyinnovation.org/wp-content/uploads/2023/01/Coal-Cost-Crossover-3.0.pdf

Subreddit Stats. (2023a). *r/politics stats* [Online]. Accessed July 05, 2024, from https://subredditstats.com/r/politics

Subreddit Stats. (2023b). *r/worldnews stats* [Online]. Accessed July 05, 2024, from https://subredditstats.com/r/worldnews

Subreddit Stats. (2023c). *Subreddit stats* [Online]. Accessed July 05, 2024, from https://subredditstats.com/

Tadesse, M. M., Lin, H., Xu, B., & Yang, L. (2019). Detection of depression-related posts in reddit social media forum. *IEEE Access, 7*, 44883–44893. https://doi.org/10.1109/ACCESS.2019.2909180

Treen, K., Williams, H., O'Neill, S., & Coan, T. G. (2022). Discussion of climate change on Reddit: Polarized discourse or deliberative debate? *Environmental Communication, 16*(5), 680–698. https://doi.org/10.1080/17524032.2022.2050776

United States Department of Agriculture. (2024). *Rural energy for America program*. https://www.rd.usda.gov/programs-services/energy-programs/rural-energy-america-program-renewable-energy-systems-energy-efficiency-improvement-guaranteed-loans

Yao, H., Rashidian, S., Dong, X., Duanmu, H., Rosenthal, R. N., & Wang, F. (2020). Detection of suicidality among opioid users on Reddit: Machine learning–based approach. *Journal of Medical Internet Research, 22*(11), e15293. https://doi.org/10.2196/15293

Zhao, J., Sinha, A., Inuwa, N., Wang, Y., Murshed, M., & Abbasi, K. (2022). Does structural transformation in economy impact inequality in renewable energy productivity? Implications for sustainable development. *Renewable Energy, 189*, 853–864. https://doi.org/10.1016/j.renene.2022.03.050

Chapter 8
The Possibilities and Perils of Research Engagement with Policymakers

Jason A. Kalmbach and Jonah J. Ralston

Throughout the 2020 election cycle, the COVID-19 pandemic dominated policy debates. The United States presidential election was no exception, with the two presidential candidates trading barbs about the severity of the virus, whether economic progress was being unduly hampered by health precautions, and the remedies available to individuals once they had contracted the virus. In some ways, the debate was a callback to America's founding when partisans fought over how to respond to outbreaks of yellow fever (Pernick, 1972; Smith, 2020). As election day drew close, then-candidate Joe Biden spoke at Gettysburg, Pennsylvania, and he called for an end to political divisiveness over the virus while also repeating the need for policymakers to "follow the science" with respect to the government's response to COVID-19 (Biden, 2020). It was a message designed to appeal to the general prestige the public holds for both science and the scientists who carry out the research (Gauchat, 2012).

However, these calls to use science in the policy process fail to recognize that scientific research is, at its most basic, a collection of data-based observations that help society understand the scope and severity of a perceived problem. Scientific research on its own does not require that the government intervene through public policy. Scientific information is one of several considerations that government officials keep in mind when they consider their policy options. An elected official is faced with a multitude of considerations when making policy: pressure from party leaders to vote in line with a political party's stated position on a policy; the interests of constituents who are important for the official's re-election; powerful people and

J. A. Kalmbach
National Coalition of Independent Scholars, Brattleboro, VT, USA

J. J. Ralston (✉)
University of Wisconsin-Whitewater, Whitewater, WI, USA
e-mail: ralstonj@uww.edu

N. Guehlstorf (ed.), *Environmental Policy Science's Exploration for Innovative Data*, Natural Resource Management and Policy NA,
https://doi.org/10.1007/978-3-031-90889-7_8

groups who financially support the official; and the official's values and beliefs. These considerations may conflict with the desires of scientific researchers who view government action as necessary. Complicating policy development in the United States is the horizontal and vertical fragmentation of the U.S. political system, which often results in more actors being involved in policy debates. Furthermore, a high degree of political polarization means limited opportunities for bipartisan policymaking. Thus, it can be rather difficult for governmental actors to simply "follow the science."

In the context of COVID-19, science can inform policymakers how the disease spreads and offer evidence for whether specific precautions, such as masking requirements, will successfully mitigate the transmission of the virus. Scientific studies even went so far as offering projections about how many lives could be saved if specific precautions were taken. However, science cannot help government officials balance the value of saving lives versus the economic impact of shutdowns or the educational impact on students who are forced to learn from home. These are human decisions that depend on the values and preferences of society. Scientific research can help officials better understand the trade-offs, but it is up to society to strike a preferred balance between that information and underlying values and beliefs.

In many ways, scientific information is akin to a classic cost-benefit analysis (CBA) that is carried out by policy analysts. A CBA can compare policy options and advise policymakers on which policy will produce the "most bang for the buck." However, a CBA primarily accounts for the cost-efficiency of policies. It does not speak to whether the policy is the most effective or the fairest. The costs and benefits of the policy may not fall on the population equally, with some paying more costs or receiving more benefits than others. Decision-makers still need to wrestle with those trade-offs, with the CBA just becoming a set of relevant facts that they use as they weigh trade-offs.

With this conceptualization of science and how it fits into the decision-making process, we will explore in more detail how science and scientists fit into the classical theories of the policy process, specifically the agenda-setting phase. A typology is then offered to help conceptualize the range of scientific disputes that may occur during these policy debates. A specific case focused on lead's use in gasoline is offered to help illustrate the typology and the role of scientists in the policy process.

The Political Arena and Science

The commentary from philosophers of science on what it means to carry out scientific research is vast and rich (e.g., Miller, 1985; Kuhn, 1996). How to perform proper research, and the interpretations associated with such research, are important discussion points given the role of science in evaluating and substantiating beliefs. In this process, scientists continually question how the world works and carry out analyses in an attempt to falsify proposed causal arguments.

Ideally, the scientific process provides a forum for scientists to debate competing theories and a systematic means by which these debates can be settled. Thomas Kuhn (1996) noted the back and forth that occurs in scientific disputes, and he noticed a pattern. Scientific advancement can be characterized as a multistage process. At an early stage, there is genuine puzzlement among scientists about a particular phenomenon. There is a candid moment where scientists agree that they cannot explain an observation. However, that does not mean the scientific process cannot be utilized to understand the event. Resources are leveraged to carry out research and scientists begin to develop a causal argument that helps society make sense of the event. This initial understanding is debated by scientists at conferences and in journal publications. Eventually, a majority of scientists agree on the proposed causal argument, establishing a paradigm from which to understand the world. Scientists can then use this understanding to explain other phenomena. Kuhn refers to this phase as normal science.

At some point, however, the initial causal argument might start to fall apart. Abnormalities or inconsistencies within the theory are observed. At first, a scientist or small group of scientists might start to question the established paradigm. This small-scale battle constitutes a crisis, as researchers start to question their understanding of the event. The crisis might escalate, with more and more scientists disagreeing with the established view. A scientific revolution can occur, where the underlying assumptions of a paradigm are re-examined and perhaps replaced with new assumptions. The old causal argument is thrown out and replaced with a new understanding. Kuhn refers to this emergence of a new paradigm as revolutionary science. The history of scientific advancement is rich with stories of new ideas dethroning previous conceptualizations of the world. This process is usually slow, as it takes time for new ideas to gain traction and become a dominant working paradigm within the scientific community (Sherwood, 2011).

The overall theme is that science is a continuous process. Our understanding of the world and how it works is constantly evolving. A conceptual challenge is integrating these scientific developments with the policy literature. This literature often gives a nod to the role of scientists, but arguably it is underdeveloped in its integration of the nuances of scientific debate and conflict. We will now summarize two main agenda-setting theories before turning to the nuances of scientific developments and how they may impact policy development.

Agenda-Setting and Scientists

Traditional policy theories in political science focus on the agenda-setting phase. What issues get the attention of decision-makers and why? It is a critical step if society expects to realize policy change. Two theories are worth mentioning given their applicability to scientists and the role they play in the policy process: the "Three Streams" theory and the "Advocacy Coalition Framework."

Kingdon's Three Streams. In his seminal study, Kingdon (1995) interviewed numerous decision-makers in Washington, D.C, in an attempt to understand what attracts their attention. From these discussions, he conceptualized three separate and independent "streams" that must converge to create a window that makes policy change happen.

The "problem stream" consists of issues that are recognized as significant problems. That is, there is a perception that a public problem exists which requires government action. Problems come to the attention of policymakers through feedback, crises, or national events. Decision-makers pay attention to indicators to help identify whether a problem is getting worse. Scientists (whether working in academia or for government agencies) are often the ones collecting data and monitoring problems. The Intergovernmental Panel on Climate Change (IPCC) is an example. The IPCC periodically convenes to discuss the state of society's knowledge about climate change. They provide reports that give decision-makers the information they need to know about humanity's impact on the climate. Scientists who engage in similar routine research that reveals potential environmental or health problems that might benefit from the implementation of policy solutions are conceivably working within the problem stream.

Separate from the problem stream is the "policy stream," which is the list of all solutions available that could solve a problem. Experts and analysts examine situations and identify potential solutions. Researchers can play a role here as they might develop and discuss solutions to problems. Examples include medical researchers studying experimental treatments for disease, academic researchers working on revolutionary improvements to existing technology, or social scientists working on effective ways to increase public compliance with government regulation.

Lastly, there is the "political stream," which consists of what is going on in the federal or state capital. Considerations of politics define this stream, including the degree to which it is politically advantageous for decision-makers to address a given problem and whether a majority of legislators can agree on a policy solution. Legislators pay attention to a number of relevant factors when deciding how to act, such as swings in the national mood, interest group arguments, specific forms of public opinion, whether they can sell the policy action to their constituents, and so forth. A focusing event, such as a crisis or a major report detailing worsening indicators, can be critical for drawing the attention of the public and policymakers to an issue.

When the streams collide, it creates a window (or opportunity) for policy development. Some windows are predictable, such as during an election year or a regular budget cycle, but other windows are due to chance or an unforeseen event. Windows as a whole are small and scarce; they do not last forever and a change in any of the streams can prevent a window from fully opening or can close it before action can be taken.

Policy entrepreneurs are often integral to opening windows and taking advantage of them. They couple solutions with problems and try to foster the necessary political momentum to enact significant changes in policy. A policy entrepreneur could be an elected official, a leader of an interest group representing industry, or a scientific expert. They possess the knowledge, resources, resolve, and oftentimes luck to be able to take advantage of policy windows. When a focusing event occurs and there is heightened attention to a public problem, they are the ones who are ready and willing to promote their ideas and solutions to policymakers.

Advocacy Coalition Framework. The Advocacy Coalition Framework was developed by Sabatier and Jenkins-Smith (1993), who focused on actors working with and against each other across a variety of subsystems. They envisioned a network, or group of people, working together because they share a set of policy goals. These groups include agencies and associations, think tanks, and the media, among others. Together they seek to influence and modify budgets, personnel, and policies to achieve their goals.

It is theorized that there are competing advocacy coalitions within each policy domain (e.g. education, environment, health, etc.). For every issue that exists, there are at least two coalitions within that group. One supports the status quo, and the others are various coalitions arguing for a change to the existing system. Actors in these coalitions share knowledge of a public problem and collectively work on solutions. They are all motivated, though, by some set of mutually shared beliefs. It is these beliefs that unite them in their cause, to either preserve the status quo or bring about change.

For policy change to happen, what is often needed is a policy broker, who is a highly trusted individual capable of bringing the two groups together and reaching a compromise. This process provides a potential opportunity for a scientist to be a broker. A scientist is likely to have the prestige and trust of the community, and they can bring their expertise to the table and help craft a new policy. In this conceptualization, scientists are part of a coalition that participates in policy battles with other coalitions. Scientists coordinate information and research evidence with lobbyists, think tanks, and legislators. They become the "trusted" voices that appear at legislative hearings and publicly testify as experts to document a problem and help rationalize the justification for a specific policy.

An example of competing coalitions in a policy domain can be found with biofuels. The coalition in favor of government policy promoting the production and consumption of biofuels is made up of corn farmers, the agricultural lobby, biofuels refiners, government agencies, and a number of powerful politicians. The coalition in opposition to these policies is made up of livestock producers, oil companies, environmentalists concerned about the pollution generated by producing biofuels, and lobbyists for food manufacturers. The coalition in favor of biofuels has been successful in securing government support for biofuels. For example, the Renewable Fuel Standard is a federal program that requires a minimum volume of renewable fuels to be blended into transportation fuel. For 2023 and after, the EPA has the statutory responsibility for setting these volume requirements, but the agency must consider several factors when doing so such as supply, costs, air and water quality, national energy security, climate change impacts, infrastructure concerns, and commodity prices. In this instance, regulators and scientists at the EPA become the default policy brokers who must work with a multitude of affected entities to gather their input before developing a policy all parties can accept. Unsurprisingly, when the EPA announced new volume requirements in 2023, environmentalists felt they were too high while biofuels producers felt they were too low, which is an indication of how the EPA was able to reach an agreement that reflected a compromise between competing coalitions.

Science as a Contact Sport. Generally speaking, these policy theories conceptualize opportunities for scientists to get involved in the policy process. However, as noted by climatologist Stephen Schneider (2010), science is a contact sport that can and often does involve scientists stepping into politics, playing more than just an advisory role in the policy process.

Pielke (2007) cautions scientists to be careful of how they get involved in the policy process. A scientist can serve as an honest broker—someone who clearly presents the evidence and does not embed their policy preferences within their scientific discussions with legislators—but there is an inherent danger when scientists use the language of science to mask their policy preferences within their advice, which Pielke calls being a stealth issue advocate. Thus, while there are opportunities for scientists to engage in the political process, there is a risk that they lose the prestige generally associated with their position.

In Pielke's framework, political context is an important determinant of the degree to which scientific information is incorporated into policy. In situations where there is a consensus of values and low uncertainty, scientific information is likely to be sought after and used in the formation and implementation of policies. Bans on public smoking are an excellent example. The preservation of health is an important value for most citizens and there is no longer any uncertainty as to the negative health effects of smoking. By convincingly demonstrating the dangers of second-hand smoke, science was able to inform the final policies that resulted from this policy debate, which in most cases did not allow any smoking within public places. It is worth noting, though, that these policies took a significant amount of time to be accepted and initially there was a great deal of resistance to these restrictions on personal freedom, indicating that even for these types of issues, policy change does not always come easily.

For issues where values are conflicting and a high degree of uncertainty exists, scientific information alone is unable to determine what policies should be pursued. So-called "designer babies" illustrate this point well. Debates over whether society should permit the genetic modification of human embryos to prevent disease and enhance desirable traits are rooted in conflicting beliefs about the ethics and morality of such an action. These are value debates to which science cannot provide a satisfactory answer. Further complicating the issue is that the science in this area is still developing and there is significant uncertainty about what is possible and what consequences may arise.

A Typology of Scientific Actions and Policy Conflicts

With this broad understanding of where scientists fit into political debates, it is important to develop a conceptualization of how scientists behave once they exit their "laboratory" and start to interact with policy actors. Relying on Kuhn's discussion, a typology of scientific conflict is developed (see Fig. 8.1). It starts with the proposition that every scientific endeavor or question has some level of consensus. The level of consensus is represented by the vertical axis in the figure, ranging from low to high consensus. The high end of the continuum represents near-consensus, which suggests the development of uncontested knowledge. Basic physics, molecular theory, and so forth are all examples of areas where scientists are in near-universal agreement, which in Kuhn's parlance is the current scientific paradigm. Researchers in these various fields have since moved on to researching other phenomena within their fields of study. Operating within the current scientific paradigm corresponds to Kuhn's idea of normal science.

At other times, scientists encounter a phenomenon that they are unable to explain. Scientists have made initial observations, but they cannot develop a causal argument that withstands scientific scrutiny.[1] At this point, scientists are genuinely puzzled and cannot adequately explain the observation. In short, there is no consensus on the issue. If the puzzle is valuable enough to society, the issue is researched intensely until, it is hoped, a state of uncontested knowledge is reached. Alone, the vertical

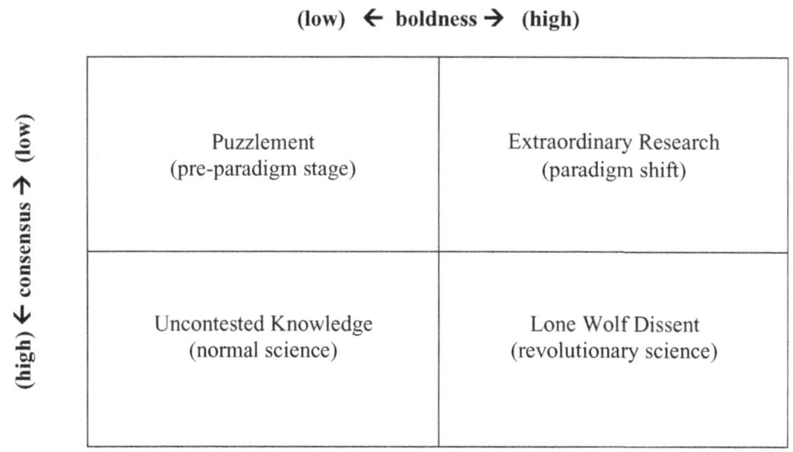

Fig. 8.1 Typology of scientific conflict

[1] For instance, the honeybee population is in decline, a phenomenon known as colony collapse disorder (CCD). For much of the 2000s, scientists struggled to explain the collapse of the bee population. Various causal arguments have been advanced, but not many have withstood the rigors of scientific inquiry. While there have been recent advances in society's understanding of CCD, the science necessary to understand the full extent of CCD is still being carried out. Scientists have admitted they are still attempting to understand the problem and that multiple factors, and perhaps even interactions, are driving the decline in the bee population.

axis representing scientific agreement might embody a limited version of Kuhn's conceptualization of scientific revolutions. On various issues, scientific information moves society from the puzzlement stage to uncontested knowledge. Eventually, research anomalies are encountered, resulting in a reversion where the state of knowledge moves from uncontested knowledge back to some level of puzzlement. At times, the reversion might involve rewriting basic scientific principles that require throwing out previously accepted knowledge.

The level of consensus represented by Fig. 8.1's vertical axis, however, is arguably not enough to fully integrate Kuhn's arguments into a typology of scientific conflict. This first dimension captures just simple disagreement. For Kuhn, revolutionary science is much more than scientists disagreeing about the cause of an observation. For a revolution to occur, recourse to an existing paradigm has failed. Scientists become emboldened on the issue and "resort to techniques of mass persuasion" (Kuhn, 1996, p. 93). As Kuhn (1996) noted about an anomaly or crisis upsetting the status quo: "The proliferation of competing articulations, the willingness to try anything, the expression of explicit discontent, the recourse to philosophy and to debate over fundamentals, all these are symptoms of a transition from normal to extraordinary research" [p. 91].

Undertaking extraordinary research outside the current paradigm of science and/or resorting to unscientific means of persuasion are conceptualized as a boldness dimension in the typology. While all scientists presumably care about their work, some are more passionate and dogmatic when it comes to debating and defending the veracity of their research, and some are more willing to accept the risk of being spurned by carrying out innovative and experimental research that does not conform to existing methods. In this conceptualization, a high degree of boldness can indicate that the debate has moved from the professional disagreement that occurs in the scientific realm to outright hostility.

It should be noted that disagreement and conflict resolution are at the heart of the scientific process. Theories are developed, hypotheses are proposed, and those hypotheses are tested using both qualitative and quantitative research methods. Conflict is often pictured as taking the form of civil debates in academic meetings and workshops, Q&A sessions at academic conferences, and the back and forth of the peer review process that is used to improve the research for publication. Whether through scientific norms, peer pressure, or the individual personalities of the researchers, the debate remains muted and technical. However, as boldness increases, these routine forms of conflict become more personal and feature elevated levels of hostility and emotion. Scientists become unwilling to compromise and become fixated on convincing others to accept their findings and conclusions. This boldness dimension is captured by the horizontal axis in Fig. 8.1, which ranges from low to high.

When bold action is observed, the conflict takes two forms depending on the level of consensus. If there is a high consensus around an issue or causal argument, then there tends to be the "lone wolf dissenter"—a single or extremely small group of scientists that challenge the status quo.[2] The tension in the discipline can be expanded as the lone wolf dissenter is capable of convincing others that a prevailing theory is incorrect and new ideas and methods are needed. The conflict might expand to such an extent that the existing consensus is called into question, which increases the likelihood that the existing paradigm will shift.

How can conflict be identified? Several behaviors on the part of scientists can be expected, although some behaviors might be considered more contentious than others. A proposed sampling of specific actions utilized by bold scientists in policy debates might include the following, which are listed in order of the increasing severity of the action:

- Developing new methods and techniques and then claiming they are superior to old ones that were reliable in the past.
- Advocating in non-scientific forums for a novel theory to replace a well-established one.
- Calling into question the published work of other scientists because they overlooked potentially relevant causal factors in their research.
- Publicly questioning the interpretations of well-respected researchers.
- Dismissing another scientist's work as "junk science" that lacks merit.
- Assigning blame rather than discussing the details of scientific research.
- Questioning the integrity and motives of one's opponents.
- Suggesting evidence in a scientific debate is deliberately fabricated.

Low boldness means the behaviors above are largely absent. In these low-boldness cases, scientists admit that they are genuinely puzzled by the event and that more research is needed to understand the phenomenon, but they do not attack the work of fellow scientists. They try to solve research puzzles through currently accepted methods. The four categories proposed in Fig. 8.1 offer one way to understand the various types of scientific conflict that might be observed during policy debates.

It is worth noting that the boldness of scientific research may depend in part on the entities funding the research endeavor. Generally speaking, most basic research is funded by the federal government while private corporations are more likely to

---

[2] The effect of the "lone wolf dissenter" can take two primary forms: history may vindicate a dissenter's work and they will be remembered as advancing society's knowledge, such as astronomer Nicolaus Copernicus developing the heliocentric model of the solar system and geologist Alfred Wegener proposing a theory of continental drift; or, history may show that the scientific community is unable to replicate the dissenter's work and thus the dissenter's bold and innovative research is rejected, as was the case for Andrew Wakefield who was part of a small team that identified an alleged relationship between the MMR vaccine and autism. Wakefield's arguments went against the consensus view that vaccines are both safe and necessary (although not without side effects). Follow-up research was unable to replicate his team's results, and allegations surfaced that Wakefield may have fabricated his data. However, Wakefield stands by his original work even though his co-authors withdrew their support for it. He continues to use the press to claim the causal relationship between the vaccine and autism is real and criticizes the government for not having the safety of the population in mind when regulating vaccinations.

carry out applied research. The boldness of a scientist's research agenda may depend on the source of the funding, but the nuances may go even further. The Defense Advanced Research Projects Agency (DARPA) is a government agency well known for funding high-risk, high-reward research. However, other public funding agencies might be more risk averse, such as NASA arguably preferring astronaut safety over bold innovation for space exploration (Simberg, 2013). Various degrees of risk tolerance and political expectations are linked to the funding, which in turn may limit the boldness of how scientists act.

Consequences of How Science Is Communicated

These types of conflicts generally occur behind the scenes between scientists. At some unpredictable point, however, an area of scientific research may become relevant to an ongoing policy debate. Non-scientists will step into the fray and offer the public their own interpretation of the debate between scientists and the societal implications of scientific research. This intervention is likely to occur when the work of scientists suggests that a public problem exists and that remedial policies may be necessary. Climate change is the most readily available example and an area of much social science research, but other areas of research make national headlines as well. The use of hydraulic fracturing to extract petroleum and natural gas, contamination from "forever chemicals" (PFAS), and the population stability of endangered species are just a small sampling of areas where non-scientists are involved in the interpretation of scientific research for the public.

Scientists, media outlets, and political personalities all attempt to frame the implications of scientific research, and scholars have rightly focused on how this information is communicated to the public. The public's views on science may or may not be consistent with the original information offered by scientists because multiple actors have attempted to convince the public of their interpretation of the science. Each actor can be expected to frame the information in a manner consistent with the actor's own values and policy preferences (Schattschneider, 1960; Jones & Baumgartner, 2005). If an issue is repeatedly discussed by media outlets, then there is more information available for the public to develop views based on that information (Krosnick & Kinder, 1990; Zaller, 1992; Barker & Knight, 2000) and to match their opinions with political leaders (Carmines & Stimson, 1982; Carmines & Stimson, 1986). Because the public often mimics what they hear within their general information environment (Zaller & Feldman, 1992; Zaller, 1992), how science is communicated or framed can shape the contours of public opinion (Nisbet & Mooney, 2007).

There are a variety of frames utilized by opinion leaders to sway public opinion. Frames might emphasize the economic costs of a policy (e.g., Pralle & Boscarino, 2011), the extent to which experts agree that a problem exists (e.g., Wood & Vedlitz, 2007), the health benefits of medical treatments (e.g., Nyhan et al., 2014), and so forth. Framing issues for the public is not always intentional. For example, exposure to negative images of scientists, such as the unethical behavior of scientists in movies, is argued to increase the public's level of reservation about scientific advancements (Nisbet et al., 2002).

Now turning to the degree of scientific agreement, there is evidence that perceptions of a scientific consensus correlate with beliefs about scientific issues. In the context of climate change, non-experimental surveys suggest that those who believe a majority of scientists think global warming is occurring are more likely to support remedial policies (Ding et al., 2011). Surveys using an experimental design reach similar conclusions: emphasizing a degree of consensus (Lewandowsky et al., 2013) or certainty (Wood & Vedlitz, 2007) among scientists corresponds with increased beliefs about the issue that are more in line with those of scientists. Thus, it matters whether individuals perceive a scientific consensus.

Political actors seek to leverage the importance of a scientific consensus to public opinion. In the context of climate change, conservatives have made efforts to frame the debate in a manner opposed to climatologists. In the 1990s, conservative think tanks suggested a coordinated theme consisting of two claims: (1) "the science of global warming appears to be growing more and more uncertain"; and (2) "the harmful effects of global warming policy are becoming increasingly certain" (McCright & Dunlap, 2000, p. 499). These arguments are inconsistent with those of the IPCC, which emphasizes areas of scientific consensus and discusses the consequences of inaction. As scientists have advanced society's understanding of climate change and more consequences have been observed (e.g., uncontrolled forest fires and record-breaking average temperatures in the modern era), the partisan discord has become more nuanced but still exists (Kennedy & Tyson, 2024; Mayer & Smith, 2023). In short, perceptions of scientific actions and the level of agreement on an issue—a consensus or a lack thereof—are found to correspond to beliefs, particularly with respect to climate change.

Climate change has been studied extensively in academia but this general pattern of scientific infighting overlapping with politics and public beliefs occurs elsewhere, such as with genetically modified foodstuffs. Generally, genetically modified products are thought of as safe by both regulatory agencies and research scientists (American Association for the Advancement of Science, 2012). However, there was a small research team acting in a manner similar to lone wolf dissenters that expressed concern about the long-term safety of consuming genetically modified foods (Séralini et al., 2012). The study was heavily scrutinized by other toxicology researchers, which included allegations that the paper should never have been published due to technical irregularities (e.g., Schorsch, 2013). While this disagreement does not seem to have a political dimension within the United States (Kahan, 2013), it has dominated political discussions in Europe at times, especially in the mid-2000s when a short-lived moratorium was put in place on the introduction of new genetically modified foods.

When politics and science intersect, partisans are more likely to follow the cues offered by their preferred party's leadership team rather than defer to experts, while non-partisans appear more likely to align their views with those of experts (Kuklinski et al., 1982). If partisans are more educated and interested in policy issues (Taber &

Lodge, 2006), then it might be inferred here that the less-informed segments of society (e.g., independents) are more likely to follow cues from scientists.

Lastly, framing does have its limitations, especially when media consumers question the credibility of the news source or the quality of the frames (Druckman, 2001). If there is no trust in the person doing the framing, the frame is likely to have a minimal impact on public opinion. Generally, scientists are seen as trusted sources of information (Miller, 1983), although even then that trust varies by partisanship and who exactly is carrying out the research (Gauchat, 2011; Gauchat, 2012). For instance, Critchley (2008) argues that the public is more likely to trust public scientists compared to corporate scientists. Greater trust in scientists can lead to more support for scientific research. In the context of climate change, there is considerable polarization in the level of trust held for the IPCC, especially after "Climategate" (Leiserowitz et al., 2013). More recently, the public was able to see the iterative nature of science in "real time" as the medical community rushed to fully understand the SARS-CoV-2 virus, which caused the COVID-19 outbreak. Scientists may agree or disagree about a specific causal relationship, but it does not follow that once agreement in the scientific community has been reached that it will then influence public opinion.

Case Study

To better illustrate the overlap between the science community and political activity, we turn to a case study on the use of lead in the United States. It is a study of how a scientist worked to affect policy change in the mid-twentieth century.

Clair Patterson was a geochemist who set out to do something that up to that point had not yet been accomplished: to precisely and accurately measure the real age of the Earth. This scientific endeavor would require novel data collection techniques involving uranium-lead dating, zircons, and meteorites. The uranium-lead dating technique would prove problematic because in the 1940s and 1950s when Patterson was carrying out this work, lead in the environment was ubiquitous: lead was a common additive in the paint used in buildings; it was in the ambient air from the burning of leaded gasoline; it was in drinking water from the use of lead pipes; and it was also in food from the use of lead solder to seal cans. Even the most minute amount of outside lead would contaminate his results, which necessitated a new method of collecting his data that ultimately led to Patterson becoming one of the first researchers to create an ultra-clean room. His newly developed methods were needed to ensure that only the lead in his sample was the lead that was being measured. His innovative methods led to other new techniques of collecting data, such as measuring lead isotope ratios. It took years of study, but Patterson was able to determine that the Earth is approximately 4.55 billion years old.

Patterson was not content to stop there. He applied his newfound ability to measure lead at the microgram and sub-microgram levels to a new problem: the widespread lead contamination that he experienced while trying to carry out his initial research on the age of the Earth. In an ironic twist, the American Petroleum Institute funded some of Patterson's work, with the oil industry at the time being a major contributor to anthropogenic emissions of lead because of the widespread use of tetraethyl lead as an anti-knocking agent in gasoline. Patterson's new work in marine chemistry revealed that the upper layers of the ocean had much higher levels of lead than the deeper layers, indicating an external source of lead deposition. His modeling suggested that the combustion of leaded gasoline and the amount of lead it was putting into the atmosphere could explain what he found.

Just a few days after publishing the results of his ocean lead analysis, the American Petroleum Institute ended its financial support and pressured Patterson's administrators to fire him. The implications of Patterson's research jeopardized the continuation of his work, but Patterson was resistant to outside pressures and refused to back down or change course even when he knew it would imperil his research funding and engender significant resistance from powerful interests. What this case indicates is that the use of novel data or techniques can often lead to greater scrutiny and skepticism of one's results, especially if they do not conform to an existing consensus. That pushback can come from within the scientific community itself, but it can also come from external actors if it is an issue of public concern with the potential to upset the status quo.

Patterson sought out new sources of revenue and was successful in securing research funding from the federal government. Financial support is worth mentioning as a potential determinant of whether or not certain exploratory research is even possible to conduct. In this case, the money supported expeditions to Greenland and Antarctica where Patterson once again constructed an unconventional dataset. He combined his techniques of ultra-clean sampling and minute measurement of lead with ice core collection and analysis. His results confirmed his previous findings that lead concentrations in the modern era were dramatically higher than in the past, and the increase correlated with the introduction of leaded gasoline. The implications were immediately clear to Patterson: humanity was poisoning itself and the environment, and this realization set him on a lifelong quest to convince others of the same. Lead was a known neurotoxin, and its toxicity had been acknowledged since the times of ancient Greece and the Roman Empire. In Patterson's time, it was known that at high levels of exposure lead could cause anemia, neurological changes, gastrointestinal problems, and, in the most extreme cases, death. What was not well known at the time was that even at low levels of exposure it could cause irreparable harm to children, affecting their mental and physical development and leading to lifelong problems like lower IQ and behavioral disorders.

Patterson was, like many scientists, more comfortable in a lab than a legislature, but it was at this time in the mid-1960s that Patterson became more involved in policy advocacy. He thought his research and its obvious implications would be powerful enough to speak for themselves, but he soon became frustrated by a lack of action in response to his research demonstrating the widespread contamination of lead caused by human activity. Patterson's work was picked up by medical doctor and editor of the *Archives of Environmental Health*, Katherine Boucot, who reached out to him to see if he would write an editorial. The journal was somewhat afield of the standard publications for his area of research but rather than simply reporting his results in a narrow subfield of his discipline, it serves as an example of extrapolating the broad implications of one's work and expanding its intended audience. In his article, Patterson estimated that the lead burden of modern people at the time could have been as much as 100 times greater than what would naturally be expected. He ended the article with a call for more research on the problem of lead pollution and his preferred solution to the problem: "It appears that the following activities deserve serious consideration and support: defining natural and toxic lead levels with greater care than has been shown in the past; investigating deleterious effects of severe chronic lead insult; investigating the dispersion of industrial lead into food chains; elimination of some of the most serious sources of lead pollution, such as lead alkyls, insecticides, food can solder, water service pipes, kitchenware glazes, and paints; and a re-evaluation by persons in positions of responsibility in the field of public health of their role in this matter" (Patterson, 1965).

It is interesting that Patterson initially chose a peer-reviewed outlet to sound the alarm about the increasing lead concentrations in the environment from human sources. Perhaps this initial foray into advocacy fit better with personal preferences he may have held at the time about a scientist's public role. But the academic debate it spurred soon made it into mainstream politics when it was covered by *The New York Times*. Patterson also did his best to try to move the article from the problem stream to the policy stream by sending it to health ministries, the Governor of California, and Massachusetts Senator Edmund Muskie, who at the time headed a Senate subcommittee on air and water pollution. The year after his editorial was published, Patterson would land himself squarely in the politics stream when he testified at a Congressional hearing organized by Senator Muskie. Patterson found himself pitted against industry scientist Robert A. Kehoe, a medical expert and apologist for the use of lead.

Patterson, taking on the role of a lone wolf dissenter, challenged the existing paradigm espoused by Kehoe. Kehoe had a monopoly on lead research up to that point, and he had helped to establish a consensus on lead that exposure to it was natural and its widespread use was not of significant concern (Needleman, 2000). Kehoe was, by training, a medical doctor, but he had long embraced an advocacy role and used his expertise and industrial backing to significantly influence government policy (Patterson was known to question the motives of scientists with strong ties to industry like Kehoe). It is just one of many examples in environmental science whereby powerful and well-financed interests seek out scientists who are willing to stake out a position friendly to their cause. This fact provides a compelling reason for advocacy on the part of objective scientists with relevant expertise to counter dangerous and misleading claims.

Patterson's work on lead and his willingness to engage in policy advocacy came at a propitious time when a window had opened for environmental policy. The Clean Air Act of 1970 provided the newly established Environmental Protection Agency (EPA) with the authority to regulate air pollution, public opinion in regard to the environment and public health was favorable toward government regulation, and the federal government's efforts to reduce urban air pollution had resulted in a requirement that beginning in 1975 new vehicle models had to be equipped with catalytic converters. Catalytic converters cannot operate properly in the presence of lead. Furthermore, a successful 1972 lawsuit from the Natural Resources Defense Council led to a court order for the EPA to establish regulations for a phase-down in the use of lead in gasoline. The agency had been interested in reducing anthropogenic contributions to lead levels in the environment and it now had the scientific (problem stream), political (politics stream), and legal (policy stream) justification it needed to phase out leaded gasoline.

Patterson's activism did eventually coincide with policy action, but his activism cut both ways and partly validates why some scientists are concerned about taking bold actions that lead to a loss of their image as unbiased researchers. Patterson was intentionally excluded at times from the committee work of federal government agencies who saw him as being uncompromising, which put him at odds with a political process that often necessitates compromise to achieve policy action. However, his steadfastness and undeniable expertise did finally lead to him being asked to serve on a Lead in the Human Environment committee for the National Research Council of the National Academy of Sciences, but his effectiveness was diminished by his combativeness and the polemic tone of what he wanted included in the committee's report. In the end, he refused to work with others on the committee and his part of the report became more of an addendum rather than an integrated section that flowed naturally with the rest of the report. It is readily acknowledged that Patterson could be abrasive and disruptive. However, throughout the years he maintained close contact with scientists at the EPA, fellow academic researchers studying the dangers of lead, senior colleagues proficient at securing research funds on his behalf, and powerful politicians such as Senator Edmund Muskie. He was not known for political shrewdness, but he was able to effectively build a coalition of actors capable of serving as policy entrepreneurs and this group of like-minded individuals helped contribute to the enactment of his preferred public policies.

Patterson's boldness was dogmatic and had the potential to hamper his efforts to effect change. When it came to research on lead, he held a Manichean view that people were either on his side (in his view, the right one) or they were not, which could alienate potential allies. But his certainty was a double-edged sword that also had its benefits. When doing extraordinary research on the frontiers of science, especially when it threatens the prestige and prosperity of powerful interests that are comfortably entrenched within the status quo, one's work is likely to be questioned, and a steely resolve can aid in fostering the patience and persistence that is often needed to successfully call into question the existing consensus. Politicians desire certainty but science is open to skepticism and scrutiny of results, with science relying on a preponderance of evidence rather than absolute truths, and one has to be prepared to see the scientific process through until their research results are validated. Utilizing innovative data and/or new techniques can make it difficult for the work to be accepted but once others have also utilized similar methods of research and demonstrated their efficacy, it is more likely that the original work will be accepted to become the new normal. Revolutionary work may initially receive a critical reception, but it does not mean it is wrong.

Clair Patterson is rightfully remembered as a trailblazer who empirically demonstrated widespread lead contamination from humanity's extensive use of the metal, and he did so by collecting novel data and using experimental research techniques that were revolutionary for their time. Part of his legacy is also his unwavering commitment to seeing that the government acted on the problem. His example illuminates not only the possibilities of engaging in policy advocacy but also the potential pitfalls. The information for this case study is common knowledge and is widely available, but Lydia Denworth's (2008) *Toxic Truth: A Scientist, a Doctor, and the Battle Over Lead* was of particular assistance in crafting it, and this book would serve as an excellent reference for anyone interested in learning more about Patterson's work on lead and his policy efforts to bring about the elimination of lead pollution.

Final Thoughts

The Patterson case study serves as an illustration of a scientist working in the political arena to bring about policy change. Relying on his research and working with a collection of like-minded actors, he worked to influence both the public and government officials to bring about a policy change that improved environmental quality for all of society. However, it is just one type of scientific conflict within one specific policy domain. Other policy issues have different levels of political cleavage and involve different sets of biases, both within legislatures and within the citizenry. The interactions and experiences of a scientist in the context of the environmental sciences may be different than one working on vaccination research, which in turn may be different from someone working on newer, safer ways to harness nuclear power. Each issue has its own political coalitions and resonates differently with the public.

When the scholarly community finds itself at the intersection of science and politics, it is important to recognize the overlap and realize that science is primarily information. It informs society of a potential problem and potential solutions. However, whether the problem is a *public* problem that merits governmental intervention is a separate calculation that is largely independent from the science. Political actors must debate the trade-offs with other (likely non-scientific) dimensions such as the effectiveness of specific policies, whether the costs are worth the potential societal improvements, the ideological values of both the public and political leaders, and so forth. It also involves at least some scientists inserting themselves into the political arena, as Patterson did. How scientists engage in the political process can influence policy change, but their engagement can also impact how the public thinks of the issue and their trust in scientists (see Section "Consequences of How Science is Communicated" above).

We encourage scholars to keep these implications in mind as they engage their community in a professional capacity as subject-matter experts. Scientists do not work in a vacuum. To truly better society while also maintaining their trust as subject-matter experts, scientists need to be aware of the possibilities and perils of engaging in the political process as well as the limits of the information they provide decision-makers. As Schneider has noted, science is a contact sport. The disagreements and conflicts within both the scientific community and the political arena are real, as are the consequences for scientific prestige and trust if science is miscommunicated. Very few policy issues can be solved by simply "following the science" to develop a policy and solve public problems. The problems are inherently more complex than such an oversimplified statement would suggest. A better understanding and appreciation for this dynamic can arguably be one step toward improving the quality of scientific and political discourse in society.

References

American Association for the Advancement of Science (2012). *Statement by the AAAS board of directors on labeling of genetically modified foods*. Accessed on August 5, 2024, at https://www.aaas.org/sites/default/files/AAAS_GM_statement.pdf

Biden, J. R. (2020). *Remarks by vice president Joe Biden in Gettysburg, Pennsylvania*. The American Presidency Project. https://www.presidency.ucsb.edu/node/345125

Barker, D., & Knight, K. (2000). Political talk radio and public opinion. *The Public Opinion Quarterly, 64*(2), 149–170. https://doi.org/10.1086/317760

Carmines, E. G., & Stimson, J. A. (1982). Racial issues and the structure of mass belief systems. *The Journal of Politics, 44*(1), 2–20. https://doi.org/10.2307/2130281

Carmines, E. G., & Stimson, J. A. (1986). On the structure and sequence of issue evolution. *The American Political Science Review, 80*(3), 901–920. https://doi.org/10.2307/1960544

Critchley, C. R. (2008). Public opinion and trust in scientists: The role of the research context, and the perceived motivation of stem cell researchers. *Public Understanding of Science, 17*(3), 309–327. https://doi.org/10.1177/0963662506070162

Denworth, L. (2008). *Toxic truth: A scientist, a doctor, and the battle over lead*. Beacon Press.

Ding, D., Maibach, E. W., Zhao, X., Roser-Renouf, C., & Leiserowitz, A. (2011). Support for climate policy and societal action are linked to perceptions about scientific agreement. *Nature Climate Change, 1*, 462–466. https://doi.org/10.1038/nclimate1295

Druckman, J. N. (2001). On the limits of framing effects: Who can frame? *The Journal of Politics, 63*(4), 1041–1066. https://doi.org/10.1111/0022-3816.00100

Gauchat, G. (2011). The cultural authority of science: Public trust and acceptance of organized science. *Public Understanding of Science, 20*(6), 751–770. https://doi.org/10.1177/0963662510365246

Gauchat, G. (2012). Politicization of science in the public sphere: A study of public trust in the United States, 1974 to 2010. *American Sociological Review, 77*(2), 167–187. https://doi.org/10.1177/0003122412438225

Jones, B. D., & Baumgartner, F. R. (2005). *The politics of attention: How government prioritizes problems*. The University of Chicago Press.

Kennedy, B. & Tyson, A. (2024, March 1). *How republicans view climate change and energy issues*. Pew Research Center. Accessed on August 15, 2024 at: https://www.pewresearch.org/short-reads/2024/03/01/how-republicans-view-climate-change-and-energy-issues.

Kahan, D.M. (2013). We aren't polarized on GM foods— No matter what the result in Washington state. *The Cultural Cognition Project at Yale Law School*. Accessed on August 17, 2024, at http://www.culturalcognition.net/blog/2013/11/5/we-arent-polarized-on-gm-foods-no-matter-what-the-result-in.html

Kingdon, J. W. (1995). *Agenda, alternatives, and public policies* (2nd ed.). HarperCollins College Publishers.

Krosnick, J. A., & Kinder, D. R. (1990). Altering the foundations of support for the president through priming. *The American Political Science Review, 84*(2), 497–512. https://doi.org/10.2307/1963531

Kuklinski, J. H., Metlay, D. S., & Kay, W. D. (1982). Citizen knowledge and choices on the complex issue of nuclear energy. *American Journal of Political Science, 26*(4), 615–642. https://doi.org/10.2307/2110965

Kuhn, T. S. (1996). *The structure of scientific revolutions* (3rd ed.). The University of Chicago Press.

Leiserowitz, A. A., Maibach, E. W., Roser-Renouf, C., Smith, N., & Dawson, E. (2013). Climategate, public opinion, and the loss of trust. *American Behavioral Scientist, 57*(6), 818–837. https://doi.org/10.1177/0002764212458272

Lewandowsky, S., Gignac, G. E., & Vaughan, S. (2013). The pivotal role of perceived scientific consensus in acceptance of science. *Nature Climate, Change, 3*, 399–404. https://doi.org/10.1038/nclimate1720

Mayer, A. P., & Smith, E. K. (2023). Multidimensional partisanship shapes climate policy support and behaviours. *Nature Climate Change, 13*, 32–39. https://doi.org/10.1038/s41558-022-01548-6

McCright, A. M., & Dunlap, R. E. (2000). Challenging global warming as a social problem: An analysis of the conservative movement's counter-claims. *Social Problems, 47*(4), 499–522. https://doi.org/10.2307/3097132

Miller, D. W. (1985). *Popper selections*. Princeton University Press.

Miller, J. D. (1983). *The American people and science policy*. Pergamon Press.

Needleman, H. L. (2000). The removal of Lead from gasoline: Historical and personal reflections. *Environmental Research, 84*(1), 20–35. https://doi.org/10.1006/enrs.2000.4069

Nisbet, M. C., & Mooney, C. (2007). Science and society. Framing science. *Science, 316*(5821), 56–56. https://doi.org/10.1126/science.1142030

Nisbet, M. C., Scheufele, D. A., Shanahan, J., Moy, P., Brossard, D., & Lewenstein, B. V. (2002). Knowledge, reservations, or promise?: A media effects model for public perceptions of science and technology. *Communication Research, 29*(5), 584–608. https://doi.org/10.1177/009365002236196

Nyhan, B. J., Reifler, S., & Richey & Freed, G.L. (2014). Effective messages in vaccine promotion: A randomized trial. *Pediatrics, 133*(4), e835–e842. https://doi.org/10.1542/peds.2013-2365

Patterson, C. C. (1965). Contaminated and natural Lead environments of man. *Archives of Environmental Health: An International Journal., 11*(3), 344–360. https://doi.org/10.1080/00039896.1965.10664229

Pernick, M. S. (1972). Politics, parties, and pestilence: Epidemic yellow fever in Philadelphia and the rise of the first party system. *William and Mary Quarterly, 3d series, 29*(4), 559–586.

Pielke, R. A. (2007). *The honest broker*. Cambridge University Press.

Pralle, S., & Boscarino, J. (2011). Framing trade-offs: The politics of nuclear power and wind energy in the age of global climate change. *Review of Policy Research, 28*(4), 323–346. https://doi.org/10.1111/j.1541-1338.2011.00500.x

Sabatier, P., & Jenkins-Smith, H. (1993). *Policy change and learning: An advocacy coalition approach*. Westview Press.

Séralini, G. E., Clair, E., Mesnage, R., Gress, S., Defarge, N., Malatesta, M., Hennequin, D., & de Vendômois, J. S. (2012). Long term toxicity of a roundup herbicide and a roundup-tolerant genetically modified maize. *Food and Chemical Toxicology, 50*(11), 4221–4231. https://doi.org/10.1016/j.fct.2012.08.005. (Retraction published Food Chem Toxicol. 2014 Jan;63:244. doi: 10.1016/j.fct.2013.11.047).

Schneider, S. H. (2010). *Science as a contact sport: Inside the battle to save Earth's climate*. National Geographic.

Schorsch, F. (2013). Serious inadequacies regarding the pathology data presented in the paper by Séralini et al. (2012). *Food and Chemical Toxicology., 53*(0), 465–466. https://doi.org/10.1016/j.fct.2012.10.043

Simberg, R. (2013). *Safe is not an option*. Interglobal Media LLC.

Sherwood, S. (2011). Science controversies past and present. *Physics Today, 64*(10), 39. https://doi.org/10.1063/PT.3.1295

Schattschneider, E. E. (1960). *The semi-sovereign people: A realist's view of democracy in America*. Illinois, The Dryden Press.

Smith, S. M.. (2020). We've Been Here Before. *Rice Magazine*. https://magazine.rice.edu/fall-2020/weve-been-here.

Taber, C. S., & Lodge, M. (2006). Motivated skepticism in the evaluation of political beliefs. *American Journal of Political Science, 50*(3), 755–769. https://doi.org/10.1111/j.1540-5907.2006.00214.x

Wood, B. D., & Vedlitz, A. (2007). Issue definition, information processing, and the politics of global warming. *American Journal of Political Science., 51*(3), 552–568. https://doi.org/10.1111/j.1540-5907.2007.00267.x

Zaller, J., & Feldman, S. (1992). A simple theory of the survey response: Answering questions versus revealing preferences. *American Journal of Political Science, 36*(3), 579–616. https://doi.org/10.2307/2111583

Zaller, J. R. (1992). *The nature and origins of mass opinion*. Cambridge University Press.

The manufacturer's authorised representative in the EU is Springer Nature Customer Service Centre GmbH, Europaplatz 3, 69115 Heidelberg, Germany. If you have any concerns regarding our products, please contact ProductSafety@springernature.com

Printed and bound by CPI Group (UK) Ltd, Croydon, CR0 4YY
30/09/2026
02225577-0011